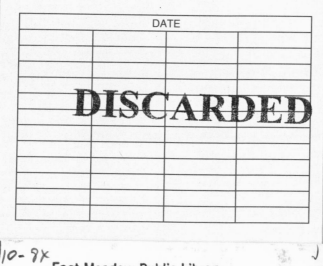

Cooking Well for the Unwell

Cooking Well for the Unwell

More Than One Hundred Nutritious Recipes

EILEEN BEHAN, R.D.

Hearst Books
New York

It is the policy of William Morrow and Company, Inc., and its imprints and affiliates, recognizing the importance of preserving what has been written, to print the books we publish on acid-free paper, and we exert our best efforts to that end.

Library of Congress Cataloging-in-Publication Data

Behan, Eileen.
    Cooking well for the unwell: More than one hundred nutritious recipes/ by Eileen Behan
    p.   cm.
    Includes bibliographical references and index.
    ISBN 0-688-11372-9
    1. Cookery for the sick.   I. Title.
  RM219.B375 1996
  641.5'631—dc20   95-39090
                               CIP

Printed in the United States of America

First Edition

1 2 3 4 5 6 7 8 9 10

BOOK DESIGN BY VERTIGO DESIGN

To John M. Behan

My father was always ahead of his time in his interest in nutrition. He saw food and nutrients as an underutilized tool in the fight against disease and in the maintenance of good health. His interest is no doubt where I obtained my own enthusiasm for the subject, and I thank him for this. I know he would have been happy to see this book finally in print.

Acknowledgments

To my mother Elizabeth Behan, Sharon, Sheila, and Kevin—thanks for your support. I am grateful to Trish Cronan and Brad Lavigne for their encouragement. I'd like to thank James Bloomer, M.D., for reading parts of the manuscript for accuracy and Judy Paige, R.D., for her contributions as a friend and nutritionist. Thanks to Marilyn Desimone, R.D., and Madeleine Walsh, R.D., for their help and ideas.

At Hearst Books I would like to thank Harriet Bell for seeing the potential in this book and for sticking with the project through its rough stages. Thanks to Kathleen Hackett for all her help. Judith Sutton is a copy editor extraordinaire. Special thanks to my agent, Carol Mann.

Finally, I would like to thank my husband, David, and daughters, Sarah and Emily, who contribute so much to my life and work.

contents

cooking well
for the unwell

Introduction

Nutrition is an underutilized tool in the fight against illness and disease. The foods a sick person eats play a tremendous role in how strongly he or she fights back against illness. At a minimum, food provides the energy for the battle; at a maximum, it may contain special nutrients research suggests may be key in fighting diseases such as cancer.

Having worked as a nutritionist for twenty years, I have a growing recognition of the role nutrition therapy has to play in medical care. Years ago, the person who approached his or her doctor about nutrition would have been dismissed as silly, hypochondriacal, or worse. Today, some physicians pay more attention to nutrition issues when designing a total care plan for managing most illnesses, but many do not. Given the public interest in nutrition, questions about fat and cholesterol, adequate calcium intake, the use of salt when cooking, and more are also likely to arise during physical exams. If special nutrition is needed, counseling with a registered dietitian is frequently recommended.

Still, nutritional care is in danger of becoming even more underutilized in these times of health care reform, when cost-cutting strategies are being sought in all areas. Many leaders in this changing system simply do not realize the value of proper nutrition in fighting and preventing illness and its complications. That value will gain greater attention at some point, given the persistent voices of those who do understand what nutrition can contribute to the effective management of disease. But it well may be after a period characterized by a lack of widely available professional nutrition services within hospitals and other health care settings. In the meantime, the onus for proper nutritional care falls largely on the patients' and their families' shoulders.

Managing that responsibility successfully will mean seeking out quality resources—perhaps working with a registered dietitian on your own outside the hospital or doctor's office, without the financial assistance of insurance coverage. Certainly it will mean using helpful guides such as this book. But regardless of how it is done, it is the tremendous potential of good nutrition for treating and preventing illness that will spur us to do it.

Cooking Well for the Unwell addresses nutrition issues that arise during illnesses and gives you the information you need to help prevent the nutrition-related complications of disease. In this book, I have condensed the enormous amount of nutrition science found in textbooks and journals into an easy-to-read reference guide that addresses the most important nutritional concerns that occur with illness and disease. The subjects I have chosen to address were arrived at based on questions and comments I have received from family, friends, and clients—questions about what to eat when ill, what to eat to prevent the progression of an illness, or how to serve foods to best treat symptoms. Traditional cookbooks, including those that emphasize healthy cooking, generally do not deal with illness-related nutrition issues such as unintended weight loss, taste changes, and the need for substantial amounts of protein.

My own insight into these issues was sharpened during my father's battle with leukemia and Wegener's granulomatosis. Despite my mother's remarkable talent as a cook, my father's problems brought changes in the way he ate that were very difficult to cope with. He was lucky to have a very resourceful and knowledgeable cook to care for him and a daughter trained in nutrition. Still, we desperately wanted a cooking guide to assure ourselves that we were using the preventive and healing powers of food to the fullest. It was during my father's illness that I began to write *Cooking Well for the Unwell.*

There is no single food prescription that can be applied to all ailments. And this book does not offer a simple approach to the eating problems an ill person may face. Instead, it spells out specific problems often unique to certain illnesses and gives insight into how to best manage them.

It's a book for people in many situations—those caring for a friend with AIDS; someone nursing a loved one with cancer, whose appetite has been zapped by chemotherapy or radiation; a parent anxiously looking after a sick child. The needs of the patient as well as the caregiver are considered, combining the two to come up with a workable nutritional plan. Cooking allows for the caregiver to express concern through the nurturing act of feeding foods the patient both needs and desires.

This book also helps you decide when to give in to your patient's whims about what to eat that may be contrary to what you consider good nutrition. Indeed, there are many factors that can affect the definition of good nutrition for an ill person. The first chapter, Food Heals, gives you initial insight into these many factors. Chapter 2, The Healing Food Guide, explains the foundation of a healthful diet and is the starting point for feeding any ill person, whether with a serious long-term illness or with a temporary one that must just be weathered. The Nutrition Prescription, Chapter 3, reviews potential nutrition problems created by diseases related to the immune system, digestive tract, and cardiovascular system, and surgery.

The following chapters then give detailed information for dealing with specific problems, whether they be getting a loved one to eat enough protein and calories, figuring out how to prepare a low-sodium diet, or serving soothing foods to someone with a sore mouth or poor appetite. Chapter 4, Protein and Calories: A Lifesaving Combination, offers guidelines for calculating the need for both these essential nutrients. In Chapter 5, Foods and Recipes to Speed Recovery, you'll find more than one hundred easy-to-prepare recipes for reducing the risk of protein-calorie malnutrition. Other chapters include recipes designed to meet the special needs of specific illnesses or diseases, whether temporary or long-term. In some cases, I intentionally developed recipes with odd yields so that you will have leftovers for those days when you're too tired or simply don't have time to cook.

For the anxious times when an ill person just doesn't feel like eating, Chapter 8, But I'm Just Not Hungry, gives ideas for supplying vital calories in the face of a nonexistent appetite.

At the end of the book, alternative therapies for many illnesses are discussed to give a basis for making decisions about whether or not to try these therapies. There is also a resource section with addresses and phone numbers for products to help meet the physical needs of some patients and for support and education groups to help you meet the physical and emotional needs of your patient as well as yourself.

Intended as a supplement to the advice you get from a doctor or a qualified nutrition professional, *Cooking Well for the Unwell* will help you make the right decisions about what to feed your patient. Use this book to become an active participant in helping your patient heal. The rewards will be personal satisfaction and, perhaps, triumph over the battle against serious illness.

Nutrition Analysis

Nutrition analysis was determined as follows:

When a choice of ingredients is given in the ingredients list, the first food listed was used for the analysis. Optional ingredients are not included. When milk is listed as an ingredient, the nutrition value for whole milk was used unless otherwise specified. When a serving size range is given, it is the first number of servings that was used for analysis.

How to use the nutrition information:

After each recipe, the calorie, protein, and fat content are given for one serving, as well as nutrient data for all the leader nutrients described in Chapter 2. If your patient is trying to gain weight, select dishes with the highest calorie value per serving. When extra protein is needed, check the protein content to find a recipe that meets your patient's needs. If fat is not being well tolerated, choose recipes with low-fat content. Note also that the fat content of some recipes can be reduced by using low-fat dairy products. For overall nutrient balance, consult Chapter 2, The Healing Food Guide. Serve the recommended servings from each food group and you will be meeting your patient's needs for vitamins and minerals.

food heals

1

Can you imagine celebrating a holiday, birthday, or other milestone without food? We certainly wouldn't anticipate the event with the same pleasure, nor would it leave the lasting impression that comes from a traditional meal of many of our favorite foods.

Food holds tremendous social, cultural, and emotional significance for most of us. We use it to show we care and to promote friendliness. When new neighbors move in, we welcome them with gifts of home-cooked fare. When tragedy strikes, we express compassion by offering food to help provide physical and emotional sustenance. When we sit down to a meal with family, friends, business associates, or strangers, it serves as a statement of equality.

Favorite foods hold even more significance. Eating them gives us a sense of security and comfort. We often reward others or express our love by offering sweet foods. Treating friends or loved ones—and ourselves—to an expensive meal helps show how much we value them and ourselves.

Yes, food helps meet our needs in a way that is very important to our emotional health, which ultimately can affect our physical health. But food plays a much more direct role physically. As the major source of the many nutrients that are key to fighting disease successfully, food often ranks as our first defense against illness, whether we are trying to prevent it or cure it.

Supplying Vital Nutrients

Food supplies more than forty nutrients that are essential to our most basic bodily functions. Individually, nutrients cannot cure disease, but without them, our bodies simply do not function optimally. As we become depleted of various nutrients because of a poor diet, we become more vulnerable to the development of a host of diseases associated with diet. A poor diet may also speed the progression of many illnesses.

For instance, vitamin B_6 is vital to our very existence as a key nutrient necessary to make red blood cells. Red blood cells carry oxygen throughout the body, delivering the very element upon which human life depends. Vitamin A helps keep lymph glands and skin healthy, which in themselves play important roles fighting off invasive bacteria and viruses.

Along with vitamins and minerals, we also need optimal amounts of calories, fat, carbohydrate, and protein. Fat supplies essential fatty acids, which are needed for normal growth in children and for healthy skin in all of us. It also contributes flavor and texture to foods, adding to the satisfaction we derive from eating.

Even more important, during illness fat is a rich source of calories, or energy. Because ounce per ounce, it contains more than twice the calories of protein or carbohydrate, fat makes a major contribution to feeding people with poor appetites. They can eat much smaller portions of high-fat foods than of others to get the calories they need.

Many people who are seriously ill lose interest in eating at some point, either because of an illness that diminishes their appetites or because of a lack of energy necessary to prepare and consume food. When too little food is consumed, Mother Nature kicks in with a wonderful emergency system that provides energy in the absence of food *for a while*. Glucose, the energy source for body cells that normally comes from carbohydrates in the diet, is released from the liver. Fat stores also release substances called fatty acids. The body can operate quite nicely on glucose and fatty acids for some time.

This adaptive system can temporarily keep a person thinking clearly and capable of carrying out routine activities. But what might seem stable is actually a time bomb waiting to go off.

As stored glucose is used up, the body begins to depend more on fatty acids derived from the breakdown of fat stores. But the brain and nervous system for the most part cannot use fatty acids. When glucose is not supplied via the diet, the body eventually breaks down the liver and muscles to get protein, which is then converted into glucose. If this protein breakdown continues, severe muscle wasting occurs. As protein reserves become depleted, the immune system becomes less effective and the chances of secondary infections and complications increase.

In most cases, protein reserves are exhausted in about three weeks, and death soon follows. If you are successful in halting this decline before it leads to serious consequences, energy and protein stores must be fully replenished before the next bout of illness or traumatic therapy, such as radiation treatments for cancer, begins to interfere with eating. Otherwise, the process is speeded up as the stores that were only partly replenished become quickly exhausted.

We also depend on protein for the amino acids that are essential to repair tissues damaged every day through normal wear and tear of the body. During illness, body tissues are broken down at a greater than normal rate, so meeting protein needs becomes even more important. Again, if we do not get enough protein in our diets, our bodies take the protein they need from our muscles, resulting in the muscle wasting commonly seen in prolonged illness.

Food Can Make a Difference

The benefits of a well-balanced, varied diet that meets our many needs are easy to see in most people. Abundant energy and a positive attitude go hand-in-hand with the good health that comes from eating well.

When we are ill, food continues to play a central role to our well-being. Indeed, what we eat may play as important a role as more traditional treatments for disease, such as medicine or surgery. In fact, there are many anecdotal cases in which orthodox medical treatment was stopped, but the patient went on to thrive following a program based on providing good nutrition.

I strongly believe in traditional medicine, and I don't want to suggest otherwise. When my children are sick, we seek advice from our pediatrician. When my husband or I have health concerns, we consult our family doctor. But I also know from my experience as a nutritionist that at present, nutritional therapy is not adequately integrated into the traditional medical system of health care.

The lack of recognition of the importance of nutrition in the treatment of disease stems in part from other health care professionals' past experiences with nutritional therapies. For example, the therapy may have required too much of the patient—such as adherence to an unrealistic diet that included none of the foods the person was accustomed to eating—or it was some bizarre regimen that had no scientific basis.

This book is based on the nuts and bolts of nutrition science. It will give you the information you need to feed your loved ones during serious illness, to give them the building materials they need to repair their bodies and provide time for medical treatments to take effect. It will show you how to use food to the best advantage when dealing with a person who is seriously ill, demonstrating the fact that food truly does help to heal.

WHAT THE COOK CAN DO

One of the most important things you can do when someone you love becomes ill is to make certain he or she is well fed. The food you prepare will nourish his or her body and soul, as well as the bond between the two of you.

- Learn which foods maintain or promote good health, then prepare and serve them. Read the Healing Food Guide (page 18).

- Listen to your patient. Concentrate on good nutrition, but indulge cravings and whims too. Calories are the most important nutrient for many ill people.

- Keep small portions of nutritious foods available to offer when your patient expresses an interest in eating.

- Handle food safely. Serious illness reduces the body's ability to fend off food poisoning. Read about food safety on page 27.

- Be your patient's advocate. Ask the health care provider about the need for special diets, food, or supplements. Also ask about the effects medication or treatments may have on appetite or nutrition.

- Alert the health care provider immediately if your patient refuses meals and loses weight.

- Be positive. Caring for a sick one is both difficult and rewarding.

- Take care of yourself too. Get plenty of rest, eat well, and find time for personal enjoyment.

WHAT THE PATIENT CAN DO

If you are both the patient and the cook, the fact that you have picked up this book indicates you already recognize that food can play an important role in your recovery.

- Learn about the foods you need to promote or regain good health. Read the Healing Food Guide (page 18). Strive to eat foods from these groups daily.

- Keep a record of the foods you eat in a day, then compare it to the recommendations in the Healing Food Guide.

- Weigh yourself once a week. Keep your health care provider aware of any unusual fluctuations.

- Ask your health care provider how your illness and the medications and/or treatments you receive may affect your need for nutrients.

- Manage symptoms that interfere with your appetite as soon as they appear—read Chapter 8, But I'm Just Not Hungry.

- Ask for help. Seek the advice of a registered dietitian. He or she can offer both practical and technical advice.

- Let friends and family help. When someone asks what he or she can do, tell them to bring you some ready-to-eat snacks or meals.

the healing
food guide

2

"What should I eat to get better?" That is a question everyone with a serious illness should ask. Any condition that interferes with regular activities or requires treatment to slow its progression and prevent possible complications can be called serious.

There is no one food that meets the many and various needs of an ill person. Rather, the goal is a balanced combination of foods that provide all the nutrients the body needs to heal itself. The Healing Food Guide, described in detail in the following pages, gives you all the information you need to select the right foods to help heal your loved one.

The Healing Food Guide features twenty-eight vital nutrients, including all of those for which Recommended Dietary Allowances (RDA) exist. RDAs are the levels of essential nutrients that, on the basis of current scientific knowledge, are judged to be adequate to meet the known nutrient needs of most healthy persons. Different diseases may affect the need for various nutrients. On page 24, I give instructions for making general modifications to the Healing Food Guide to meet special needs. I've outlined more specific instructions for the special nutrition needs brought on by specific diseases in later chapters.

Food Groups with Leader and Secondary Nutrients

Don't try to memorize the nutrients in each food group; just be aware that any food within a group contains a variety of essential nutrients. By preparing meals that feature all these groups over the course of each week, you'll serve the right mix of nutrients your loved one needs.

When a food is listed in parentheses following a nutrient, it means the nutrient is found specifically in that food and not in other foods within the group. For example, fish is rich in iodine, but most other protein foods are not. Wheat germ is a good source of chromium, but other fats and oils are not.

Protein Group
LEADER NUTRIENTS: Protein, iron

SECONDARY NUTRIENTS: Vitamins A, B12, B6, D (eggs), and K (meat and eggs), biotin, riboflavin, pantothenic acid, niacin, phosphorus, copper, iodine (fish), selenium, zinc

Calcium Group
LEADER NUTRIENTS: Calcium, protein

SECONDARY NUTRIENTS: Vitamins A, K, D, and B12, phosphorus, molybdenum

Vegetable Group
LEADER NUTRIENTS: Vitamins E, A, and C, carbohydrates, calcium (green leafy vegetables)

SECONDARY NUTRIENTS: Vitamin K, folate, magnesium, potassium

Fruit Group
LEADER NUTRIENTS: Vitamins A and C, carbohydrates

SECONDARY NUTRIENTS: Vitamin K, potassium

Grain/Starch Group

LEADER NUTRIENTS: Carbohydrates, iron (fortified foods)

SECONDARY NUTRIENTS: Thiamin, riboflavin, niacin, vitamin B6, biotin, manganese (whole grains), pantothenic acid

Fat/Oil Group

LEADER NUTRIENTS: Fat, vitamin E

SECONDARY NUTRIENTS: Vitamin D, magnesium (whole seeds), copper (nuts and seeds), chromium (wheat germ)

Estimated Safe and Adequate Daily Dietary Intakes of Select Vitamins and Minerals

These are not included in the main 1989 RDA table because there is less information on which to base allowances. The recommended intakes listed below are published by the Food and Nutrition Board of the National Research Council.

	Age (years)	Biotin (mg)	Pantothenic Acid (mg)	Copper (mg)	Manganese (mg)	Fluoride (mg)	Chromium (mg)	Molybdenum (mg)
Infants <6 mos.	0–0.5	10	2	0.4–0.6	0.3–0.6	0.1–0.5	10–40	15–30
6–12 mos.	0.5–1	15	3	0.6–0.7	0.6–1.0	0.2–1.0	20–60	20–40
Children and adolescents	1–3	20	3	0.7–1.0	1.0–1.5	0.5–1.5	20–80	25–50
	4–6	25	3–4	1.0–1.5	1.5–2.0	1.0–2.5	30–120	30–??5
	7–10	30	4–5	1.0–2.0	2.0–3.0	1.5–2.5	50–200	50–150
	11+	30–100	4–7	1.5–2.5	2.0–5.0	1.5–2.5	50–200	75–250
Adults		30–100	4–7	1.5–3.0	2.0–5.0	1.5–4.0	50–200	75–250

To ensure adequate intake of these nutrients, the Healing Food Guide focuses on foods that are rich in the leader nutrients: protein, calcium, fat, carbohydrate, vitamin A, vitamin E, vitamin C, and iron. By concentrating on getting enough leader nutrients, you virtually guarantee an adequate intake of other essential, or secondary, nutrients: vitamin D, vitamin K, thiamin, riboflavin, niacin, vitamin B6, folate, vitamin B12, phosphorus, magnesium, zinc, iodine, selenium, biotin, pantothenic acid, copper, manganese, fluoride, chromium, and molybdenum.

To simplify the process of eating to get enough of these many nutrients, nutritionists have grouped foods into six groups according to the leader nutrients they contain. The foods in each group are listed in the Healing Food Guide on page 19.

1989 Recommended Dietary Allowances

The Recommended Dietary Allowances are published by the Food and Nutrition Board of the National Research Council. These are the most recently published figures.

Fat-Soluble Vitamins

	Protein (g)	Vitamin A (m g RE)	Vitamin D (m g)	Vitamin E (mg a TE)	Vitamin K (m g)	Vitamin C (mg)	Thiamin (mg)	Riboflavin (mg)
Infants <6 mos.	13	375	7.5	3	5	30	0.3	0.4
Infants 6–12 mos.	14	375	10	4	10	35	0.4	0.5
Children 1–3	16	400	10	6	15	40	0.7	0.8
4–6	24	500	10	7	20	45	0.9	1.1
7–10	28	700	10	7	30	45	1.0	1.2
Males 11–14	45	1000	10	10	45	50	1.3	1.5
15–18	59	1000	10	10	65	60	1.5	1.8
19–24	58	1000	10	10	70	60	1.5	1.7
25–50	63	1000	5	10	80	60	1.5	1.7
51+	63	1000	5	10	80	60	1.2	1.4
Females 11–14	46	800	10	8	45	50	1.1	1.3
15–18	44	800	10	8	55	60	1.1	1.3
19–24	46	800	10	8	60	60	1.1	1.3
25–50	50	800	5	8	65	60	1.1	1.3
51+	50	800	5	8	65	60	1.0	1.2

The realities of illness do not always make it possible to eat a balanced diet every day. On good days, encourage your patient to eat the most nutritious food possible, making up for days when appetite is diminished. Try not to become discouraged if the food you prepare is refused. In all likelihood, it's not the food or your ability as a cook that is at fault, but the illness. Indeed, illness can be a challenge to even the best cook, and, in most cases, preparing meals for someone who is sick requires a great deal of trial and error. What works one day may not be appealing the next week, or even at the next meal, but keep trying, keep experimenting. Take comfort in the fact that you are doing the best you can do— and in the body's wonderful ability to heal itself.

Water-Soluble Vitamins / Minerals

Niacin (mg NE)	Vitamin B_6 (mg)	Folate (m g)	Vitamin B_{12} (m g)	Calcium (mg)	Phosphorus (mg)	Magnesium (mg)	Iron (mg)	Zinc (mg)	Iodine (m g)	Selenium (m g)
5	0.3	25	0.3	400	300	40	6	5	40	10
6	0.6	35	0.5	600	500	60	10	5	50	15
9	1.0	50	0.7	800	800	80	10	10	70	20
12	1.1	75	1.0	800	800	120	10	10	90	20
13	1.4	100	1.4	800	800	170	10	10	120	30
17	1.7	150	2.0	1200	1200	270	12	15	150	40
20	2.0	200	2.0	1200	1200	400	12	15	150	50
19	2.0	200	2.0	1200	1200	350	10	15	150	70
19	2.0	200	2.0	800	800	350	10	15	150	70
15	2.0	200	2.0	800	800	350	10	15	150	70
15	1.4	150	2.0	1200	1200	280	15	12	150	45
15	1.5	180	2.0	1200	1200	300	15	12	150	50
15	1.6	180	2.0	1200	1200	280	15	12	150	55
15	1.6	180	2.0	800	800	280	15	12	150	55
13	1.6	180	2.0	800	800	280	10	12	150	55

Why Leader and Secondary Nutrients Are So Important During Illness

The leader and secondary nutrients found in the food groups listed here are vital to health. Each nutrient has at least one and usually several specific functions that it performs to help the body fight illness. If any of these nutrients is not consumed on a regular basis, a deficiency will occur and negative consequences will follow.

For instance, in the case of iron, a deficiency leads to decreased resistance to infection. A zinc deficiency manifests itself in the form of diarrhea, vomiting, and even a reduced number of white blood cells, which are crucial to fighting infection.

How Leader and Secondary Nutrients Help the Body Heal and Resist Disease

Leader Nutrients

PROTEIN: Builds and repairs tissues, such as skin and muscles. Part of antibodies that fight off disease; helps make enzymes essential for digestion of food

CALCIUM: Keeps bones and teeth strong and healthy. Helps in muscle contraction and blood clotting. Plays a key role in the immune system. May help prevent high blood pressure and colon cancer

FAT: Provides energy, carries fat-soluble vitamins and essential fatty acids, insulates the body to maintain temperature, and pads vital organs to protect against trauma

CARBOHYDRATE: Supplies energy; spares protein to be used for more vital functions than as energy source

VITAMIN A: Helps maintain vision, healthy skin, and mucous membranes. Involved in production of essential hormones. May help protect against and control cancer

VITAMIN E: Helps prevent cell damage that may lead to cancer. Protects red blood cells and vitamin A

VITAMIN C: Helps keep blood vessels strong, makes scar tissue, metabolizes protein, boosts the immune system, and absorbs iron

IRON: Carries oxygen throughout the body as part of red blood cells; any loss of blood increases need for iron

Secondary Nutrients

THIAMIN (VITAMIN B_1): Helps metabolize energy and maintain appetite and properly functioning nervous system

RIBOFLAVIN (VITAMIN B$_2$): Essential to energy metabolism; helps keep skin and eyes healthy

NIACIN: Helps release energy; helps keep skin, nervous system, and digestive system functioning properly

FOLATE: Essential to make new cells

VITAMIN B$_{12}$: Essential to make new cells and keep nerve cells healthy

BIOTIN: Vital to metabolize energy, produce fat, and use amino acids

PANTOTHENIC ACID: Helps metabolize carbohydrates, protein, and fat

VITAMIN D: Vital for strong, healthy bones

VITAMIN K: Essential for proper blood clotting

POTASSIUM: Helps maintain fluid balance in cells and helps muscles contract

PHOSPHORUS: Helps keep bones and teeth healthy

MAGNESIUM: Helps build protein; helps keep muscles working and teeth strong

ZINC: Aids in healing wounds; necessary for sense of taste

IODINE: Makes up part of thyroid hormones; prevents goiter

COPPER: Vital for proper iron absorption; makes up part of blood and membranes that cover and protect nerve tissue

MANGANESE: Part of enzymes necessary for cell functioning

CHROMIUM: Necessary to release energy from storage

SELENIUM: Works with vitamin E to prevent important body compounds from being destroyed

MOLYBDENUM: Necessary to several enzymes that help ensure proper cell function

Nutrient deficiencies are rare in most people because the body stores nutrients in reserve for times when the diet does not supply enough. The body also has backup systems for producing essential nutrients from parts of other nutrients. These backup systems work best, however, in healthy people eating healthful diets.

During illness, when medical treatments may rob an individual of the desire to eat or may even increase the need for certain nutrients, it becomes more difficult to avoid deficiencies. This means that during illness every bite of food must count toward meeting the body's nutrient needs. Even if you believe your patient eats well, use the Healing Food Guide to evaluate how balanced his or her diet actually is. Use it, too, to plan a balanced diet containing at least the minimum recommended number of servings daily from each food group.

Can Vitamin-Mineral Supplements Replace Food?

Taking a vitamin-mineral supplement does not eliminate the need for a well-balanced diet. As we have seen, twenty-eight substances are currently recognized as, or suspected to be important to health, and supplements contain many of these nutrients. But foods contain a huge number of other substances for which there are no supplements. In the future, these may be identified as crucial to our health. For example, researchers continue to discover fascinating connections between health and substances found naturally in foods, such as the phytochemicals in plants. Future research may illuminate a role for them in healing. But these substances are not found in vitamin-mineral supplements.

Supplements do, however, play a role in fighting illness. They can ensure that at least the RDA for many nutrients is met. A study published in the medical journal *Lancet* revealed that the use of an ordinary vitamin-mineral supplement by older people helped keep them healthy. The supplement appeared to boost the immune system, thereby helping to fight off infections.

A good vitamin-mineral supplement should contain roughly 100 percent of the RDAs for a wide array of essential vitamins and minerals, and it should include vitamin E, vitamin C, and beta carotene. You can read more about selecting vitamin-mineral supplements in Chapter 19.

How to Use the Healing Food Guide

The Healing Food Guide shows how to plan a diet that provides the nutrients your patient needs. If he or she eats according to it over a period of days or weeks, you can rest assured that he or she is eating well.

The guide lists the types of food that fall within each food group, along with the minimum number of servings needed daily to meet the RDAs for the leader nutrients supplied by the foods. It outlines a diet that supplies approximately 1600 to 2200 calories, 80 grams protein, 40 to 50 grams fat, 250 to 350 grams carbohydrate, 8 to 10 milligrams (mg) vitamin E, 20 to 25 mg iron, 800 to 1200 mg calcium, 1000 retinol equivalents (RE) vitamin A, and 60 mg vitamin C (providing at least one citrus food is eaten daily).

The actual nutrient and calorie content of an individual menu will vary depending on the food selected. Over time, however, if the basic plan is followed, intake of leader nutrients will average the amounts listed above. (If an increased calorie intake is necessary to prevent or reverse weight loss, refer to Chapter 4.)

To use the Healing Food Guide, first familiarize yourself with the foods within each group. In some cases, you may be surprised to find very different foods are grouped together. For example, both milk and green leafy vegetables are good calcium sources, and they are listed together in the Calcium Group.

Next, look at the daily number of servings recommended for each group and plan menus accordingly. Also pay attention to serving sizes. An ounce of milk in coffee does not count as a serving of milk, but eight ounces of milk added here and there over the course of a day do add up to a full serving.

Count each serving only once. For example, if you serve cheese, don't count it as a serving from the Calcium Group and from the Protein Group. If you "double count," the total food intake may be too low.

If you have trouble determining your patient's food intake, keep a diary of what he or she eats and drinks over the course of twenty-four hours. Count the number of servings that fit into the different groups, then compare what he or she ate with what is recommended to identify where he or she is falling short. Once you know the gaps, you can plan menus to feature foods that fill in where necessary.

This food group system may seem tedious at first. But like anything else, the more you use it, the easier it will become. Remember this is a guide, with room for dietary indiscretions such as occasionally eating chocolate cake instead of fresh fruit or opting for a milk shake at dinner instead of a three-course meal. The Healing Food Guide is intended to help you select a menu for several days, not just one meal. Meeting emotional needs, such as providing the comfort of a favorite food (such as chocolate cake) can be as important as providing nutritional needs, as long as those needs are met at some point.

You can use the Healing Food Guide for children by simply decreasing the amount of food served. In general, a serving size for a child under eleven years of age is approximately half the serving size suggested for an adult. For more information about feeding children during illness, read Chapter 18.

The Healing Food Guide

Protein Group

COMPLETE PROTEINS: Meat, fish, poultry, cheese, eggs

INCOMPLETE PROTEINS: Beans, peas, nuts

AMOUNT OF LEADER NUTRIENTS IN ONE SERVING: 21 grams protein; 1 to 4 mg iron

RECOMMENDED DAILY SERVINGS: At least two

SERVING SIZES: 3 ounces beef, pork, poultry (chicken, duck, or turkey), lamb, fish, or hard cheese, such as Cheddar, mozzarella, Swiss, or Colby longhorn; ³/₄ cup cottage or ricotta cheese; 3 whole eggs; 1¹/₂ cups cooked beans or peas, such as kidney, black, or pinto beans, lentils, split peas, or garbanzos; 1 cup cooked soybeans; 8 ounces soy tempeh; 8 ounces tofu; ¹/₂ cup nuts or seeds, such as chopped cashews, walnuts, peanuts, or pistachios, sunflower seeds, pumpkin seeds, or sesame seeds; 5 tablespoons peanut butter

COMMENTS: Protein foods are either *complete* or *incomplete.* Complete proteins contain the eight essential amino acids needed by the body to make new protein. Complete proteins naturally come from animal foods such as meat, fish, chicken, eggs, and cheese. Plant proteins such as those in beans and nuts are incomplete; incomplete proteins are also found in small amounts in grain foods, such as bread, pasta, rice, and cereal. To make a complete protein using plant proteins, combine foods containing all the essential amino acids. For example, together beans and rice make a complete protein. Likewise, a peanut butter sandwich provides complete protein. When appetite is poor and food intake low, complete proteins from animal foods may be better choices. For example, rather than trying to get down half a cup of cooked beans, an ill person may more easily eat one small egg to meet his or her protein needs.

Three ounces of red meat and half a cup of cooked beans both supply about 2 to 3 milligrams of iron, but iron from animal sources is better absorbed. One egg supplies about 1 milligram of iron. Dairy products, such as cheese, are poor sources of iron.

Calcium Group

Milk, cheese, tofu, green leafy vegetables

AMOUNT OF LEADER NUTRIENTS IN ONE SERVING: 300 mg calcium; 8 grams protein (milk products and tofu only)

RECOMMENDED DAILY SERVINGS: At least two for adults, three for teens and young adults to age twenty-four

SERVING SIZES: 1 cup milk (all types), kefir (cultured milk), yogurt (all varieties), pudding or custard made with milk, or hot chocolate made with milk; 1¹/₂ cups cottage cheese, ice cream or ice milk, or cream soup made with milk; 1¹/₂ ounces Cheddar, other hard cheeses, or American cheese; 3 cups soy milk; 4 to 5 ounces canned salmon (with bones); 8 ounces tofu; 3 cups cooked Swiss chard or broccoli.

COMMENTS: While nondairy foods such as broccoli do provide calcium, note how much must be eaten to get the same amount there is in one cup of milk. The recommended number of servings provides 600 to 900 milligrams calcium; small amounts of it found in vegetables, grains/starches, and protein foods contribute the remaining calcium needed to meet the RDA. Anyone who cannot eat the recommended amounts of these foods will need a calcium supplement.

Dairy products such as milk and yogurt also provide significant amounts of complete protein and so can contribute significantly to protein intake. Protein needs, however, can be met entirely by foods from the Protein Group.

Vegetable Group
All vegetables and their juices

AMOUNT OF LEADER NUTRIENTS IN ONE SERVING: Varies

RECOMMENDED DAILY SERVINGS: Two to three

SERVING SIZES: $1/2$ cup cooked or 1 cup raw chopped vegetables; $3/4$ cup vegetable juice

COMMENTS: Good sources of vitamin A include deep-green or yellow-orange vegetables such as broccoli, carrots, romaine lettuce, sweet potatoes, pumpkin, and winter squash. Good sources of vitamin C include broccoli, Brussels sprouts, cauliflower, green peppers, and potatoes. Cruciferous vegetables such as broccoli, Brussels sprouts, and cauliflower also contain components that may be important in preventing diseases such as cancer. Vegetable juice is an easily consumed source of the many valuable nutrients found in vegetables. If sodium is a concern, look for low-sodium varieties.

Fruit Group
All fruits and their juices

AMOUNT OF LEADER NUTRIENTS IN ONE SERVING: Varies

RECOMMENDED DAILY SERVINGS: Two to three

SERVING SIZES: $1/2$ cup chopped, cooked, or canned fruit; 1 medium piece fresh fruit; $3/4$ cup fruit juice

COMMENTS: Aim for one source of the important healing nutrient vitamin C daily; choose blueberries, blackberries, raspberries, strawberries, grapefruit, lime, lemons, or oranges. Yellow-orange fruits such as apricots, cantaloupes, mangoes, papayas, and peaches are good sources of vitamin A. Select 100 percent fruit juices: orange, grapefruit, pineapple, or apple juice fortified with vitamin C.

Grain/Starch Group
Bread, cereal, rice, pasta, tortillas

AMOUNT OF LEADER NUTRIENTS IN ONE SERVING: Varies

RECOMMENDED DAILY SERVINGS: Seven or more

SERVING SIZES: 1 slice bread (all types); 1 small roll, biscuit, or muffin, tortilla, or small pancake or waffle; ½ bagel or English muffin; ¾ cup dry cereal; ½ cup cooked cereal, rice, bulgur, barley, or pasta; 6 Saltine-type crackers or 3 graham crackers; 3 tablespoons wheat germ; ⅓ cup cooked beans or peas; ½ cup mashed potatoes or 1 medium potato; 2 cookies; 1 small slice cake

COMMENTS: This highly palatable group of foods supplies plenty of carbohydrates and can be valuable in preventing or stopping weight loss if appetite is poor.

Fat/Oil Group

Cooking oils, butter, margarine, wheat germ, nuts and seeds

AMOUNT OF LEADER NUTRIENTS IN ONE SERVING: Varies

RECOMMENDED DAILY SERVINGS: Five

SERVING SIZES: 1 teaspoon oil, butter, margarine, or mayonnaise; 1 tablespoon salad dressing, cream, nuts, or seeds; 10 large peanuts; 10 small olives

COMMENTS: An adequate fat intake helps ensure an adequate calorie intake because fat contains twice the calories of protein or carbohydrate. Perhaps more important, however, fat adds taste appeal to food. A meal containing fat is also digested more slowly than a fat-free meal, thereby staving off hunger for a longer period of time.

Water

Because we cannot survive without it for more than a few days, many nutritionists consider water a nutrient. Adults need eight to ten cups of water or other fluid each day. This may sound like a lot to swallow, but, fortunately, we don't need to down that much in the form of water each day. Coffee, tea, milk, juice, soups, and fruits and vegetables with high water contents all contribute to the recommended daily intake.

Encourage your patient to drink whenever he or she is thirsty. However, the body's thirst mechanism cannot be entirely depended on to tell us when we're not getting enough fluid. In fact, the body is already slightly dehydrated by the time the thirst signal kicks into action. As a result, to make certain your patient consumes enough fluid, serve plenty of tasty liquids and fluid-rich foods such as those listed above. Soup, which is particularly appealing to many people when they are ill, can be a good way to supply fluids.

Seasonings, Condiments, and Beverages

Many foods, beverages, and other ingredients are of little nutritional benefit, yet the enjoyment they add to eating makes them important to many well-balanced plans for eating, whether a person is healthy or ill.

Spices and herbs, for example, enhance flavor and can be particularly useful when your patient must limit salt or sodium in the diet. Seasonings added to stews, soups, casseroles, and other baked dishes often make them more appealing, especially for those whose medications and symptoms decrease the sense of taste. On the other hand, strong flavors may turn off the appetites of those with gastrointestinal illnesses and nausea. Experiment with them, incorporating them into dishes gradually. Read more about cooking with herbs and spices in Chapter 11.

Salt can always be used in cooking unless your patient has been specifically advised to avoid it. The treatment of high blood pressure or fluid retention may require salt restriction. Pepper is allowed too, unless a prescribed diet prohibits it, such as the diet used in treating some gastrointestinal disorders.

Condiments such as mustard, catsup, horseradish, and relish do not provide significant nutrients, but they may make food appealing and increase the appetite. Most condiments are high in salt. If a salt-restricted diet has been advised, discuss the use of these foods with the health care provider or a registered dietitian.

Coffee and the caffeine it contains have been the subject of much research in recent years. The conclusion: Moderate consumption of either, or both, appears safe for most people. Excessive consumption, however, can create problems. Too much coffee, for example, can increase stomach acid, which runs contrary to appropriate treatment for ulcers. A heavy intake of caffeine, which stimulates the nervous system, can produce shaky, jittery symptoms even in healthy people. If your patient enjoys coffee and it is not contraindicated in the treatment of his or her illness, two cups a day are allowed.

Tea contains less caffeine than coffee and can be a wonderfully soothing way to consume fluid. If served with milk, it becomes more nutritious. Many people find herbal teas, which come in many flavors, very soothing. Beverages such as soda and fruit drinks carry little, if any, nutrients but are a good source of calories.

Whether your patient should consume alcohol is an issue that must be discussed with the health care provider. If the illness affects the liver or levels of blood sugar or triglycerides, drinking alcohol will make matters worse. Alcohol can also interfere with the effectiveness of some medications.

On the other hand, a glass of wine before bed or a meal helps some people sleep better and often boosts a frail appetite. I once had a client who enjoyed a coffee brandy mixed with heavy cream each evening, supplying him with 300 much-needed calories. While alcoholic beverages should not take the place of food, one to two drinks a day can be part of a healthy diet. One drink is defined as a twelve-ounce beer, one and a half ounces of liquor, or five ounces of dry red or white wine. Mixers such as sodas and juices used with liquors also add calories, which some patients may need.

Modifying the Healing Food Guide to Meet Special Needs

It's not unusual for an ill person to have different needs when it comes to food and nutrients. When this is the case, it's necessary to modify the recommended servings and choices suggested in the Healing Food Guide. The following adaptations to the Healing Food Guide are very general. For specific diseases, consult later chapters. If you are not certain whether or not your patient needs any special modifications, ask the health care provider.

- *To increase calories,* select whole-milk products. Increase the servings of the Fat/Oil Group to at least six per day and of the Grain/Starch Group to nine or more.

- *To increase protein,* increase Protein Group servings to three daily. At least one serving should be a complete protein. From the Calcium Group, select dairy foods instead of nondairy choices, which contain less protein.

- *To decrease fat,* select nonfat dairy foods. Choose lean meats, poultry, fish, eggs, and beans. Trim all excess fat from meat and remove skin from poultry. Do not serve more than three servings from the Fat/Oil Group per day. Bake, broil, or steam foods instead of frying. To satisfy appetite, serve more foods from the Grain/Starch, Vegetable, or Fruit groups.

- *To avoid lactose,* select dairy products that have been specially processed to lower the lactose content, e.g., lactose-reduced milk. Aged cheeses and yogurt with live, active cultures contain less lactose than regular milk. Read ingredients labels on foods (including breads, cereals, frostings, salad dressings, drink mixes, sauces and gravies, and more) and select those made without milk. Some people may tolerate lactose-containing foods if they are given in small amounts—e.g., one half cup milk at a time.

- *To increase fiber,* select whole-grain breads and cereals, rice, and pasta from the Grain/Starch Group. Serve at least three servings each from the Vegetable and Fruit groups every day.

- *To restrict sodium,* do not use salt in cooking or at the table. Buy and cook only fresh foods, those frozen without added salt, or packaged foods that are labeled *low*-sodium. *Reduced*-sodium foods may contain significant amounts of sodium, as is the case with reduced-sodium soups. Serve homemade soups and casseroles instead of canned or frozen.

Shopping for Good Food

Shopping wisely is the first step to ensuring that your patient gets the most nutrients possible in every bite of food. Many times that means buying foods that have been minimally processed. Indeed, the more food is trimmed, peeled, stewed, or otherwise processed, the more likely it is to have fewer nutrients than its fresh counterpart. One baked potato contains 20 milligrams of vitamin C; the equivalent amount of canned potatoes contains only 14 milligrams, and the same amount of French fries yields less than 1 gram of this valuable nutrient.

Similarly, in most cases, skip the sugar substitutes, nondairy creamers, and bottled fruit drinks. Instead, use the real thing to supply calories and add—even if minimally—to the nutrient intake. Choose sugar, honey, or molasses if it's permitted on your patient's diet. Use milk or cream instead of nondairy substitutes. Buy only 100 percent fruit juice, or make your own using a juicer or blender.

However, sometimes processing may offer certain benefits. Frozen vegetables contain more nutrients than vegetables that have spent days traveling from farm to warehouse to supermarket before languishing in your refrigerator.

Although the grain in breads and cereals must be processed before it's edible, whole-grain choices provide much more nutrition than white varieties. People raised on white breads and flour, however, often dislike whole grains, even more so when they are ill. If this is the case, try to use whole grains in a way that your patient does find appealing—for example, cookies made with oatmeal and whole wheat flour. Buy good-tasting whole grain cereals rather than their more refined cousins.

READ THE LABEL

Use the Nutrition Facts panel, carried on most food products, when you're shopping. Serving sizes are given in household measures and the list of nutrients covers most that are important to our health. The % Daily Value is based on a daily diet of 2000 calories and is intended to show how a food fits into the overall diet. I find the labels most helpful when I'm concerned about the amount of calories, protein, fat, sodium, or fiber in a particular food product.

Serving sizes are now more consistent across product lines, stated in both household and metric measures, and reflect the amounts people actually eat.

The list of nutrients covers those most important to the health of today's consumers, most of whom need to worry about getting *too much* of certain items (fat, for example), rather than too few vitamins or minerals, as in the past.

The label now tells the number of calories per gram of fat, carbohydrates, and protein.

Nutrition Facts

Serving Size ½ cup (114 g)
Servings Per Container 4

Amount Per Serving

Calories 90	**Calories from Fat 30**

	% Daily Value*
Total Fat 3 g	**5%**
Saturated Fat 0 g	**0%**
Cholesterol 0 mg	**0%**
Sodium 300 mg	**13%**
Total Carbohydrate 13 g	**4%**
Dietary Fiber 3 g	**12%**
Sugars 3 g	
Protein 3 g	

Vitamin A	80%
• Vitamin C	60%
Calcium	4%
• Iron	4%

*Percent Daily Values are based on a 2000-calorie diet. Your daily values may be higher or lower, depending on your calorie needs:

		Calories	**2000**	**2500**
Total Fat	Less than		65 g	80 g
Sat Fat	Less than		20 g	25 g
Cholesterol	Less than		300 mg	300 mg
Sodium	Less than		2400 mg	2400 mg
Total			300 g	375 g
Carbohydrate				
Fiber			25 g	30 g

Calories per gram:

Fat 9 • Carbohydrates 4 • Protein 4

Source: U.S. Food and Drug Administration, 1993.

New title signals that the label contains the newly required information.

Calories from fat are now shown on the label to help consumers meet dietary guidelines that recommend people get no more than 30 percent of their calories from fat.

% Daily Value shows how a food fits into the overall daily diet.

Daily values are also something new. Some are maximums, as with fat (65 grams *or* less); others are minimums, as with carbohydrates (300 grams *or more*). The daily values on the label are based on a daily diet of 2000 and 2500 calories. Individuals should adjust the values to fit their own calorie intake.

Preserving the Nutrients in Fruits and Vegetables

Even if you buy the most nutritious foods available, unless you store and cook them properly, your good efforts may be wasted. Follow these basic tips for preventing unnecessary loss of nutrients and flavor.

- Handle produce carefully. Bruising destroys nutrients and texture.

- To preserve moisture and nutrients, store vegetables in the refrigerator, wrapped in plastic or in the vegetable bin.

- Store root vegetables, such as potatoes, in a cool, dark, well-ventilated spot.

- Keep most fruits cold to preserve nutrients. To enhance flavor, bring to room temperature just before serving.

- Do not place tomatoes, peaches, or pears in a sunny window to ripen; they get too hot and become watery. Keep them at room temperature in a clean paper bag, then refrigerate when ripe.

- Shell green peas and lima beans just before cooking.

- Use as little water as possible when cooking vegetables. Quick-cooking methods, such as steaming or microwaving, preserve more nutrients than slow-cooking methods, such as stewing.

- Use the outer leaves of lettuce if possible; that's where the nutrients are concentrated.

- Use broccoli stems and leaves—they're packed with vitamins and minerals. But trim the stems from green leafy vegetables such as spinach and kale—most of the nutrients are in the leaves.

Handling Food with Care

The last thing a person with a serious illness needs is food poisoning. Yet illness increases the risk of food poisoning by lowering resistance to infection.

The potential for unnecessary food poisoning is great. Contamination from salmonella alone, just one source of this problem, causes about forty thousand cases of food poisoning each year, according to the Centers for Disease Control. Unreported cases may make the actual total closer to one to two million cases.

Most cases of food poisoning arise from improper storage and handling of food. Foods of animal origin, such as meats, fish, poultry, and eggs, are the most likely to harbor dangerous bacteria. They must be stored at cold temperatures before cooking to keep bacteria from multiplying and producing poisons. Additionally, these foods must be thoroughly cooked before serving to destroy the bacteria.

Vegetables and fruits are not as likely to be dangerous. Produce that has come in contact with the soil, however, has the potential to carry harmful bacteria. For example, an article in a 1991 issue of the *Journal of the American Medical Association* reported more than four hundred confirmed cases of salmonella poisoning from eating cantaloupe. Cutting the melons for serving apparently transferred the bacteria on the outside of the melons to the edible portion.

Produce can also be contaminated during storage or preparation if it comes in contact with bacteria from other sources. Store it in its own bin in the refrigerator, away from raw meats and poultry. All fruits and vegetables should be thoroughly washed before eating. To prevent food poisoning, follow the guidelines below.

Meat

- Cook beef and pork until well-done, 160°F. Cook lamb and veal to 170°F.
- Cook meat at oven temperatures of 325°F. or above.
- Store uncooked meats away from vegetables or fruits that are to be eaten uncooked; raw meat juices should never touch other foods.
- Avoid raw or undercooked meat (this includes hot dogs).
- Refrigerate uncooked roasts, steaks, and ribs for no longer than three days.
- Use leftover cooked meat within three days.
- Use ground meats and presliced or shaved deli meats within twenty-four hours; they are most prone to spoilage.
- Marinate meats, poultry, and fish in the refrigerator. Discard the marinade, or bring it to a boil before serving. Do not taste an uncooked marinade that has been used.

Poultry

- Rinse all poultry before cooking. Assume it carries the salmonella bacteria; at least one third of the chicken we buy does. Always wash your hands after contact with raw poultry. Prevent cross-contamination by washing cutting boards, knives, and any other surface that the poultry or its juices have touched with hot, soapy water immediately after handling poultry.
- Cook to 180° to 185°F.; the juices should run clear when the poultry is pierced at its thickest point.
- Don't store stuffed raw poultry; stuff just before putting it into the oven.
- Cook poultry within forty-eight hours of purchase, or freeze it.

Fish

- Cook fish until opaque throughout and flaky, about eight to ten minutes per inch of thickness.
- Avoid raw fish, including shellfish, sushi, or uncooked marinated seafood, such as ceviche.
- Cook fresh fish within a few hours of purchase.

- Wash cutting boards, knives, and any other surface that the fish has touched with hot, soapy water after each use.

Eggs
- Discard any cracked eggs.
- Avoid eating raw eggs. Do not use them in eggnog and other drinks, mayonnaise, or homemade ice cream and refrain from eating raw cookie dough or cake batters made with eggs.
- Cook eggs until the yolks and whites are firm; avoid soft-boiled eggs.
- Keep eggs refrigerated, in their original container, for no longer than four to five weeks.

Dairy
- Refrigerate milk and cheese.
- Use milk within five days of the "sell by" date marked on the carton.
- Use only pasteurized milk products; avoid raw milk and raw-milk cheese.
- People who are ill should avoid soft cheeses such as Camembert, Brie, or soft Mexican-style cheeses. They may be contaminated with the bacteria *Listeria*. People with impaired immune systems can be two hundred to three hundred times more susceptible than healthy individuals to poisoning from this organism.

Microwave Cooking
- Stir foods for even cooking.
- Follow all cooking instructions: The resting periods called for in recipes are critical to reach the required temperatures.
- Check for doneness in the center of the food; microwave ovens cook from the outside in.
- Reheat foods until hot inside.

General Kitchen Tips
- Discard any prepared food that has been held at room temperature for two hours or longer.
- Keep the refrigerator temperature at 34° to 39°F. (bacteria can multiply even in cold temperatures of 40° to 50°F.).
- Keep freezer temperatures at 0°F. or less.
- Clean refrigerators and countertops with warm soapy water or a mixture of one teaspoon of bleach and one quart of warm water.
- Use a food thermometer to take the guesswork out of determining when a food is cooked. They are available at most department and kitchenware stores.

the nutrition prescription

A healthy diet plays a crucial role in the treatment of illness and disease by supplying the energy and nutrients needed for recovery. Some medical conditions can be controlled or improved with a specific diet. For example, a high-fiber diet is often prescribed for gastrointestinal diseases. Sodium restriction often serves as an effective tool for controlling high blood pressure. When the immune system is impaired, a diet rich in protein and nutrients such as vitamin C and iron may give it a boost.

This chapter reviews specific conditions that require additional nutrition therapy not covered in the Healing Food Guide. All the nutrition therapies, however, build upon the Healing Food Guide as the basis for supplying the nutrients necessary for good health. If you are cooking for someone with one of these medical conditions, read the appropriate section.

The information in this chapter is not a substitute for a health care provider's nutritional advice. The course of an illness and any complications may vary from person to person. For this reason, it is not possible to give exact dietary recommendations for each disease or condition. Instead general guidelines for nutritional care are reviewed to help support and explain the information received from a health care provider. He or she has complete access to the appropriate medical information regarding the person you are caring for, which may be essential to develop the best diet for healing.

AIDS/HIV

AIDS is a viral disease that attacks the body's immune system. It knows no limits, infecting babies, children, men, and women alike. There is no cure yet, and we still don't know how best to treat it nutritionally. We do know that malnutrition and muscle wasting caused by poor appetite is a serious problem. Furthermore, if malnutrition can be controlled, the immune system may be able to work longer and better to fight the life-threatening complications of AIDS.

Providing the proper nutrition for an AIDS patient can be tricky. AIDS affects the central nervous system, lungs, liver, and kidney, all of which are essential to the way the body uses nutrients. Fever, diarrhea, and mouth sores that make eating uncomfortable often accompany the disease as it progresses, increasing the chances of malnutrition. Many of the powerful drugs used to treat AIDS patients can cause nausea and loss of appetite, taking the patient further down the road to malnutrition.

Many people with HIV (the human immunodeficiency virus that causes AIDS) can live symptom-free for years. While good nutrition doesn't prevent HIV from developing into full-blown AIDS, it does make a difference, a point that should be recognized from the day of diagnosis. Because a person with HIV who is also malnourished is more likely to be susceptible to colds, flu, pneumonia, and other illnesses, often he or she progresses faster to full-blown AIDS.

Even when symptom-free, HIV-infected people may experience mild zinc, copper, selenium, vitamin B_6, and vitamin B_{12} deficiencies. Left untreated, these deficiencies can compromise the immune system. Thiamin deficiency may also be a complicating factor.

Furthermore, research suggests that intake of certain nutrients in amounts above that needed by healthy persons may be beneficial. A recent study in the *American Journal of*

Epidemiology found that the risk of developing AIDS after testing HIV-positive was 40 to 50 percent lower over a seven-year period among people who consumed the following amounts of nutrients daily, either in food or supplements: 61 milligrams niacin (RDA is 20 mg), 9000 to 20,000 IU vitamin A (RDA is 5000 IU), and 715 milligrams vitamin C (RDA is 60 mg). But twenty milligrams of zinc per day (RDA is 15 mg) appeared to increase the rate at which AIDS developed.

In most cases, HIV-infected people need to eat more than the recommended minimum amounts listed in the Healing Food Guide, particularly if fever or weight loss occurs. Fever increases the need for calories by about 7 percent for each degree above normal body temperature. That's about 175 additional calories for a man who normally needs about 2500 calories daily.

Severe diarrhea, a potential complication of HIV/AIDS, may occur because of intestinal infections, reactions to medical treatments, or malabsorption syndromes brought on by the disease. Whatever the reason for it, diarrhea can lead to poor absorption of nutrients and weight loss.

If the disease results in confusion, dementia, or immobility, food intake may decline with further weight loss. All HIV-infected persons should strive to maintain ideal body weight to help ensure an adequate stockpile of nutrients and calories that may be needed when food intake is poor or nutrient demands increase.

Specific recommendations for determining your patient's calorie needs can be found on page 71. If he or she is not able to eat enough, tube feedings may be used to supply complete nutrition. The perception that tube feedings signal the beginning of the end is totally false. Indeed, they may be just what the patient needs to gain enough strength to resume a normal diet. A 1991 issue of the *American Journal of Nursing* featured three case studies showing how malnutrition and its serious effects can be reversed through aggressive nutrition therapy. In two of the cases, parenteral feedings (through the veins) were effective, and the patients were released from the hospital within two weeks.

Difficulty in chewing and swallowing—obviously an enormous obstacle to eating—may also prevent proper nutrition in the person with AIDS. Oral candidiasis and herpes simplex in the mouth, throat, and esophagus commonly affect those with AIDS and cause significant pain during eating. Modifying the texture of foods, serving liquid foods, and/or avoiding spicy or strong seasonings can help prevent pain and increase the amount of food consumed.

Medications used to treat the complications of AIDS may also cause nutrition problems. Pentamidine, used to treat *pneumocystis carnii* pneumonia (PCP), can interfere with the regulation of blood sugar and cause hypoglycemia, which requires specific nutritional steps for treatment. On the other hand, some foods improve the effectiveness of certain medications. Stomach acid must be present for the antibiotic Ketoconazole to be properly digested, but the disease can reduce stomach acid. It is often recommended that this medication be taken with an acidic beverage, such as orange juice or cola.

The American Dietetic Association Task Force on Nutrition Support in AIDS suggests that all people diagnosed with HIV get a complete nutrition assessment and individual nutrition counseling. The Task Force also recommends that aggressive nutrition support be instituted when indicated and that intake of calories become a priority.

To care adequately for someone who has HIV or AIDS, work with a medical team that includes a registered dietitian or other qualified nutritionist. AIDS can be complicated by many conditions that impose additional nutrient requirements or restrictions. As the symptoms of the disease change, so will the food choices to deal with it.

What to Eat
- A balanced diet based on the Healing Food Guide.

- Enough calories to maintain an ideal weight. Use the formula on page 73 to determine the number of calories needed. Consider using the 100-calorie-an-hour meal plan discussed in Chapter 6.

- Regular meals and snacks. Replace any missed meals with high-calorie snacks or liquids, as suggested in Chapter 6.

- Low-fat, low-fiber foods, if diarrhea is a symptom.

- Soft, bland foods or liquids for a sore mouth or throat. Use a straw to ease swallowing. Frozen pops ease mouth soreness and provide calories and fluid.

- Liquids or medical nutrition supplements if solid foods are refused.

- Vitamin-mineral supplements as directed by the health care provider.

What to Avoid
- Any food not well tolerated.

- Caffeine, if diarrhea is a symptom. It acts as a diuretic, removing water from the body.

- Lactose (milk sugar), if diarrhea is a symptom. See Chapter 16 for information on cooking without milk.

What Else to Do
- Write down the foods eaten on a typical day and compare the result to the recommendations in the Healing Food Guide. Concentrate on providing any missing food groups.

- Keep a record of weight gain and loss. Alert the health care provider of substantial changes.

- Manage symptoms that affect food intake as soon as they arise. Read Chapter 8, But I'm Just Not Hungry.

- Discuss with the health care provider how prescribed medications may affect the digestive system.

- Read about fat in Chapter 15, fiber in Chapter 10, and soft foods in Chapter 9.

Alzheimer's Disease

Alzheimer's disease is characterized by irreversible degeneration of the brain and causes premature and progressive senility. It affects 4 percent of all Americans by the age of sixty-five. By age eighty, the number increases to 20 percent. Some experts believe nutrition plays a role in Alzheimer's. But it's not necessarily what the patient eats; it's the nutrition the brain receives. Normally, blood flow to the brain decreases with age, but the brain compensates by increasing its rate of absorption of oxygen and blood glucose, which it uses for energy. In Alzheimer's, this compensation doesn't seem to take place and may contribute to declining brain function.

Aluminum in the diet has long been linked to Alzheimer's because high levels of the metal have been found in the brains of people who had the disease. But high levels have not been found in other parts of the body, such as the blood, spinal fluid, or hair of Alzheimer's patients. This suggests that aluminum ingestion is not a cause of the elevated brain concentrations, but rather that they are a result of the disease. However, the subject is still controversial. If you will sleep better knowing you are cooking with glass or stainless steel pots and pans instead of those made with aluminum, then by all means do so. At this point, however, avoiding aluminum—which is found abundantly in our soil, water, and food—has not been recommended as a way to prevent Alzheimer's.

In three South Carolina counties, researchers found an inverse relationship between the levels of fluoride in the drinking water and the incidence of Alzheimer's. This suggests that the fluoridated water we drink to help protect our teeth may also help prevent Alzheimer's.

Once Alzheimer's has been diagnosed, nutritional therapies involve keeping the patient in the best health possible. There is no known nutritional method to help cure the disease.

A major problem with Alzheimer's patients is that they often forget to eat, or they eat poorly. If you are caring for someone with the disease, focus on providing enough food and calories to meet nutritional needs. Restlessness, which often accompanies the illness, may increase the need for calories. Forgetfulness may require reminding your patient about meals. Behaviors such as gorging, or refusal to eat and cravings for sweets are not uncommon either. Allow for individual desires, but keep the health care provider informed of any prolonged eating problems.

Safety becomes a serious issue as the disease progresses. Patients can confuse a non-food item like soap with something to eat.

What to Eat
- A balanced diet based on the Healing Food Guide.

- Small, frequent meals at regular times.

- Easy-to-eat finger foods.

- Liquid meals or commercial supplements to help the forgetful, distracted eater.

What to Avoid
- Tough, crunchy foods, to minimize the possibility of choking.

- Changes—in meal schedules, place settings, or utensils—that increase confusion.

What Else to Do
- Maintain family or group meals for as long as possible.

- Serve meals at the same place.

- Keep the table setting simple, with only the required utensils.

- Use a plate that is a different color from the place mat.

- Put catsup, mustard, dressings, and so forth on food before serving it.

- Offer one food at a time. Try not to overwhelm with large servings.

- Stay with the person during meals for safety and companionship. Your patient may mimic your behavior if you eat too.

- Learn what to do if choking occurs. Ask the health care provider how to do the Heimlich maneuver.

- Inform the doctor if swallowing difficulties develop. Read about swallowing problems on page 207.

- Contact the Alzheimer's Association for more information (see Resources, page 340).

Arthritis

Joints may be affected by inflammatory or degenerative changes that cause the pain and stiffness described as arthritis. Over one hundred separate conditions can cause arthritis, including infection after injury, aging, rheumatic fever, gout, psoriasis, and diseases of the nervous system.

The symptoms of *osteoarthritis* are pain in the fingers, thumbs, neck, spine, and/or knees. It results in the progressive breakdown of the joints. Athletes who repeatedly injure a joint face high risk for osteoarthritis, but everyone over the age of fifty-five is likely to experience some form of the disease.

Rheumatoid arthritis can occur from infancy to old age, and it can be the most serious form of arthritis. The exact cause is unknown, but it appears that the immune system actually attacks the joints, causing debilitating inflammation.

Gout, also known as gouty arthritis, can also cause severe pain. It develops when crystals of uric acid form in the joints. The big toe is almost always the first site of occurrence. If left untreated, gout can affect other joints, such as those in the hands, and cause permanent damage.

There are many unproven nutrition remedies suggested for treating arthritis. They range from vegetarian diets to "cleanse" the body or fasting to "rest" it to regular consumption of an elixir of honey and vinegar to "thin" joint fluids and relieve pain. No evidence exists to prove the effectiveness of these remedies. This does not mean, however, that these therapies are all without substance. A study reported in *Lancet* found that patients with rheumatoid arthritis who fasted and then followed a vegetarian diet experienced less joint pain and other negative symptoms than patients following a regular diet. Do not adopt a nutritionally risky regimen such as fasting, however, without the guidance and approval of the health care provider.

Good nutrition, regardless of the form it takes, may also help manage other aspects of the disease. Thiamin levels have been found to be lower in patients with rheumatoid arthritis, perhaps because the body uses thiamin less efficiently. Thiamin-rich diets, with plenty of breads and cereals, help reduce the risk for thiamin deficiency, which can lead to mental confusion, muscular weakness, and more. Aspirin, a drug commonly used to treat arthritis symptoms, may irritate the stomach and cause blood loss, requiring an iron-rich diet to build up the blood.

Other medications prescribed to manage arthritis place their own nutritional demands on the body. For example, researchers found that the diets of fifty-two rheumatoid arthritis patients were low in folic acid, pyridoxine, zinc, and magnesium. In fact, not only were their intakes of these nutrients low, they were taking drugs to treat their disease that are known to interfere with the utilization of the nutrients, magnifying the potential for ill effects.

In at least one study, researchers found fish oil supplements to be helpful in treating arthritis. Patients with rheumatoid arthritis who received high-dose fish oil supplements (41 milligrams omega-3 fatty acids per pound per day) experienced improvement in twenty-one of forty-five clinical measures, such as swollen and tender joints. In comparison, patients receiving low-dose supplements (20 milligrams omega-3 fatty acids per pound per day) experienced improvement in only eight clinical measures. Patients receiving olive oil supplements showed improvement in only five measures.

The bottom line for nutrition therapy in arthritis is that we just don't know enough at this point. Until further studies illuminate the fine points, nutrition therapy should center around healthy eating. No nutrition therapy should ignore the body's need for basic nutrition. An adequate diet can help maintain the integrity of the immune system and relieve symptoms. A poor diet may only make the situation worse.

What to Eat
- A balanced diet based on the Healing Food Guide.

- Eat a variety of fish 2 to 3 times per week.

What to Avoid
- Gout sufferers should avoid beer, which has a higher purine content than wine or liquor, as well as other foods high in purine (see box).

What to Do
- Lose weight if overweight. This may help relieve joint pain.

- Follow medical advice regarding exercise and medications.

- Talk to the health care provider about the use of fish oil supplements in the case of rheumatoid arthritis.

Cancer

Cancer is a family of diseases characterized by the uncontrolled growth of cells in any organ of the body, resulting in tumors or tumor-like growths. With the exception of leukemias, certain lymphomas, and multiple myelomas, cancers usually originate in a single isolated growth; at this early stage, removal of the solitary tumor will cure the disease. Once the cancer cells spread to the bones, liver, or other major organs, however, the disease

PURINE CONTENT OF SELECTED FOODS

Excessive intake of purine may make gout symptoms worse. The American Dietetic Association recommends eliminating all foods that contain more than 150 milligrams of purine per three-ounce serving.

High-Purine Foods (approximately 150 to 825 mg per 3-ounce portion)
Anchovies
Game meats
Gravies
Herring
Mackerel
Meat extracts
Organ meats (brains, kidney, liver, and sweetbreads)
Sardines
Scallops

Moderate-Purine Foods (approximately 50 to 150 mg per 3-ounce portion)
VEGETABLES: Asparagus, cauliflower, mushrooms, green peas, and spinach

BREADS AND CEREALS: Whole-grain breads and cereals, oatmeal, wheat germ, and bran

FISH AND SHELLFISH: All fresh water and saltwater finfish, including eel; crab, lobster, and oysters

LEGUMES: All dried beans, peas, and lentils

MEAT: Beef, lamb, pork, veal, and meat soups and broths

POULTRY: Duck, chicken, and turkey

Low-Purine Foods (approximately 0 to 50 mg per 3-ounce portion)
Cheese and milk
Coffee, tea, and soda
Eggs
Fats
Fish roe (caviar)
Fruits and fruit juices
Gelatin
Most vegetables, except those listed above
Nuts
Refined white bread and cereals
Sugar, syrup, sweets

is not controllable by surgery alone. Carried in the bloodstream or in the network of lymphatic channels to distant parts of the body, cells from the primary tumor "seed" themselves and grow, infiltrating and eventually destroying the healthy tissues around them.

Many of the two hundred and fifty forms of cancer are curable, but the disease as well as the treatment may affect food and nutrient needs at any point during treatment. Loss of appetite, taste changes, increased metabolism rate, and bowel obstructions may occur and, if significant, interfere with good nutrition. Experts believe that the person who is able to stay well nourished significantly increases his or her chances for fighting cancer, reducing side effects and improving a sense of well-being along the way. Taking an active role in maintaining good nutrition can also be a positive way for cancer patients to participate in their care.

The effects of cancer treatment, rather than the cancer itself, often create the biggest challenge to good nutrition. Any form of surgery increases the need for calories and protein to build and repair tissue. Radiation treatments, depending on where the cancer is located, affect nutrition. Radiation of the neck, head, or mouth, for example, can affect taste, smell, and appetite and make swallowing painful. It may also reduce saliva flow, resulting in dental problems, which can in turn increase eating difficulties. Radiation of the stomach or bowels can cause diarrhea and vomiting—two problems that can affect the body's ability to store and use nutrients.

Chemotherapy treatments use powerful medications to stop the growth of cancer cells. Unfortunately, the medications don't distinguish between healthy and cancerous cells, which causes side effects ranging from loss of appetite and stomach upsets to vomiting and diarrhea. People receiving chemotherapy may develop aversions to specific foods, particularly any foods eaten within hours of undergoing treatment. Read more about this on page 203.

As with any illness, effective nutrition therapies to treat cancer must be matched to the symptoms. For example, a person suffering from cancer of the mouth or throat may require a change in the consistency and types of foods eaten. Soft, bland foods, frozen pops, cold fruit juices, and milk shakes may be more appealing and easier to eat.

In general, the person battling cancer needs extra calories and protein to aid in the fight. In most cases, protein needs will be met just by selecting foods from the Healing Food Guide as recommended. Additional protein may be necessary if surgery takes place or weight loss occurs.

The goal of nutrition management in cancer is to achieve and maintain a good body weight and to prevent and correct any nutritional deficiencies. If the person with cancer has never eaten well, now is the time to start. Follow the Healing Food Guide and aim for weight maintenance. If side effects interfere with eating, manage them as soon as possible. Try to replace any lost meals with snacks, liquid drinks, or commercial supplements. Since malnutrition usually increases risk for complications, it makes sense to prevent it.

What to Eat
- A balanced diet based on the Healing Food Guide.

- Small frequent meals, if better tolerated.

- Adequate calories.

- Foods that taste good, even unusual food combinations.

- If food aversions occur, select a replacement within the same food group.

- Soft, bland, and cold foods, if swallowing or mouth discomfort is a problem.

What to Avoid
- Foods with unappealing flavors and smells, even if they have previously been favorites.

- Nontraditional nutrition therapies that do not provide foods from all groups.

- Large meals, if premature fullness is a problem.

What Else to Do
- Manage symptoms that affect eating as soon as they appear. Read Chapter 8, But I'm Just Not Hungry.

- Read about calories and protein in Chapter 4.

- Read Chapter 6, When Every Calorie Counts, if boosting calorie intake is necessary.

- Read about soft diets in Chapter 9.

- Get proper dental care.

- Indulge food cravings if they promote a better food intake.

- Discuss with the health care provider any effects the cancer treatment may have on eating and nutrition. Inquire about the effects of medication on food and appetite.

- Monitor weight and keep the doctor informed of any unwanted changes.

Chronic Obstructive Pulmonary Disease

Chronic bronchitis and pulmonary emphysema are the primary forms of chronic obstructive pulmonary disease (COPD), a disease in which airflow to the lungs is limited. People with COPD are frequently short of breath and quick to fatigue. The effort required to breathe means the person with COPD may need 400–700 calories more than a healthy person, to meet the demands of breathing.

This significant increase in calorie requirements can lead to significant weight loss, and, in turn, decrease in lung function and lower resistance to infection. Other side effects include bloating, an uncomfortable feeling of fullness, and loss of appetite.

On the other hand, in some people COPD can lead to excessive weight gain, as a result of reduced activity levels caused by breathing difficulties and/or increased appetite brought on by medications. As with weight loss, weight gain can increase breathing problems.

The nutritional goal for the patient with COPD, then, is to maintain adequate nutrition without unwanted weight changes. Optimal nutrition intake has been shown to promote improved lung function.

In severe cases, carbohydrates such as sugar and starches may need to be limited. The digestion of carbohydrates produces more CO_2 than digesting protein or fat, placing additional demands on the lungs. The ideal carbohydrate intake differs for each person with COPD and should be discussed with the health care provider.

What to Eat
- A balanced diet based on the Healing Food Guide.

What to Avoid
- More carbohydrate-rich foods than advised by the health care provider.

What Else to Do
- Discuss appropriate eating strategies with the physician or registered dietitian. Ask about your patient's risk for weight loss or gain, as well as about potential drug-nutrient interactions.

- Determine calorie needs (see page 71).

- Monitor weight and respond appropriately.

Coronary Heart Disease

Coronary heart disease is our nation's leading disease killer, accounting for about six hundred thousand deaths each year. Although the condition may develop slowly over many years, its impact is instantaneous in nearly a third of all cases—death is its first manifestation. The blood vessels that provide oxygen and nutrients to the heart are normally elastic and smooth. In coronary heart disease, there is a buildup of plaque—cholesterol, scar tissue, calcium, and other substances—in the lining of these arteries. Excessive amounts of these substances block the flow of blood to the heart muscle, eventually resulting in a heart attack. Angina pectoris, a gripping chest pain, is an early warning sign.

High blood cholesterol ranks as one of the major risk factors for coronary heart disease. Cholesterol is a fatlike substance made in the liver; it is also found in the animal foods, such as eggs and meat, we eat. Interestingly, however, for as many as two thirds of adults, it is not the amount of cholesterol in the diet that contributes to heart disease, but the amount of saturated fat that determines an increased risk for heart disease. The confusion stems from the fact that saturated fat and cholesterol are usually found together in foods such as meat, poultry, cheese, and whole-milk products. Thus, cutting back on sources of saturated fat automatically cuts intake of cholesterol.

A heart-healthy low-fat, low-cholesterol diet features plenty of foods from the Grain/Starch Group, such as breads, rice, pasta, and cereal, along with fruits and vegetables. Animal foods from the Meat Group such as beef, lamb, and pork are more accompaniment than the entrées they usually serve as in traditional Western diets.

High blood cholesterol levels are only one risk factor for heart disease. Others include age (men over forty-five, women over fifty-five, and women of any age who have had an early menopause without estrogen replacement therapy face higher risks), heredity (if heart disease runs in your family, your risk is higher), smoking, high blood pressure, low HDL-cholesterol level (HDLs are the "good" cholesterol; levels are increased through regular exercise and, in smokers, by quitting smoking), and diabetes.

If primarily low-fat foods are selected, the minimum number of servings from each group in the Healing Food Guide provides about 40 to 60 grams of fat and 165 to 220 milligrams of cholesterol. This meets the guidelines for a heart-healthy diet. To satisfy appetite and additional calorie needs, select low-fat foods, particularly those from the Grain/Starch, Vegetable, and Fruit groups. Foods from the Protein and Calcium groups should be lean and low-fat choices, such as lean ground beef, beef and pork loin, veal, poultry without skin, fish, skim and 1 percent milk, and low-fat yogurt and cheeses.

What to Eat

- A balanced diet based on the Healing Food Guide.

- Food prepared using low-fat techniques such as baking, broiling, and steaming.

- Fish two to three times a week.

- Fiber-rich foods.

What to Avoid

- Fried foods.

- Fatty meats and poultry skin.

- More than six ounces of meat or poultry a day.

- Excessive amounts of fats and oils; limit intake to one or two servings at each meal; choose unsaturated fats such as olive, corn, or safflower oil more often than saturated fats such as butter or shortening.

What Else to Do

- Follow a regular exercise program approved by the health care provider.

- Take medications as advised.

- Monitor blood cholesterol levels.

- Read Chapter 15 for more information on low-fat eating.

KNOW YOUR CHOLESTEROL LEVELS

The National Cholesterol Education Program from the National Heart, Lung, and Blood Institute specifies the following healthy levels for different types of blood cholesterol. Check with your health care provider to have your blood levels measured.

Type of Cholesterol	Healthy Levels
Total cholesterol	Less than 200 mg/dl
LDL-cholesterol (the "bad" kind)	Less than 130 mg/dl
HDL-cholesterol (the "good" kind)	From 45 to 75 mg/dl

Diabetes Mellitus

Diabetes develops when the body does not make enough insulin or cannot use the insulin it does make. Insulin is the hormone that helps glucose (blood sugar) enter body cells to be used as energy. If this process does not take place, levels of blood sugar rise to unhealthy levels and can cause fatigue, thirst, and even hunger. Over time, if blood sugar levels remain too high, risk increases for complications such as heart, kidney, and eye disease. Results from the Diabetes Control and Complication Trial (DCCT), released in 1994, unequivocally demonstrate that maintaining blood sugars in an optimal range (80 to 120 mg/dl when fasting, 100 to 140 mg/dl at bedtime, after a day of regular meals) will delay the onset and slow the progression of these long-term diabetic complications.

There are two major types of diabetes. Type 1, also called insulin-dependent diabetes, requires daily insulin injections because the body makes very little or no insulin. In Type 2, or non–insulin-dependent diabetes, the body does make insulin but cannot use it properly. Often oral hypoglycemics (pills) are used instead of injected insulin to help reduce blood sugar levels in Type 2 diabetes. Diet is an essential part of the treatment for both forms of diabetes.

In 1994 the American Diabetes Association released revised nutrition recommendations. There is no longer a general diet prescribed for all diabetics, and sugar is no longer off-limits but can be eaten in moderation in the context of a healthful diet. New research has shown that simple sugars from foods such as candy do not raise blood sugar any faster than other carbohydrate foods, such as the starch from beans, potatoes, or bread. The revised guidelines recommend that the amount of carbohydrate and fat in the diet be tailored to the individual, based on treatment goals. The more important aspects of a diabetic diet include regular timing of meals with a controlled carbohydrate, fat, and calorie intake. Of course, obtaining adequate nutrients for good health is essential.

A cholesterol-lowering diet is also frequently recommended because of the increased risk for heart disease that accompanies diabetes. Foods rich in fiber, such as whole grains, fruits, and vegetables, also may help regulate blood sugar. What's more, whole grains provide chromium; deficiencies of chromium can produce symptoms that mimic diabetes.

People taking pills or insulin to manage diabetes can experience the undesirable symptoms of low blood sugar known as hypoglycemia: headaches, shakiness, and dizziness. Hypoglycemia can be prevented by eating meals on time, taking medications as directed, and snacking before exercise. To treat the symptoms of hypoglycemia when they occur, physicians often recommend consuming a high-sugar food such as orange juice, sweetened soda, or candy.

DIABETES AND SICK DAYS

When illness strikes and appetite declines, the person with diabetes must make adjustments in his or her usual menu. This may be the time when foods containing sugar become a major part of meals. Ginger ale or custard may be appealing and act as temporary meal replacements.

For the person taking insulin or other diabetes medication, an adequate intake of calories is very important to keep blood sugar levels from dropping too low. Check blood sugar levels frequently with a home glucose monitor, and alert the health care provider if levels rise too high or fall too low, or if meals are refused.

The Healing Food Guide recommendations for healthy eating are similar to those suggested in the American Diabetes Association's diabetic exchange diet.

What to Eat
- A balanced diet based on the Healing Food Guide.
- Foods high in fiber.

What to Avoid
- Foods with sugar as the main ingredient, including sweetened sodas, jam, jelly, candy, and syrups. For good nutrition use them only once or twice a week.
- Alcohol; it should be used only as advised by the health care provider or dietitian.
- Foods high in saturated fat and cholesterol.

What Else to Do
- See a registered dietitian affiliated with the health care provider to design an individualized eating plan.
- Eat meals at regular times.
- Exercise regularly and maintain healthy weight or lose weight if overweight.
- Monitor blood sugar as instructed by the doctor. Be prepared for hypoglycemia, keeping a source of sugar in the car, wallet or purse, or desk.
- Read about high-fiber eating in Chapter 10.

HYPOGLYCEMIA

Hypoglycemia occurs when blood sugar levels drop too low. Symptoms include dizziness, headaches, weakness, and trembling. Hypoglycemia may occur in people with diabetes who take insulin or oral hypoglycemics when regular meal patterns are not followed or if too much medication is taken. People with diabetes should work closely with the health care provider and registered dietitian to develop an eating plan that reduces the chances for hypoglycemia to occur.

Reactive hypoglycemia is a rare condition that sometimes occurs in people without diabetes. After they consume sugar-rich foods like sweetened sodas and candy, their blood sugar levels rise and the pancreas releases excess insulin. This causes a drop in blood sugar and accompanying negative symptoms. To prevent hypoglycemia in sugar-sensitive people, a sugar-free diet is often advised. Read more about sugar-free cooking in Chapter 14.

Diseases of the Digestive Tract

The digestive tract includes all the organs that turn food into fuel for the body. If you understand how food becomes assimilated into the body, you will have a better appreciation for the importance of good nutrition when the stomach and intestines are afflicted.

After food is swallowed, it travels down the throat and esophagus into the stomach. In the stomach, food is partially digested and changed into a liquid; it then passes into the small intestine. Most nutrients are absorbed into the body there, as various substances such as bile, enzymes, and hormones work to break food down into its smallest components.

The small intestine is divided into three parts, the duodenum, jejunum, and ileum. The duodenum is attached to the stomach; the ileum is the end of the small intestine, which is attached to the large intestine. The large intestine is wider than the small intestine and consists of six parts, called the cecum, ascending colon, transverse colon, descending colon, sigmoid colon, and rectum.

Nondigestible substances such as fiber pass into the large intestine, where excess moisture is absorbed into the body. The remaining waste is stored there until it is eliminated.

Diseases such as Crohn's disease, ulcerative colitis, hepatitis, cirrhosis, pancreatitis, ulcers, and gallbladder disease all negatively affect the gastrointestinal tract. Because many of the involved organs are located near the digestive tract, poor diet is often thought to be the cause of many of these illnesses. Rarely is this the case, but of course the diet can affect the symptoms and course of the illness.

Diverticulosis

The disease called diverticulosis is characterized by small pouches or sacs protruding through the intestinal membranes. The pouches usually appear toward the end of the large intestine in the sigmoid colon and are caused by pressure in the intestine, which herniates the intestinal wall. The contents of the digestive tract—food waste—may get caught in these small pouches, causing diverticulitis, or inflammation that can lead to bleeding.

A low-fiber diet increases the pressure needed to move the stool through the intestines, whereas foods that leave large amounts of residue in the colon decrease pressure. That makes a high-fiber diet the best nutritional therapy for diverticulosis. It both helps prevent the pouches from forming and reduces the chances that they will become filled with waste and inflamed.

If the pouches become inflamed, the health care provider may advise a clear liquid diet, progressing to a diet low in residue or fiber until inflammation subsides. High-fiber diets are then recommended for the general management of the diverticulosis. If the patient is not accustomed to eating a high-fiber diet, start slowly to avoid problems with gas and cramping. Increase fiber in the diet gradually and make sure the patient drinks plenty of liquids.

What to Eat
- A balanced diet based on the Healing Food Guide.

- Foods high in fiber: unpeeled choices from the Vegetable Group, whole fruits from the Fruit Group, whole-grain cereals and breads and brown rice from the Grain/Starch Group, and beans from the Protein Group.

- Plenty of fluids.

What to Avoid
- Small nuts, seeds, popcorn, strawberries, blueberries, raspberries, and blackberries, if so advised.

What Else to Do
- Follow the doctor's advice if a low-fiber diet is temporarily recommended to treat diverticulitis (inflammation).

- Read about high-fiber eating in Chapter 10.

Gallbladder Disease

The gallbladder's main purpose is to concentrate and store bile, a bitter green liquid that is needed to digest fat. When high-fat foods are eaten, the gallbladder releases bile into the small intestine, where it emulsifies the fat so enzymes can break it down for absorption. If the chemical balance of bile is upset, gallstones may develop.

Gallstones form in the gallbladder and block the flow of bile, inflaming the gallbladder and causing pain, bloating, nausea, and vomiting. Women run a higher risk for developing gallstones than men, but both African-American women and men have a lower rate of gallstones than whites. The disease is commonly linked with obesity.

Gallstone sufferers usually complain of a sharp, steady pain on the right side of the body. If it is severe, the pain can radiate through the chest, shoulders, or back; it is not uncommon to confuse the symptoms with a heart attack.

During acute attacks, patients may be advised to eat nothing at first and then to progress to clear fluids. A soft, fiber-restricted diet often follows, with fat limited to 20 to 30 grams a day.

Otherwise, a diet containing no more than 50 to 60 grams of fat a day, divided into small meals, may best manage symptoms. Some people may experience discomfort after eating spicy foods and should avoid them.

A recent study published in the *Journal of the American Medical Association* revealed a greater incidence of gallstones in obese individuals who were following very low calorie and low fat diets—500 to 1000 calories and only 1 gram of fat. It is thought that such a diet may result in underuse of the gallbladder, allowing the bile to concentrate and form gallstones.

What to Eat
- A balanced diet based on the Healing Food Guide.

- Small, frequent meals.

- No more than two daily servings of animal foods from the Protein Group.

- Only nonfat or low-fat dairy foods from the Calcium Group.

- Low-fat foods from other food groups.

- No more than two to three servings daily from the Fat/Oil Group.

- Foods recommended by the health care provider during periods of acute attack.

What to Avoid
- Spices or seasonings known to cause symptoms.

- Very low calorie and low-fat diets.

What Else to Do
- Lose weight if overweight.

- Read about low-fat cooking in Chapter 15.

Heartburn

Heartburn occurs when some of the acids that normally stay confined to the stomach travel up into the esophagus. Once there, the acids cause a burning feeling in the area of the esophagus that is close to the heart.

A "lazy" esophageal sphincter usually lies at the root of this problem. This sphincter normally acts as a one-way door, allowing entry into the stomach but blocking exit. Sometimes, however, it doesn't work properly, and acids escape upwards, with heartburn the result. Eating low-fat meals and avoiding known irritants may help control symptoms.

What to Eat
- A balanced diet based on the Healing Food Guide.

- Low-fat foods; bake, broil, or boil instead of frying.

- Small, frequent meals.

- Adequate fiber and fluids, to prevent constipation.

What to Avoid

- Chocolate, alcohol, mints, hot peppers, carbonated beverages, citrus and tomato juices, coffee (regular and decaffeinated), and tea, if not well tolerated.

- Smoking.

What Else to Do

- Lose weight if overweight.

- Relax and eat slowly at mealtimes and eat small meals and avoid overeating.

- Avoid eating within three hours before bedtime, do not lie down immediately after eating.

- Elevate the head of the bed.

- Avoid clothing that is tight in the abdominal area.

- Take antacids or medications as prescribed.

- Read about low-fat cooking in Chapter 15.

Inflammatory Bowel Disease

The term *inflammatory bowel disease* refers to several diseases that affect the intestines, including Crohn's disease (or regional enteritis) and ulcerative colitis.

Crohn's disease is a chronic, long-term inflammation of the intestines, usually the lower reaches of the small intestine. It most frequently affects young adults; the cause is unknown. The wall of the small or large intestine—sometimes both—becomes inflamed and can ulcerate. In its active stages, Crohn's disease can cause severe pain, diarrhea, steatorrhea (fatty stool), weight loss, fever, and weakness. It can interfere with appetite and absorption of nutrients and lead to vitamin and mineral deficiencies, protein loss, and even anemia, from blood loss.

In ulcerative colitis, also called simply colitis, the mucous membranes of the colon become inflamed. Again, this disease most often affects young adults, and its cause is unknown. It often leads to frequent urges to defecate, abdominal cramps, diarrhea, weight loss, dehydration, and anemia. During an attack, significant amounts of protein and blood can be lost.

A diet high in calories and protein, along with a vitamin-mineral supplement, helps prevent the serious nutritional deficiencies that can occur with inflammatory bowel disease. When inflammation is present, a diet very low in fiber and residue is usually prescribed; some physicians even recommend total bowel rest, feeding patients parenterally (through the veins) instead. A different type of fat, called medium-chain triglycerides, or MCT oil, which is more easily absorbed, may also be prescribed for a time.

Injections of vitamin B_{12} may be needed if the ileum area of the intestine that absorbs B_{12} is damaged. The doctor can measure B_{12} levels with a simple blood test.

What to Eat
- A balanced diet based on the Healing Food Guide.

- Small, frequent meals including at least one protein-rich food.

- A fiber-rich diet when the disease is inactive, to help keep bowel movement regular. Eat whole-grain foods from the Grain/Starch Group, beans from the Protein Group, and recommended amounts of fruits and vegetables.

What to Avoid
- Milk, hot spices, and alcohol.

- Foods that are not easily digested, such as corn, nuts, and popcorn.

What Else to Do
- Work closely with the health care provider to establish the appropriate nutrition prescription to manage symptoms.

- Stress management may be helpful in ulcerative colitis. So encourage the patient to read the Mind/Body suggestions under Resources.

Irritable Bowel Syndrome

Also known as spastic colon, mucous colitis, or irritable colon syndrome, irritable bowel syndrome (IBS) is characterized by irregular bowel patterns with alternate bouts of constipation and diarrhea. There is no inflammatory process, as in inflammatory bowel disease, but there can certainly be significant discomfort.

IBS affects 15 to 20 percent of children and adults. The cause is unknown, although stress may be a factor. Laxative abuse, inadequate fluid intake, excessive caffeine, and irregular sleep, rest, and bowel habits have all been linked to the syndrome.

Pain most often occurs in the individual's lower left side, caused by spasm-like contractions of the colon, accompanied by alternating periods of constipation and diarrhea. In some cases, the colon may undergo a spasm that temporarily stops the bowel from moving. Bloating, heartburn, and headache may also occur.

Allergies to food may exacerbate or even cause IBS. Studies show that IBS symptoms improve with an allergy-elimination diet (a diet that excludes foods to which the person is allergic). Lactose (milk sugar) and sorbitol (a sugar alcohol commonly found in sugar-free candies) may also cause problems for some people. Eating a menu lower in fat may be helpful too.

There are no clear nutritional guidelines that can help all people with IBS. The appropriate diet must be highly individualized to help treat symptoms specific to the person.

What to Eat

- A balanced diet based on the Healing Food Guide.

- Regularly scheduled meals.

- Appropriate amounts of fiber (when diarrhea strikes, a reduction in fiber may be helpful; when constipation occurs, increase fiber intake by eating high-fiber foods).

- Plenty of fluids.

What to Avoid

- Overeating.

- Lactose and sorbitol, if not well tolerated.

- Laxatives.

- Excessive caffeine intake.

What Else to Do

- Stress management may be helpful.

- Gets adequate rest.

- Exercise regularly; it affects intestinal motility and reduces stress.

- Read about high-fiber eating in Chapter 10 and managing stress in Chapter 19.

Ulcers

An ulcer is a sore that develops in the lining of the digestive tract. All ulcers are referred to collectively as peptic ulcers, although they may also be named by location. For example, a gastric ulcer occurs in the stomach and a duodenal ulcer in the duodenum.

An ulcer develops when there are weak spots in the lining of the stomach or duodenum that have no mucus coating to protect them. Without this protection, anything that touches the eroded area, such as the contents of the digestive tract, can cause a great deal of pain. These acidic gastric juices burn into capillaries, causing the ulcer to bleed. Left untreated, an ulcer can erode the wall of the stomach and lead to perforation of the stomach wall.

Excessive stomach acid or the digestive chemical pepsin may trigger an ulcer in some people, but recent research shows many ulcers may result from a bacterial infection that can be treated with antibiotics. (Not that stress, poor diet, smoking, and alcohol no longer play roles.) Treatment may include the use of antacids, antibiotics, and medications that limit acid production and proper diet.

For many years, a patient with an ulcer was placed on a bland diet of milk, cream, and refined cereals and grains. Fruits and vegetables were limited. This therapy was eventually proven unnecessary, but old traditions die hard. The bland diet continues to be prescribed by health care providers who lack up-to-date knowledge about the role of nutrition and diet in treating ulcers.

We now know that milk, which was once the cornerstone of the bland diet, can actually add to ulcer symptoms by causing an increase in the production of stomach acids. In a study published in the *British Medical Journal,* sixty-five patients hospitalized for ulcer disease were given their choice of an unrestricted menu or a diet consisting primarily of milk. After four weeks, researchers found that more of the people who had chosen from the unrestricted menu had healed ulcers than these on the milk-based diet.

Indeed, people with ulcers who drink milk before bedtime often complain of a sharp gnawing or burning pain that wakes them about two or three hours after going to sleep. While milk does have an initial calming effect, as the night wears on, the proteins, fats, and sugars in milk require digestion—and that calls for more stomach acid. The acid digests the milk but can then inflame the ulcer.

It's not even accurate to say that spicy or high-fiber foods cause trouble for people with ulcers. Another study from the *British Medical Journal* revealed that patients with ulcers who ate cayenne pepper with their meals for four weeks healed at the same rate as patients who did not eat cayenne. And in another experiment described in *Lancet,* the rate at which ulcers recurred was compared in people who ate low-fiber diets versus those who ate fiber-rich diets. The fiber-rich group showed fewer new ulcers.

What to Eat

- A balanced diet based on the Healing Food Guide.

- At least three meals a day, or small, frequent meals for those who gain relief with food (duodenal ulcer pain is often relieved by the presence of food, whereas gastric ulcer pain may be increased).

What to Avoid

- Alcohol.

- Bedtime snacks.

- Beverages that stimulate acid secretion, such as caffeinated and decaffeinated beverages, including coffee and tea.

- Any food that repeatedly causes discomfort.

- Smoking.

- Stress.

What Else to Do

- Eat slowly, chew food thoroughly, and relax at mealtimes.

- Follow the health care provider's advice regarding medication and the use of antacids.

- Read about managing stress in Chapter 19.

Geriatric Conditions

As many as 15 to 20 percent of people over the age of sixty-five may be malnourished. The reasons vary from a decline in taste function, which affects the desire for food, to isolation and depression, which results in a lack of interest in eating. Drug-induced malnutrition also ranks high on the list of possible causes.

As with all people, regardless of age, malnutrition can lead to poor health, in part because it weakens the immune system. In a study of ninety-six independently living, healthy elderly individuals, researchers showed that supplementation with vitamins and minerals significantly reduced the occurrence of illnesses from infections. The supplement included 100 percent of the RDA for most nutrients, with more vitamin E (44 milligrams) and beta carotene (16 milligrams).

Another study of elderly patients hospitalized with hip fractures showed that supplementation with 20 grams of protein daily speeded healing and discharge from the hospital. The patients also had fewer complications and deaths than patients not taking the additional protein.

It's easy to get this small amount of additional protein. A single serving from the Protein Group supplies about 20 grams. A homemade milk shake, eggnog, or commercial liquid supplement (see Chapter 7) also contains the requisite amount of protein.

There are other strategies that may help improve nutrition for the elderly. Eating with others increases the amount of food we eat, no matter what our age. For the person living alone, it's worth the effort to invite others to dinner; the guests can reciprocate at another time. An attractive table set with good china, silver, and place mats or table linens can also stimulate the appetite. Community meal services provide both meals and socialization. Small meals or nourishing liquid meals can help the person with a poor appetite.

Consider the situation carefully before restricting sodium or cholesterol, even when it is recommended by the physician. For the elderly person who is not eating much, the advice to eat less sodium or cholesterol may not apply. If food intake is already low, chances are both cholesterol and sodium intake are also low. Eliminating eggs or favorite salty foods may not be necessary. Furthermore, they may be among the few foods your patient truly likes to eat. Unnecessary restrictions can lead to even lower food intakes and unintended harm.

What to Eat
- A balanced diet based on the Healing Food Guide.

- Small meals, if better tolerated.

- Nutritious snacks based on foods from the food groups.

What to Avoid
- Dieting that limits food intake or eliminates whole food groups.

- Isolation.

What to Do
- Ask the health care provider about the potential effect of any medications on appetite and nutrition.

- Enroll in a community eating program or sign up for Meals-on-Wheels.

- Monitor weight and inform the health care provider of unexpected changes.

- Stay active; exercise strengthens muscles and stimulates appetite.

Hypertension (High Blood Pressure)

High blood pressure and hypertension are interchangeable terms that refer to the fact that blood is traveling through the arteries at a pressure that is too high for good health. Although high blood pressure is symptomless, this does not mean that it is not dangerous. High blood pressure, "the silent killer," affects about sixty million Americans, though only half know they have it.

It's not clear why some people develop high blood pressure. Hypertension can cause long-term damage to the heart, blood vessels, and kidneys, leading to stroke, heart attack, and kidney failure. While it may vary according to age, height, and weight, a normal blood pressure generally falls below 140/90; levels for children are even lower.

High blood pressure is often treated with medication, but proper nutrition can replace drug therapy for some people. Weight loss, reduced alcohol and sodium intake, and a nutritious diet that contains plenty of potassium and calcium can sometimes eliminate the need for medication.

Excess weight carried in the upper half of the body—the classic "spare tire" look—may significantly increase blood pressure. If the individual with hypertension is overweight, even a loss of ten pounds can lower blood pressure. Alcohol intake (liquor, beer, and wine) should not exceed one to two drinks per day.

We now know that too much salt or sodium does not cause high blood pressure, but reducing sodium may help control it. Furthermore, some blood pressure medications work best when sodium intake is low. Some studies have indicated that adequate potassium helps improve blood pressure, perhaps because it helps the body excrete sodium.

Extra calcium may also help reduce blood pressure in some people. The National Health and Nutrition Examination Survey, a periodic survey conducted by the federal government, has found a link between low-calcium diets and high blood pressure in black males.

Blood pressure medications can be expensive and inconvenient and may produce negative side effects. For example, a diuretic pill prescribed to increase fluid elimination to control blood pressure may increase blood cholesterol, raise blood sugar, and lower blood potassium levels. Considering the alternative of a lifetime of drug therapy, good nutrition ranks as the first line of attack against high blood pressure.

What to Eat
- A balanced diet based on the Healing Food Guide.
- Recommended servings from the Vegetable and Fruit groups to meet potassium and fiber needs.

What to Avoid
- Excessive sodium. Read food labels to choose foods low in sodium and prepare foods without adding salt.
- Excessive alcohol, or more than one or two drinks a day; a drink is defined as one and a half ounces of liquor, four ounces of wine, or twelve ounces of beer.

What Else to Do
- Lose weight if overweight and exercise as advised by the physician.
- Control stress.
- Ask the health care provider about cholesterol, diabetes, and other factors that increase risk for heart disease.
- Read Chapter 11 for more information about low-salt cooking.
- Read Chapter 12 for more information on potassium.
- Read about managing stress in Chapter 19.

Kidney Disease

The kidneys are so critical to health that the body comes equipped with two of them; if one kidney quits, the other takes over. Every two minutes, the kidneys completely filter the blood supply, removing wastes and eliminating them into the urine. These organs also help control the amount of fluid in the body and blood pressure.

Severe kidney problems fall into two categories. *Acute renal failure* is the term used to describe a rapid deterioration of the kidneys' ability to remove waste products from the blood. It is brought on quickly by infection or injury. Acute renal failure often can be corrected once the damaging trauma is eliminated or improved.

Unlike acute renal failure, *chronic kidney disease* generally occurs over a number of years as the kidneys' nephrons are destroyed slowly and almost imperceptibly. A number of diseases imitate the chronic kidney failure process, including polycystic disease, high blood pressure, and diabetes.

Diet is extremely important in treating any type of kidney disease. In controlling the types of foods consumed, you also control the amount of wastes, fluid, sodium, and other substances that the kidney must process. If the kidneys do not function properly, these various substances build up in the body, creating serious problems. For example, an accumulation of waste can cause a dangerous internal imbalance that results in lack of appetite, nausea, and fatigue. Toxic waste products can build up to the point where they become life-threatening.

A diet to treat kidney disease must take into account intake of protein, calcium, sodium, potassium, phosphorus, and fluids as well as the type of kidney problem and how quickly the condition is progressing. To determine the exact diet recommendations, the physician must conduct an arsenal of blood tests.

Nutrition goals include supplying the body with the calories and nutrients it needs while not overburdening it with too much of any nutrient that may tax the kidneys. Only the medical team can tailor the diet that is right for anyone with kidney disease.

Before dialysis is prescribed—in which a machine substitutes for the kidneys to cleanse the blood—a diet to help treat kidney problems is often very strict. After dialysis is begun, the diet may be more liberal, but still must be closely controlled according to the individual.

What to Eat
- A diet based on the recommendations of a registered dietitian who specializes in treating kidney disease.

What to Avoid
- Protein, sodium, fluids, potassium, and phosphorus all may need to be controlled based on recommendations from the physician.

What Else to Do
- Discuss the potential benefits of a protein-controlled menu to prevent progression of your patient's form of kidney disease. Read about low-protein diets in Chapter 13 if applicable.

- Refer to Resources (page 340) for organizations from which you can get more information about kidney disease.

Kidney Stones

One in ten Americans develops kidney stones. They can be the size of grains of sand or as big as pennies. When a stone passes through the tubes meant to carry only urine, excruciating pain can result, along with nausea and vomiting.

Most kidney stones contain varying amounts of calcium, oxalate, and phosphorus. Nutrition therapy is aimed at both reducing the saturation level of these minerals in the urine, by increasing fluid intake, and limiting consumption of sodium, calcium, oxalate, and protein. Specific dietary modifications should be individualized according to the type of and cause of the kidney stones.

What to Eat
- A balanced diet based on the Healing Food Guide, limited in the foods outlined below.

- Plenty of fluid: If stones are primarily calcium, the patient should drink at least three quarts of fluid daily; half of the fluid should be water.

What to Avoid
- If stones are primarily calcium, limit calcium-containing foods as well as sodium, oxalate, and protein as advised by the health care provider.

- If stones are primarily oxalate, limit oxalate intake to 50 to 60 milligrams daily (see box).

What Else to Do
- Ask the patient to retrieve a stone from the urine if possible and have it analyzed if not certain of the composition.

- Read Chapter 11 on low-sodium cooking if applicable.

- Review the Calcium Group (page 20) to learn about high-calcium foods if applicable.

- Review the Protein Group (page 19) to learn about high-protein foods if applicable.

FOODS RICH IN OXALATE

The following foods must be used in limited amounts when following an oxalate-restricted diet.

Use in Moderation (contain 2 to 10 mg oxalate per ½ cup)

BEVERAGES: Coffee (limit to 8 ounces daily)

GRAINS/STARCH: Cornbread, sponge cake, canned spaghetti in tomato sauce

FRUITS: Apples, apricots, black currants, peaches, pears, plums, prunes, pineapples, cranberry juice, grape juice, orange juice

MEATS: Sardines

VEGETABLES: Asparagus, broccoli, carrots, corn, cucumber (peeled), iceberg lettuce, lima beans, parsnips, tomato (1 small), turnips; tomato juice

MISCELLANEOUS: Dehydrated chicken noodle soup

Use in Limited Amounts (contain more than 10 mg per ½ cup)

BEVERAGES: Draft beer (bottle beer is okay), Ovaltine and other chocolate beverage mixes, cocoa, tea

GRAINS/STARCH: Grits, soybean crackers, wheat germ, sweet potatoes, fruitcake

FATS: Nuts of any kind

FRUITS: Berries (blackberries, blueberries, dewberries, gooseberries, raspberries, strawberries), Concord grapes, currants, fruit cocktail, lemon, lime and orange peels, rhubarb, tangerine

MEATS: Baked beans with tomato sauce, peanut butter, tofu

VEGETABLES: Beans (green, wax, and dried), beets (roots and greens), celery, chives, eggplant, escarole, greens of any kind, leeks, okra, green peppers, rutabagas, summer squash, watercress

MISCELLANEOUS: Vegetable soup, tomato soup, chocolate, cocoa, marmalade

Liver Disease

While most of us may realize that the liver helps metabolize alcohol, we're not so aware of the many other vital roles it plays in our good health. A diseased liver is a critical situation.

For example, the liver converts carbohydrates into a stored form of energy known as glycogen, to be used when meals are skipped or energy needs are high—for example, during intense exercise. The liver also acts as a giant filter to remove potentially harmful toxins from the blood. And the liver makes bile, which it secretes into the gallbladder for storage and delivery into the intestinal tract when fat is eaten.

The goal of nutrition therapy in liver disease is to provide vital nutrients while allowing the liver to rest and heal. Except in liver failure, providing generous amounts of protein, carbohydrates, vitamins, and minerals is wise.

Cirrhosis

In cirrhosis, healthy liver cells are damaged and replaced by scar tissue that cannot perform the functions of normal liver tissue. It may result from inadequately treated hepatitis, problems such as hemachromatosis (iron overload), poisoning, or prolonged biliary stasis, in which bile does not flow normally and stagnates. Most often, however, it results from chronic alcoholism accompanied by its frequent partner, malnutrition.

Symptoms include loss of appetite, nausea, vomiting, and jaundice. In advanced stages, edema (fluid retention), ascites (fluid retention in the abdomen), and liver failure may occur.

Nutritional therapy is based primarily on the Healing Food Guide, although poorly nourished patients may need a high-calorie diet. To prevent liver failure, protein intake should be appropriate to the stage of the disease. Excessive amounts of protein may lead to a buildup of ammonia, a by-product of protein digestion that must be removed from the body by the liver. With less protein, less ammonia is produced, and the liver has less work to do.

In general, protein intake should not exceed 60 to 70 grams per day. You should work closely with the health care provider to determine the amount that is right for your patient. In advanced stages of the disease, the patient may even require special prescriptions for amino acids, medications to help control ammonia production, and special formulas to increase calorie intake. Patients with edema or ascites may also be advised to restrict sodium and fluid.

Vitamin deficiencies are common in patients with liver disease. Vitamin supplements, particularly those that include folic acid, vitamin B_{12}, and thiamin, may be required.

What to Eat

- A balanced diet based on the Healing Food Guide.

- A vitamin supplement containing folic acid, vitamin B_{12}, and thiamin if nutritional intake was poor prior to development of the disease. Vitamin supplements may also be required if protein intake is less than 50 grams per day; check with the health care provider.

What to Avoid

- Alcohol.

- Protein, sodium, and fluids in excess of that advised by the health care provider.

What Else to Do

- Make sure the patient takes medications as prescribed.

- Read about sodium sources in Chapter 11 if applicable.

- Read about fluid restriction in Chapter 17 if applicable.

- Read about low-protein diets in Chapter 13 if applicable.

Fatty Liver

Too much alcohol on a consistent basis can cause a fatty liver. When the liver must focus on metabolizing alcohol, the normal chemical balance in the body is disrupted and leads to a buildup of fatty acids in the liver.

The condition can be very serious, because a fatty liver cannot carry out the many vital functions a normal liver performs. For example, a fatty liver cannot activate vitamin D, which is necessary to enable this nutrient to do its work. A fatty liver cannot produce or excrete the bile essential to the digestion of fat. It may also fail to make some amino acids, which can lead to a less effective immune system.

A fatty liver is only the first phase of alcohol-related liver disease. If left untreated, it can progress to fibrosis of the liver. Ultimately, if alcohol abuse continues, cirrhosis occurs—a life-threatening and irreversible condition. Good nutrition alone will not prevent or reverse a fatty liver—abstinence from alcohol is essential.

What to Eat

- A balanced diet based on the Healing Food Guide.

What to Avoid

- Alcohol.

What Else to Do

- Join an alcohol support group.

Hepatitis

Viruses, poisons, and even medicines a doctor prescribes can cause hepatitis. Type A (infectious hepatitis) is transmitted through personal contact with contaminated drinking water or food that has been contaminated by someone with the disease (who does not wash his hands) after using the bathroom. Type B (serum hepatitis) occurs more commonly and is passed on through unsterilized needles, blood transfusions, and contact with bodily fluids such as saliva, tears, and blood.

Symptoms include inflammation and degeneration of the liver, loss of appetite, nausea, vomiting, fever, abdominal pain, diarrhea, weight loss, and jaundice. In the acute stages, patients may be fed parenterally (via the veins) or by tube feedings. Otherwise, meals are designed to regenerate tissue and stop further destruction.

What to Eat
- A balanced diet based on the Healing Food Guide.
- Six small daily meals, if appetite is poor.
- Adequate protein, calories, and carbohydrate; if weight loss and other signs of malnutrition are significant, the patient may need to eat at least 3000 calories and 100 grams of protein each day.

What to Avoid
- Alcohol.
- Protein-rich foods, if the condition progresses to hepatic encephalopathy. Seek the help of a doctor or registered dietitian.
- Strongly flavored vegetables, rich desserts, and highly seasoned foods, if not well tolerated.

What Else to Do
- Make sure your patient gets plenty of rest.
- Read about eating adequate protein and calories in Chapter 4.

Multiple Sclerosis

Multiple sclerosis (MS) is a disease marked by patchy loss or destruction of the protective myelin covering of the nerve fibers of the brain and spinal cord. Many people with multiple sclerosis turn to unproven nutritional therapies to help treat this disease. Yet according to the National Multiple Sclerosis Society, there are no special diets that will improve the signs and symptoms of MS.

Probably the best documented, but still controversial, dietary treatment for MS is a low-fat diet. Dr. R. L. Swank studied 144 MS patients following low-fat diets for thirty-four years. He found that those who ate 20 grams or less of fat per day showed significantly less deterioration and lower death rates than those who consumed more fat. The greatest results were seen in patients who had only minimum disabilities when they began the low-fat diet. Other researchers report that decreasing intake of saturated fat (found in foods such as meat and milk products) and increasing intake of polyunsaturated fats seems to help treat mild cases of MS. The Multiple Sclerosis Society does not endorse extremely low fat diets to treat the disease, but does state that well-balanced low-fat diets may be beneficial to everyone.

Indeed, proper nutrition, which includes a diet not overly rich in fat, is undeniably important. The right foods can help prevent anemia, protein deficiencies, obesity, and constipation and can aid in the fight against complications by keeping the immune system healthy. Urinary tract infections can be common, and foods that acidify the urine may help prevent and treat such infections.

In a 1990 issue of *Lancet,* several physicians from the Cleveland Clinic recommended that all patients diagnosed with MS be screened for deficiencies of vitamin B_{12}. The recommendation came after a patient had been treated for MS for fifteen years, only to find that she suffered from a deficiency of B_{12}, which can mimic MS symptoms.

What to Eat
- A balanced diet based on the Healing Food Guide.

- Foods rich in fiber, to help prevent constipation.

- Acidic foods, including cranberry juice, plums, prunes, and prune juice, to help prevent and treat urinary tract infections.

- Adequate fluids.

What to Avoid
- Nutritional therapies that do not provide adequate nutrition.

- Excessive weight gain, which can in itself hamper mobility.

What Else to Do
- Maintain a healthy body weight.

- Read about high-fiber eating in Chapter 10.

- Follow the health care provider's recommendations for treating complications such as constipation, urinary tract infections, and weight gain. Ask about the benefits of a low-fat diet, and read about low-fat cooking in Chapter 15.

Pancreatitis

When pancreatitis occurs, it blocks the flow into the intestine of enzymes that are necessary to digest food. Without these enzymes, fat, protein, and carbohydrate cannot be completely broken down and absorbed. Undigested fat in the stool in particular interferes with the absorption of fat-soluble vitamins and may cause nausea and diarrhea.

In acute attacks, patients may initially be fed parenterally (via the veins) in order to stop all pancreatic secretions and to allow the pancreas to rest. When eating is resumed, clear liquids are given first, progressing to a soft fiber-restricted diet. Over the long term, a diet high in protein, moderate to high in carbohydrate, and low in fat ranks as the best nutritional therapy to help prevent or reverse malnutrition and improve digestion and absorption of protein and carbohydrate. Because the amount of fat tolerated is often specific to the individual, you should discuss the level of fat restriction your patient needs with the health care provider. A supplement of medium-chain triglycerides (MCT), a form of fat that is more easily digested, may be necessary to increase calories.

What to Eat
- A diet based on the Healing Food Guide.

- A low-fat diet including only nonfat or low-fat dairy products from the Calcium Group and no more than two servings of animal foods from the Protein Group and two servings from the Fat/Oil Group each day.

- Foods from the Vegetable, Fruit, and Grain/Starch groups.

- MCT oil to add calories, if recommended by the health care provider (see page 186).

What to Avoid
- Fried foods or foods prepared with added fats such as creams, sauces, gravies, butter, margarine, or regular salad dressings.

What Else to Do
- Keep a food diary to determine which foods cause diarrhea or other discomfort. Use it to help the health care provider determine the amount of fat your patient can tolerate.

- Read about low-fat eating in Chapter 15.

Parkinson's Disease

Parkinson's disease is a progressive, degenerative illness characterized by jerky tremors, slow movement, and rigid muscles. The disease results from a loss of the nerve cells that produce dopamine, which is necessary for control of voluntary movement and regulation of muscle tone. While there is no cure for Parkinson's disease, it is not fatal. People with the disease, however, face greater risk for infections, pneumonia, blood clots, and malnutrition.

The risk for malnutrition exists because the once-simple task of eating—getting food from the plate to the mouth—becomes a challenge. Tremors frustrate the process and the patient, often reducing the amount of food consumed as shakiness becomes more pronounced. Difficulties with chewing and swallowing also occur, as well as changes in appetite and digestive disturbances such as constipation. Caloric requirements may be higher because of muscle tremors or lower because of decreased activity.

Fortunately, most people with Parkinson's rarely suffer all these problems. Because the problems do vary from person to person, however, there is no one diet for all patients with the disease. Nutrition care must be matched to the needs of the individual patient, and a registered dietitian can help design a plan to meet each person's needs.

One nutrition program that has drawn much attention for the treatment of Parkinson's disease is known as the Protein Redistribution Diet. In 1986, Dr. Jonathan Pincus reported a study conducted at Yale New Haven Hospital of eleven patients who suffered crippling fluctuations in their ability to move caused by Parkinson's. On a dietary regimen that contained almost no protein during the day, but unlimited protein between seven in the evening and midnight, the patients experienced improved symptoms and a reduced need for medication.

If dietary protein is controlled, the medicines used to treat Parkinson's act more effectively. These medicines—L-dopa and Sinemet (a drug containing L-dopa)—lose their effectiveness as the disease progresses, because of competition for pathways into the brain from amino acids found in protein. Limiting protein to the evening hours leaves the pathways free for the medication to enter the brain during the day.

The Protein Redistribution Diet is not an easy regimen. It limits protein to 10 grams throughout the day. That means no foods from the Protein Group, no dairy from the Calcium Group, and a very limited and careful selection from the Grain/Starch Group; nuts must also be excluded. Unlimited amounts of fruits and low-protein vegetables, such as cucumbers and lettuce, can be eaten, as well as most items from the Fat/Oil Group.

The diet does not offer a cure, but it may be helpful to people who respond unpredictably to their medications. The downside seems to be that symptoms improve during the day, only to return in such force as to immobilize the patient at night. Meeting nutritional needs can be tough too, but not impossible.

A study reported in the *American Journal of Clinical Nutrition* found that otherwise healthy and motivated individuals with Parkinson's will maintain adequate intakes of most nutrients while restricting protein intake during the day. Calcium was the hardest nutrient to get in recommended amounts, and intakes of protein, iron, phosphorus, riboflavin, and niacin were decreased while on the diet. This potential decrease is of no concern, provided the patient's normal food patterns supply plenty of these nutrients. But anyone considering undertaking such a regimen should talk first with the health care provider and a registered dietitian.

What to Eat
- A balanced diet based on the Healing Food Guide.

- Soft and liquid foods, if chewing or swallowing is a problem.

- Appropriate number of calories (determined by activity level, type and degree of movement disorder, and weight).

- Small, frequent meals, if better tolerated.

- Low to moderate fat intake.

What to Avoid
- Substantial weight change.

- Inadequate nutrition intake.

What Else to Do
- Discuss the appropriateness of the Protein Redistribution Diet with the health care provider. Read about low-protein eating in Chapter 13.

- If extra calories are needed, read ways to increase calorie intake in Chapter 6.

- Read about soft foods in Chapter 9 and liquid meals in Chapter 7.

- Get special utensils to help make eating easier (see Resources, page 340).

Surgery

Research clearly shows that well-nourished patients experience fewer complications and heal faster after surgery than poorly nourished ones. Malnutrition among hospitalized patients, however, is not uncommon. A groundbreaking study reported in 1974 in the

Journal of the American Medical Association found that more than 50 percent of general surgery patients had moderate to severe protein-calorie malnutrition (see Chapter 4). It is likely that increased recognition of the importance of nutrition since that study has significantly decreased this percentage, yet malnutrition continues as a common and serious problem for surgical patients.

Along with protein and calories, many other nutrients play vital roles in the healing process that takes place following surgery. For example, vitamin K is necessary for blood clotting, and vitamin C and iron boost the immune system, thereby affecting rate of healing. An adequate diet generally supplies sufficient amounts of these nutrients even for someone who has undergone surgery. But the common pre- and postoperative practices of allowing a patient no food or prescribing a clear liquid diet severely jeopardize adequate intake. If a patient must abstain from food or drink only clear liquids for a prolonged period of time, nutritional supplements are clearly called for.

Obviously there is little that can be done before an emergency operation, other than to eat healthfully as a regular habit. But for the chronically ill person who faces possible future surgery, good nutrition should form the very basis for treatment, to ensure that the body is ready to repair and heal surgical wounds if need be.

What to Eat

- A balanced diet based on the Healing Food Guide.

- Additional foods from the food groups to meet protein and calorie needs.

- One serving of vitamin C–rich food daily.

What to Avoid

- Unwanted weight loss.

- Missed meals.

What Else to Do

- Monitor the patient's weight; help him or her within a healthy weight range. Inform the health care provider of unwanted changes.

- Read more about meeting protein and calorie needs in Chapter 4.

- Replace missed meals with liquid meals or high-protein desserts. See Chapters 6 and 7.

protein and calories

A LIFESAVING COMBINATION

4

Alzheimer's disease, cancer, liver disease, lung disease, and AIDS are just a few of the many illnesses that can interfere with food intake and cause life-threatening weight loss. The most serious nutrition condition that occurs when someone is unwilling or unable to eat is protein-calorie malnutrition, caused by a chronically inadequate intake of calories, and leading to muscle wasting, loss of fat stores, and generalized weakness. Protein is part of the equation because, without enough calories, the body uses protein as an energy source. This can create a deficiency of protein, disturbing the vital functions of tissue repair and immunity.

Protein-calorie malnutrition develops gradually during illness: A meal is missed here and there, a dinner is left unfinished, nerves and anxiety rob the appetite. In the beginning, the changes that occur are so subtle they may go unnoticed. These changes show up as weight loss, less luster in the hair, dry skin, brittle nails, and longer healing times for cuts and scratches. Most people expect some weight loss to accompany illness and aren't surprised or alarmed when it does happen—at least not initially.

But waiting until malnutrition sets in before taking action only increases the challenge of providing adequate nutrition for a person with a serious illness. At that point, all sorts of bad side effects can add to existing problems. At the very least, malnutrition can prolong the time it takes to heal and interfere with the success of treatments. It definitely decreases resistance to secondary infections (those to which the body has less resistance because of the initial illness).

Too often, when weight loss starts, the only nutrition recommendation you may hear from the health care provider is the woefully inadequate advice to "eat a little more." As crazy as it seems, everyone agrees that nutrition matters, but rarely is the traditional health care system aggressive about it until the situation becomes so serious it can't be ignored.

Don't wait until the health care team decides nutrition is important. Take action as soon as the individual is diagnosed with a disease or illness. Learn the potential nutrition complications and move to prevent them immediately.

The information in this chapter will help you calculate and evaluate your patient's intake of protein and calories to help him or her avoid the serious complication of protein-calorie malnutrition and its consequences.

Who Is at Risk for Protein-Calorie Malnutrition?

Anyone who experiences unwanted weight loss from illness or following surgery runs the risk of developing protein-calorie malnutrition. In general, a loss of 5 to 10 percent of normal body weight signals risk.

Once protein-calorie malnutrition has occurred, the health care provider can gauge the severity of the malnutrition using blood tests that measure substances such as albumin, transferrin, and lymphocyte count. While these laboratory tests help identify the presence of malnutrition, the ideal situation is to prevent it before it occurs.

Preventing Protein-Calorie Malnutrition

Providing adequate protein along with enough calories in the form of carbohydrate and fat at meals and snacks will prevent protein-calorie malnutrition. When adequate calories are supplied in this manner, the protein in the diet is spared performing the critical tasks of healing and repairing the body.

To determine individual needs for protein and calories, use the calculations in this section, based on general guidelines for intake. Then use these calculated figures to evaluate whether the minimum number of servings from the different groups in the Healing Food Guide meet your patient's needs. On page 75, I've listed the average protein and calorie content in one serving from each food group for this purpose. If your patient's needs aren't met by the minimum number of servings, add more servings to reach the necessary level. Some medical conditions, such as kidney and liver disease, may make it necessary to adjust these guidelines even further; discuss this possibility with the health care provider.

Monitoring Weight

To enable you to monitor weight accurately, ask that weight be recorded at every doctor's visit, and check it once a week at home. Fluctuations of one to two pounds are usually insignificant in someone who is at or near his or her normal weight. Look instead for a trend in weight patterns. If a person loses weight steadily month after month, even if it is only a small amount, the weight loss is an indicator that not enough food is being consumed.

Recording and monitoring weight in this manner can reassure and help you as the caregiver. Your concern for the amount of food your patient eats may sometimes give rise to conflict over the patient's lack of desire to eat. Using weight records as an objective measure may help ease such conflict or prevent it from arising.

Determining Calorie Needs

Calorie requirements in healthy persons are a function of body size, musculature, and weight. Body weight, however, is most frequently used to calculate calorie requirements.

Often weight charts such as the one on page 72 are used to compare present weight with what is considered normal or "ideal" for men or women in a given age group. While these charts do not tell the whole story, they can be a useful resource.

During illness, conditions such as fever and infection can increase calorie needs above those based on weight alone. Follow the steps below to roughly calculate your patient's needs. Check with the health care provider if you have any questions.

STEP 1: Check the weight chart below to determine ideal body weight.

STEP 2: Multiply the ideal body weight by
13 if your patient is sedentary,
15 if your patient is moderately active,
20 if your patient performs hard labor or other strenuous activity.

NOTE: If fever or infection is present, use the activity level just above your patient's. For example, multiply by 15 if your patient is feverish and confined to bed.

STEP 3: If your patient needs to gain weight, an additional 500 calories per day should be sufficient to gain one pound per week. An additional 1000 calories per day should ensure a gain of two pounds per week.

Suggested Weights for Adults

Height[1]	Weight in pounds[2]	
	19 to 34 years	35 years and over
5'0"	97–128[3]	108–138
5'1"	101–132	111–143
5'2"	104–137	115–148
5'3"	107–141	119–152
5'4"	111–146	122–157
5'5"	114–150	126–162
5'6"	118–155	130–167
5'7"	121–160	134–172
5'8"	125–164	138–178
5'9"	129–169	142–183
5'10"	132–174	146–188
5'11"	136–179	151–194
6'0"	140–184	155–199
6'1"	144–189	159–205
6'2"	148–195	164–210
6'3"	152–200	168–216
6'4"	156–205	173–222
6'5"	160–211	177–228
6'6"	164–216	182–234

[1]Without shoes.

[2]Without clothes.

[3]The higher weights in the ranges generally apply to men, who tend to have more muscle and bone; the lower weights more often apply to women, who have less muscle and bone.

Source: *Dietary Guidelines for Americans,* 3rd Edition, 1990, U.S. Department of Agriculture, U.S. Department of Health and Human Services.

DETERMINING CALORIE NEEDS—AN EXAMPLE

A sedentary 5'9" man at his desirable weight of 160 pounds needs approximately 2080 calories each day to maintain his weight:

160 (weight) x 13 (activity level) = 2080 (calorie requirement)

If he needs to gain weight, add 500 calories per day to gain one pound a week:

2080 (calories needed to maintain weight) + 500 (extra calories) = 2580 (daily calories needed to gain 1 pound a week)

Calorie Worksheet

To maintain weight: Ideal weight ____ x activity level ____ = ____ calories needed daily

To gain weight: Daily calories needed ____ + ____ extra calories* = ____ daily calorie goal

*Add 500 extra calories per day to gain one pound per week; 1000 extra calories per day to gain two pounds per week.

What about the person who is underweight to start with? If your patient has always weighed less than the ideal weight suggested on the chart, try to build up his or her weight to within the suggested range. This can be particularly important if the disease he or she is battling is likely to be long and debilitating. Padding the body with extra fat holds fuel in reserve for days when meals are missed. A weight gain usually indicates an improved nutrient intake as well.

Determining Protein Needs

In healthy men and women, the RDA for protein ranges from 44 to 63 grams a day. This amount is easily reached and often exceeded by most Americans. During illness, however, weight loss, surgery, or a disease that increases protein needs may mean your patient needs about 100 grams of protein each day. A more accurate protein requirement can be calculated based on body weight.

Multiply body weight in pounds by:

.364 to maintain protein stores

.68 if a high-protein diet is ordered (often needed when fever, infection, surgery, or weight loss has occurred; check with the health care provider)

DETERMINING PROTEIN NEEDS—AN EXAMPLE

A 160-pound man needs approximately 58 grams of protein each day to maintain protein stores.

160 (pounds) x .364 = 58 (grams of protein needed daily to maintain protein stores)

If he has lost weight due to illness, or suffered prolonged fever or infection, his need for protein may increase to about 110 grams of protein each day.

160 (pounds) x .68 (grams protein) = 110 (grams of protein needed daily)

Your Protein Worksheet
____ Ideal body weight (pounds) x ____ (protein requirement*) = ____ grams of protein needed daily

*Multiply by .364 to maintain protein stores; by .68 if high-protein diet is needed.

Eating to Provide Protein and Calories

Together, the minimum number of servings recommended from each food group in the Healing Food Guide supply the body with approximately 80 grams of protein and 1600 to 2000 calories, depending on the particular foods selected. As discussed above, this amount of protein meets the needs of most people, although special situations such as fever, infection, surgery, or weight loss can increase needs to about 100 grams per day. Many people who have lost weight and need to stop further loss require a high-calorie, high-protein menu containing about 2500 calories each day.

To help you modify the Healing Food Guide to meet your patient's individual needs, I give the approximate calorie and protein content of one serving from each food group. To make it easier, I've also listed the minimum number of servings from each group that, when eaten over the course of a day, will together provide a menu containing 100 grams of protein and 2500 calories.

Protein Group

ONE SERVING PROVIDES: 21 grams protein, 150 to 300 calories. Include at least three servings daily in a 100-gram-protein, 2500-calorie diet. Select at least one serving of a *complete* protein food each day. Try to include one egg daily, because eggs are a superb protein source.

Calcium Group

ONE SERVING OF DAILY FOOD PROVIDES: 8 grams protein, 160 calories; one serving of nondairy food provides: 1 to 2 grams protein, 25 calories.

Include at least three servings dairy foods daily in a 100-gram-protein, 2500-calorie diet. Choose whole milk, eggnog, custard, and fruited yogurts for both protein and calories. Low-fat dairy foods do not provide sufficient calories.

Vegetable Group

ONE SERVING PROVIDES: 2 grams protein, 25 calories. Include at least three servings daily in a 100-gram-protein, 2500-calorie diet. Vegetables carry important nutrients but not much protein; increase their protein value by serving them with a protein-rich cheese or a milk-based white sauce.

Fruit Group

ONE SERVING PROVIDES: 0 to 1 gram protein, 60 calories. Include at least three servings daily in a 100-gram-protein, 2500-calorie diet. Fruits carry important nutrients but not many calories. If your patient's appetite is poor, serve the minimum number of servings from this group, then offer other higher-calorie foods.

Grain/Starch Group

ONE SERVING PROVIDES: 2 to 3 grams protein, 80 calories. Include at least eight servings in a 100-gram-protein, 2500-calorie diet. Add fats such as butter, mayonnaise, and sour cream to increase calories if needed.

Fat/Oil Group

ONE SERVING PROVIDES: 0 to 1 gram protein, 45 calories. Include at least six servings in a 100-gram-protein, 2500-calorie diet. Most foods in this group provide plenty of calories but little protein. When consumed in adequate amounts, nuts contribute a significant amount of protein (1 ounce of dry-roasted peanuts contains about 6 grams protein).

Other Foods

Seasonings, condiments, coffee, and tea contain little protein and few calories. Avoid filling your patient up with these relatively low calorie foods. Soups and casseroles made with hearty amounts of meat, fish, poultry, eggs, or cheese are good protein sources. Desserts made with milk and/or eggs contribute valuable amounts of protein and calories.

SAMPLE MENU FOR A 100-GRAM-PROTEIN, 2500-CALORIE DIET

Breakfast
1 scrambled egg
1 English muffin (white or whole wheat) with 1 tablespoon butter
³/₄ cup orange juice

Midmorning snack
1 cup fruit yogurt

Lunch
Turkey sandwich made with 2 ounces sliced turkey and 1 tablespoon
  mayonnaise
1 cup vegetable soup
1 cup whole milk
2 oatmeal cookies

Afternoon snack
1 tablespoon peanut butter spread on 3 graham crackers

Supper
4 ounces beef
¹/₂ cup buttered rice
¹/₂ cup buttered mixed vegetables
1 small roll
¹/₂ cup fruit cocktail with 1 tablespoon whipped cream

Evening snack
Milk shake (1 cup) and 3 small cookies

FAT, CHOLESTEROL, AND PROTEIN AND ILLNESS

Most Americans eat too much protein, fat, and cholesterol; hence all the advice to eat less meat and cut back on eggs, which contain large amounts of these substances. During illness, however, low-cholesterol, low-fat eating recommendations may not be to your patient's best advantage. When the appetite is poor or the need for protein and calories increases, eggs and meat can be a valuable addition to the diet. Keep in mind that the risk of malnutrition is of more immediate concern than the risk created by a high-cholesterol level. When the critical phase of the illness has passed, a more prudent diet may once again be appropriate.

foods and recipes to speed recovery

My philosophy on cooking for someone who is ill is simple: Make every bite count. These recipes are meant to help you do just that. They give you ideas for easy-to-prepare yet nutritious and good-tasting meals.

The recipes feature foods suggested in the Healing Food Guide. Some lend themselves to batch cooking and can be prepared and frozen in individual portions for use at a later time. Others are written with smaller portions in mind: one for eating when the recipe is prepared, one or two for reheating later. I've also included recommendations for how long to refrigerate or freeze each dish based on food safety guidelines from the U.S. Department of Agriculture.

My experience has taught me that unseasoned foods become boring. To keep foods interesting, many of these recipes call for garlic, onions, herbs, and spices. Yet taste changes frequently occur when someone is ill, and seasonings may need to be adjusted or eliminated if they become unappetizing to your patient. Garlic may taste too strong, and you might want to eliminate it entirely. Sugar may taste too sweet; you can often cut the amount called for in half without making much difference in the quality of the food. Don't be afraid to experiment. In fact, reducing the sugar or seasonings in any of these recipes will have little effect on the dish. The calories in the dish will be affected minimally and the protein not at all.

I've used fruits and vegetables in many of these recipes. These foods contain vitamins, minerals, and other components that may promote healing. They should be included whenever possible.

A Word About Fat

As you thumb through this chapter, you may be surprised to see so many recipes that include rich sauces, meat, fish, chicken, and even eggs. Certainly, the trend today is to avoid a high-fat diet. But remember that the person who isn't eating much needs to make every bite count. The fat in a white sauce made with butter provides extra calories, allowing the protein the patient eats to be used to keep the immune system healthy and repair worn or damaged tissues. The much-maligned egg is actually an inexpensive and efficient way to get a significant amount of complete protein.

When milk is called for in the ingredients, choose whole milk rather than low-fat versions. One cup of whole milk contains 160 calories; skim milk has only about 90 calories. Low-fat dairy products are recommended only if your patient has been advised to limit the amount of fat in his or her diet or if the fat in the whole milk causes digestive problems.

Many of the recipes use butter, olive oil, and canola oil. It may surprise you to see that I recommend butter over margarine. But butter has a superb taste, and this fact alone might improve interest in eating. While butter does contain saturated fatty acids that can be partly responsible for raising blood cholesterol to undesirable levels in healthy people, this possibility is a less immediate concern during serious illness than meeting calorie and protein needs.

I also use olive oil for extra flavor. Most of the fat in olive oil is monounsaturated, the type that research indicates may be helpful in preventing several diseases, including heart disease and cancer.

Canola oil is a less flavorful but still highly monounsaturated fat. It has the same cooking qualities as vegetable and corn oils. If you prefer other oils such as vegetable, corn, or safflower, these can be substituted for the canola with no change in flavor or the final quality of the dish. These polyunsaturated oils can also be part of a healthy diet.

While oil and butter are an easy way to add calories, fatty foods are often not well tolerated in illness. As a result, I have tried to keep the fat content of the recipes moderate.

You'll notice I list canned broth first, followed by homemade stock, in the ingredient list. Homemade stock is lower in sodium but canned broth is more convenient and most people can handle the sodium it carries. I use very little salt in the recipes simply because I prefer the natural taste of food. In some cases, salted butter or canned broth is the only source of added salt. In general, the only people who must restrict salt are those who retain fluid or have high blood pressure. If the health care provider has not specifically advised limiting salt, and if a food tastes better to your patient when sprinkled with salt, by all means use it. You can read more about salt-free cooking in Chapter 11.

How to Use the Recipes

After reading Chapter 4, Protein and Calories: A Lifesaving Combination, use the following recipes to meet these needs. There are recipes for breakfast foods, soups, vegetables, pasta, bean, and grain dishes, chicken, fish and shellfish, beef, lamb, and pork dishes, and desserts. These are the foods that my clients with illnesses request most often. Read the introductions to each section to learn how to create an appealing menu from these recipes and meet the nutrition needs of your patient at the same time. Using the nutrient information that follows each recipe, select dishes that will meet the recommended requirements for protein and calories.

The recipes that follow are intended to guide you. While they are designed to be nutritious and appetizing, they may not appeal to your patient's personal preferences. Use them as a starting point and prepare tailor-made dishes.

Breakfast

If breakfast is the favorite meal of the day, use it as an opportunity to serve protein-rich foods. Better yet, serve traditional breakfast foods three times a day if that's what your patient enjoys. Good choices are usually cooked foods, such as pancakes, French toast, ham, or sausage. Bacon contains more fat than protein, making it a good calorie source (one slice contains 30 calories). Eggs prepared in any manner are a superb morning food when calories and protein are needed. Cereals, both hot and cold, contain only a third of the protein of one egg. To add protein, serve cereals with Fortified Milk (page 172). Make toast, bagels, or muffins richer in protein by topping them with peanut butter, a slice of cheese, Luscious Lemon Curd (page 170), or Creamy Yogurt Cheese (page 171). Some of these recipes, such as Brown Sugar Breakfast Rolls (page 93) and Fluffy French Toast (page 89) can be assembled ahead of time and cooked later.

Sheila's Egg Puff

MAKES 2 SERVINGS

This is my sister's quick protein-rich breakfast. Combining eggs and milk with fruit results in a fluffy, soufflé-like omelet. I prepare this when I want to serve a hot breakfast but don't have the time to flip pancakes or tend eggs. If extra servings are needed, don't double the recipe—it won't work. Make two separate batches instead.

1 tablespoon salted butter

2 large eggs

½ cup milk

½ cup all-purpose flour

½ cup thawed fresh or frozen blueberries

Maple syrup

Preheat the oven to 400°F. Place the butter in a 1-quart baking dish and put it in the hot oven for 1 to 2 minutes, until it melts. Remove the dish from the oven and swirl the butter so that it evenly coats the bottom and sides of the dish.

In a medium bowl, combine the eggs, milk, and flour and beat well, using a wire whisk or a fork. Pour the batter into the warm dish and scatter the fruit over the top.

Bake for 20 minutes, or until puffy and golden brown around the edges. Serve immediately with maple syrup.

NUTRIENTS PER SERVING: 296 calories, 32 g protein, 13 g fat, 33 g carbohydrate, 2 mg iron, 174 RE vitamin A, 0.8 mg vitamin E, 5 mg vitamin C, 106 mg calcium.

Basic Omelet

MAKES 1 SERVING

Eggs are a superb and economical way to consume protein. Always be sure to cook eggs until the yolks are no longer runny. Omelets offer the opportunity to fold in additional healthy ingredients such as fruit and vegetables or extra cheese for more protein.

2 large eggs

2 tablespoons milk or water

Salt and pepper to taste

1 to 2 teaspoons salted butter

In a medium bowl, beat together the eggs, milk, and salt and pepper.

Melt the butter in a small omelet pan or skillet over medium-high heat. Add the egg mixture and cook for 1 minute. With a fork, draw the cooked edges of the eggs away from the pan, allowing any raw egg to slide beneath the omelet. Then cover the pan and cook for 1 minute, or until the eggs are completely cooked and no longer runny.

With a spatula, fold the omelet in half and turn out onto a warm plate. Serve immediately.

NUTRIENTS PER SERVING: 218 calories, 13 g protein, 17 g fat, 2 g carbohydrate, 1.5 mg iron, 254 RE vitamin A, 1.5 mg vitamin E, 88 mg calcium.

Cheese Omelet: Sprinkle with ¼ cup grated Cheddar or Swiss cheese over the omelet before folding it in half.

Tomato Omelet: Chop 1 small tomato and scatter it over the omelet before folding it in half.

Herb Omelet: Sprinkle 1 tablespoon chopped fresh herbs, such as parsley, basil, or chives, over the omelet before folding it in half.

Vegetable Omelet: Sprinkle 2 tablespoons very finely chopped cooked mushrooms, snow peas, carrots, or other vegetables over the eggs while they are still a bit runny, then cover and proceed as directed.

Orange Omelet: Replace the milk with 2 tablespoons orange juice. Spread 1 tablespoon orange marmalade over the omelet before folding it in half.

Vegetable Quiche

MAKES 6 TO 8 SERVINGS

This quiche combines protein-rich eggs, cheese, and vegetables to make a complete meal. Serve it for breakfast, lunch, or dinner.

1 tablespoon olive oil

1 carrot, chopped

1 small onion, chopped

1/2 cup chopped broccoli

1/2 cup chopped zucchini

1/2 cup chopped mushrooms

4 large eggs

2 cups milk

1 tablespoon chopped fresh chives

Pepper to taste

1/2 cup grated Swiss cheese

1/2 recipe unbaked Easy Pie Crust (page 136) or one 9-inch prepared pie crust

Preheat the oven to 375°F. In a large skillet, heat the oil, then add the vegetables. Sauté the carrot, onion, and broccoli in the oil until tender, about 5 minutes. Stir in the zucchini and mushrooms and cook for 2 minutes more. Remove from the heat.

In a large bowl, beat the eggs. Add the milk, chives, and pepper, and whisk until combined. Fold in the cooked vegetables and the cheese.

If using homemade pie dough, roll out the dough to a 12-inch circle on a lightly floured board. Fit it into a 9-inch pie plate and crimp the edges.

Pour the filling into the pie crust and bake for 25 minutes, or until the top is golden brown and a knife inserted into the center comes out clean. Serve warm. Cover leftovers and refrigerate up to 3 days.

NUTRIENTS PER SERVING: 378 calories, 14 g protein, 21 g fat, 33 g carbohydrate, 2.2 mg iron, 565 RE vitamin A, 1 mg vitamin E, 12 mg vitamin C, 226 mg calcium.

Banana Buttermilk Pancakes

MAKES TEN 4-INCH PANCAKES

If you don't have buttermilk on hand, substitute plain yogurt. Buttermilk and yogurt provide similar nutrients and taste, and they both make the pancakes delicate and tender. Top with syrup and butter or flavored yogurt for more calories.

1 cup all-purpose flour

¼ cup dry milk powder

1 tablespoon sugar

1 teaspoon baking powder

½ teaspoon baking soda

1¼ cups buttermilk

1 large egg

½ banana, cut into small pieces or mashed

2 tablespoons salted butter, melted

Sift the dry ingredients into a large bowl.

In another bowl, combine the buttermilk, egg, and banana and stir until blended. Pour the mixture over the dry ingredients and mix with a fork. Stir in the melted butter, breaking up any lumps with a fork; don't overmix.

Lightly butter a griddle or large skillet and heat over medium heat. Pour small portions of the batter, about ¼ cup, onto the griddle and cook until the pancakes are lightly browned on the bottom and a few bubbles begin to appear on top. Turn and cook until lightly browned on both sides. Serve hot. Leftover pancakes can be frozen, well wrapped, for 1 month. Reheat in the microwave or toaster oven before serving.

NUTRIENTS PER PANCAKE: 102 calories, 4 g protein, 3 g fat, 15 g carbohydrate, 0.6 mg iron, 46 RE vitamin A, 0.3 mg vitamin E, 62 mg calcium.

Ginger Griddle Cakes with Blueberry Sauce

MAKES TEN 4-INCH PANCAKES

I add ginger to these pancakes to give them a unique flavor—and because of its reputation for settling upset stomachs. If you like gingerbread cookies, you'll enjoy these on your breakfast table too.

1 cup all-purpose flour	**³⁄₄ cup Fortified Milk (page 172)**
1¹⁄₂ teaspoons baking powder	**1 tablespoon honey**
¹⁄₂ teaspoon ground cinnamon	**1 tablespoon molasses**
¹⁄₂ teaspoon ground ginger	**1 tablespoon vegetable oil**
2 large eggs	**Blueberry Sauce (recipe follows)**

Combine the dry ingredients in a large bowl.

In another bowl, beat the eggs. Add the milk, honey, molasses, and oil and beat until well blended. Pour the mixture over the dry ingredients and gently stir with a fork until just combined; don't overmix. It is okay to have a few small lumps in the batter.

Lightly butter a griddle or large skillet and heat over medium heat. Add the batter by quarter cupfuls and cook until the pancakes are lightly browned on the bottom and a few bubbles begin to appear on top. Turn and cook until lightly browned on both sides. Serve warm with the Blueberry Sauce. Leftover pancakes can be frozen for 1 month, well wrapped. Reheat in the microwave or toaster oven before serving.

NUTRIENTS PER PANCAKE: 100 calories, 4 g protein, 3 g fat, 14 g carbohydrate, 1 mg iron, 35 RE vitamin A, 1.2 mg vitamin E, 2.4 mg vitamin C, 58 mg calcium.

Blueberry Sauce

MAKES 1 CUP

This sauce is a more nutritious alternative to maple syrup because it contains real fruit. It tastes good too!

1 cup fresh or frozen blueberries

1 tablespoon molasses

1 tablespoon water

2 tablespoons salted butter (optional)

Combine the blueberries, molasses, and water in a small saucepan and bring to a simmer. Cover and simmer for 5 minutes more, or until the berries have burst. For a richer sauce, stir in the butter until melted. Serve with pancakes, French toast, or waffles. Refrigerate leftover sauce and use within 3 days.

NUTRIENTS PER ¼ CUP: 32 calories, 8 g carbohydrate, 0.2 mg iron, 3 RE vitamin A, 4 mg vitamin C, 10 mg calcium.

Fluffy French Toast

MAKES 2 SERVINGS

Assemble this dish ahead, refrigerate, and bake the next morning while the coffee brews. The more texture the bread has, the better the French toast will be. Thick slices of home-made bread, hand-sliced bakery bread, and whole wheat or multi-grain breads are all good choices. Serve with butter, syrup, Blueberry Sauce (page 88), or flavored yogurt to boost the calorie count.

2 large eggs

¼ cup milk

1 tablespoon sugar

½ teaspoon ground cinnamon

2 thick slices bread, cut into quarters

In a medium bowl, combine the eggs, milk, sugar, and cinnamon and mix well.

Lightly butter a medium baking dish. Arrange the bread quarters in the dish in a single layer, overlapping the edges if necessary. Pour the egg mixture over the bread and press down on the bread with a fork so it is completely submerged. Cover and refrigerate for at least 1 hour or overnight.

Preheat the oven to 375°F. Bake, uncovered, for 20 minutes, or until the bread has absorbed all the liquid and is lightly browned on top and puffy. Serve warm, with syrup, butter, fresh fruit, or flavored yogurt. Cover leftovers and refrigerate up to 2 days.

NUTRIENTS PER SERVING: 175 calories, 9 g protein, 7 g fat, 19 g carbohydrate, 1.4 mg iron, 107 RE vitamin A, 1 mg vitamin E, 90 mg calcium.

Savory Breakfast Sausage

MAKES 16 PATTIES

Ground chicken or turkey is used to make a high-protein, lower-fat sausage. Both traditional and nontraditional sausage seasonings are used for flavor. Entice a failing appetite with these well-seasoned sausages. Keep individually wrapped sausages in the freezer for a quick breakfast. Thaw in the refrigerator and cook as directed.

1 pound ground chicken or turkey	**1/4 teaspoon poultry seasoning**
1 1/2 cups seasoned bread crumbs	**1 large egg**
1 tablespoon finely minced onion	**1 tablespoon fresh lemon juice**
1 clove garlic, minced	**1/2 teaspoon salt**
1/2 teaspoon dried rosemary, crumbled	**Pepper to taste**

Combine all the ingredients in a large bowl. With your hands or a wooden spoon, mix until very well blended. Divide the mixture in half and roll each portion into an 8-inch-long log, about 2 inches thick. Wrap each log in plastic wrap and place in the freezer for 5 minutes to make slicing easier. The sausage mixture can also be refrigerated overnight.

Slice each log into 8 sausage patties. Lightly grease a large skillet with butter or spray with nonstick cooking spray. Add the sausages, without crowding, and cook, turning once, until well browned on both sides and completely cooked, about 15 minutes. Serve hot. Freeze any uncooked sausages, well wrapped, up to 3 months.

NUTRIENTS PER PATTY: 84 calories, 6 g protein, 3 g fat, 7 g carbohydrate, 0.8 mg iron, 6.5 RE vitamin A, 17 mg calcium.

Crispy Potato Cakes

MAKES 6 SMALL PANCAKES

A client's Italian grandmother brings a batch of these pancakes to friends or family whenever they are sick. The dry milk powder adds protein; eliminate it if milk cannot be tolerated.

3 medium red-skinned potatoes	**Salt and pepper to taste**
1 large egg	**¼ cup to ½ cup all-purpose flour**
2 tablespoons dry milk powder	**1 tablespoon salted butter**
Dried oregano to taste, approximately ¼ teaspoon	**Applesauce, maple syrup, catsup, or tomato sauce for serving**

In a large saucepan of salted boiling water, cook the potatoes just until tender enough to be pierced with a fork but still firm, 4 to 5 minutes. Drain and put in a bowl of cold water to cool slightly.

When the potatoes are cool enough to handle, coarsely grate into a bowl lined with paper towels. Fold the towels over the potatoes and gently blot to remove excess moisture. Remove and discard the towels.

Add the egg, dry milk, and seasonings to the potatoes and beat well. Stir in just enough flour so the mixture holds together. Shape into 6 small patties, using about ¼ cup of the mixture for each one.

Melt the butter on a griddle or in a large skillet over medium-high heat. Add the pancakes and cook until golden brown on both sides, about 2 to 3 minutes per side. Serve with applesauce, maple syrup, catsup, or tomato sauce. Cover leftovers and refrigerate up to 2 days or freeze up to 3 months. Reheat in a 350°F. oven for 15 minutes until hot.

NUTRIENTS PER PANCAKE: 85 calories, 3 g protein, 3 g fat, 12 g carbohydrate, 0.6 mg iron, 43 RE vitamin A, 0.1 mg vitamin E, 7 mg vitamin C, 26 mg calcium.

Cinnamon Coffee Cake

MAKES ONE 10-INCH BUNDT CAKE (12 SLICES)

This makes a large cake that can also double as a good snack. It is a concentrated source of calories and protein because of the butter, eggs, and yogurt. One slice has almost five times the amount of calories contained in a slice of toast.

3½ cups all-purpose flour

½ cup wheat germ

2 teaspoons baking powder

2 teaspoons baking soda

1 teaspoon ground cinnamon

½ teaspoon grated nutmeg

1½ cups (3 sticks) salted butter, softened

1 cup packed brown sugar

½ cup granulated sugar

4 large eggs

1 teaspoon vanilla

1 cup plain whole-milk yogurt

Topping

¼ cup packed brown sugar

¼ cup wheat germ

1 teaspoon ground cinnamon

Preheat the oven to 350°F. Lightly grease a 10-inch Bundt pan. In a large bowl, combine the flour, wheat germ, baking powder, baking soda, cinnamon, and nutmeg.

In a large bowl, cream the butter and both sugars until smooth and creamy. Beat in the eggs one at a time. Beat in the vanilla, then beat in the yogurt until well blended. Gradually stir in the dry ingredients just until blended; do not overmix. The batter will be thick.

In a small bowl, mix together the topping ingredients. Spread one third of the batter evenly in the Bundt pan. Sprinkle with half of the topping mixture. Spread another one third of the batter on top and sprinkle with the remaining topping. Spread the remaining batter on top.

Bake 1 hour to 1 hour and 10 minutes or until a cake tester inserted in the middle of the cake comes out clean. Let the cake cool for 5 to 10 minutes.

Place a cake plate over the cake and invert the cake onto the plate. Let it cool for 5 minutes before slicing. The cake can be refrigerated, covered up to 3 days, or frozen up to 2 months.

NUTRIENTS PER SLICE: 516 calories, 8 g protein, 26 g fat, 64 g carbohydrate, 2.6 mg iron, 249 RE vitamin A, 0.6 mg vitamin E, 72 mg calcium.

Cinnamon Coffee Cake

MAKES ONE 10-INCH BUNDT CAKE (12 SLICES)

This makes a large cake that can also double as a good snack. It is a concentrated source of calories and protein because of the butter, eggs, and yogurt. One slice has almost five times the amount of calories contained in a slice of toast.

3½ cups all-purpose flour

½ cup wheat germ

2 teaspoons baking powder

2 teaspoons baking soda

1 teaspoon ground cinnamon

½ teaspoon grated nutmeg

1½ cups (3 sticks) salted butter, softened

1 cup packed brown sugar

½ cup granulated sugar

4 large eggs

1 teaspoon vanilla

1 cup plain whole-milk yogurt

Topping

¼ cup packed brown sugar

¼ cup wheat germ

1 teaspoon ground cinnamon

Preheat the oven to 350°F. Lightly grease a 10-inch Bundt pan. In a large bowl, combine the flour, wheat germ, baking powder, baking soda, cinnamon, and nutmeg.

In a large bowl, cream the butter and both sugars until smooth and creamy. Beat in the eggs one at a time. Beat in the vanilla, then beat in the yogurt until well blended. Gradually stir in the dry ingredients just until blended; do not overmix. The batter will be thick.

In a small bowl, mix together the topping ingredients. Spread one third of the batter evenly in the Bundt pan. Sprinkle with half of the topping mixture. Spread another one third of the batter on top and sprinkle with the remaining topping. Spread the remaining batter on top.

Bake 1 hour to 1 hour and 10 minutes or until a cake tester inserted in the middle of the cake comes out clean. Let the cake cool for 5 to 10 minutes.

Place a cake plate over the cake and invert the cake onto the plate. Let it cool for 5 minutes before slicing. The cake can be refrigerated, covered up to 3 days, or frozen up to 2 months.

NUTRIENTS PER SLICE: 516 calories, 8 g protein, 26 g fat, 64 g carbohydrate, 2.6 mg iron, 249 RE vitamin A, 0.6 mg vitamin E, 72 mg calcium.

Crispy Potato Cakes

MAKES 6 SMALL PANCAKES

A client's Italian grandmother brings a batch of these pancakes to friends or family whenever they are sick. The dry milk powder adds protein; eliminate it if milk cannot be tolerated.

3 medium red-skinned potatoes	**Salt and pepper to taste**
1 large egg	**1/4 cup to 1/2 cup all-purpose flour**
2 tablespoons dry milk powder	**1 tablespoon salted butter**
Dried oregano to taste, approximately 1/4 teaspoon	**Applesauce, maple syrup, catsup, or tomato sauce for serving**

In a large saucepan of salted boiling water, cook the potatoes just until tender enough to be pierced with a fork but still firm, 4 to 5 minutes. Drain and put in a bowl of cold water to cool slightly.

When the potatoes are cool enough to handle, coarsely grate into a bowl lined with paper towels. Fold the towels over the potatoes and gently blot to remove excess moisture. Remove and discard the towels.

Add the egg, dry milk, and seasonings to the potatoes and beat well. Stir in just enough flour so the mixture holds together. Shape into 6 small patties, using about 1/4 cup of the mixture for each one.

Melt the butter on a griddle or in a large skillet over medium-high heat. Add the pancakes and cook until golden brown on both sides, about 2 to 3 minutes per side. Serve with applesauce, maple syrup, catsup, or tomato sauce. Cover leftovers and refrigerate up to 2 days or freeze up to 3 months. Reheat in a 350°F. oven for 15 minutes until hot.

NUTRIENTS PER PANCAKE: 85 calories, 3 g protein, 3 g fat, 12 g carbohydrate, 0.6 mg iron, 43 RE vitamin A, 0.1 mg vitamin E, 7 mg vitamin C, 26 mg calcium.

Brown Sugar Breakfast Rolls

MAKES 24

The aroma of freshly baked cinnamon rolls can stimulate even the weakest appetite. These rolls can be assembled the night before and allowed to rise in the refrigerator overnight before baking. When making bread dough, I like to mix in the flour with my hands to give me a better feel for the dough. To reduce stickiness, I coat my hands with a little flour before kneading.

2 packages active dry yeast

1/2 cup warm water (105° to 115°F.)

1 1/2 cups milk, scalded

1/4 cup salted butter, softened

1/2 cup honey

2 teaspoons salt

6 to 8 cups all-purpose flour

2 large eggs, beaten

Filling

2/3 cup packed brown sugar

1 cup wheat germ

1 cup bran flakes, crushed

1 apple, cored and thinly sliced (optional)

1 teaspoon ground cinnamon

2 tablespoons salted butter, softened

In a small bowl, sprinkle the yeast over the warm water. Stir and set aside for 5 minutes until foamy.

In a large bowl, combine the hot milk, butter, honey, and salt and stir until the butter melts. Let cool to lukewarm.

Add 2 cups flour to the milk mixture and beat well. Add the dissolved yeast and eggs and stir with a wooden spoon until well combined. Using the spoon or your hands, gradually add 4 more cups flour and mix until a soft dough forms; if necessary, add up to 2 more cups flour. Transfer the dough to a lightly floured surface and knead until smooth, 4 to 5 minutes.

To make the filling, combine the brown sugar, wheat germ, bran flakes, apple, if using, cinnamon, and butter. Mix with your fingers until the butter is well distributed. It will look crumbly.

Divide the dough into 2 equal portions. With a floured rolling pin, roll one portion into a rectangle about 14 by 20 inches. Sprinkle half the filling over the dough. Roll up the dough like a jelly roll. Starting at one end, cut into 12 slices about 1 inch thick. Arrange slices cut side up on a lightly oiled cookie sheet. For a crisp crust, space 1 inch apart; for softer rolls, arrange the rolls so the sides just touch. Repeat with the remaining dough and filling. (You can leave one roll uncut, wrap well, and freeze to bake later.) Freeze for up to 6 months. Thaw in the refrigerator and proceed as directed above. Cover with plastic wrap and refrigerate for 4 hours or overnight. It will increase in size by about one third.

Place the cookie sheet(s) in a cold oven. Turn the oven temperature to 400°F. and bake for 20 to 25 minutes, until the rolls are lightly browned and sound hollow when tapped on the bottom. Serve warm. Cover leftovers and refrigerate up to 3 days or freeze up to 6 months.

NUTRIENTS PER ROLL: 240 calories, 6 g protein, 4 g fat, 45 g carbohydrate, 2 mg iron, 63 RE vitamin A, 0.2 mg vitamin E, 23 mg calcium.

Sunday Breakfast Bread

MAKES 2 LOAVES (12 SLICES EACH)

Milk and eggs give this bread a tender, delicate, almost cakelike texture, and add valued nutrients and calories as well.

2 packages activated dry yeast

½ cup warm water (105° to 115°F.)

¼ cup honey

½ cup warm milk

5 tablespoons salted butter, melted and slightly cooled

3 large eggs, beaten

5 to 6 cups all-purpose flour

1 teaspoon salt

In a small bowl, combine the yeast, warm water, and honey. Set aside in a warm spot for 5 minutes, or until the yeast is foamy.

In a large bowl, using a wooden spoon, mix together the warm milk, butter, and eggs, blending well. Stir in the yeast mixture. Stir in 2 cups of the flour and the salt. Stir in the remaining flour 1 cup at a time until a soft dough forms.

Turn the dough out onto a floured board and knead until smooth and elastic, 5 to 7 minutes. Place in a buttered bowl and turn to coat with butter. Cover and let rise in a warm spot until doubled in size, 45 to 60 minutes.

Punch down the dough. Divide the dough in half. Shape each half into a loaf and place in a lightly oiled 8- by 4-inch loaf pan. Cover and let rise 30 minutes until doubled in size.

Preheat the oven to 375°F. Bake for 25 minutes, or until the loaves are golden brown on top and sound hollow when tapped. Remove from the pans and let rest for at least 5 minutes on a wire rack before slicing. Serve hot with butter or slice and toast. Once the bread is thoroughly cooled, it can be frozen, well wrapped, for up to 2 months.

NUTRIENTS PER SLICE: 150 calories, 4 g protein, 3 g fat, 25 g carbohydrate, 1.3 mg iron, 35 RE vitamin A, 15 mg calcium.

Soup

Soup is a traditional sick-day food for good reason. Illness can cause symptoms such as fever or excessive coughing, and there is an increased need for fluids. Not only are soups a superb way to replenish these fluids but they are also psychologically satisfying, perhaps because they were comfort foods served to us as children.

While a clear broth soup, such as consommé or bouillon, may settle an upset stomach, it is a poor choice during prolonged illness because it contains little or no protein and very few calories. When your patient needs additional protein and calories to stop weight loss or fight infection, encourage the consumption of soups made with protein-rich ingredients such as milk, cream, cheese, beans, eggs, meat, poultry, and/or tofu.

To boost the protein content of soups, add small pieces of chicken, beef, or lamb. You can also puree leftover beef, chicken, or lamb with broth or stir in a jar of pureed beef baby food. Make egg drop soup by stirring a beaten egg into simmering chicken broth. Continue stirring with a fork so thin threads of cooked egg swirl through the broth. Make canned broth or cream soups richer in vitamins A and C by stirring in additional cooked or pureed vegetables before serving. To add calories, top a bowl of hot soup with a pat of butter or a spoonful of yogurt before serving.

Cure-all Chicken Soup

MAKES **6** SERVINGS

Chicken soup is thought to cure colds, soothe aching tummies, and boost the body's ability to fight off illness, and there are as many claims and recipes for chicken soup as there are cooks. The key to a nourishing and tasty chicken soup is the ingredients: Don't be stingy with them. Use the best and freshest available, then let time and gentle simmering develop the flavors. I like to add a bit of thyme to my chicken soup, but you can omit it.

One 3-pound stewing chicken

5 cups cold water

1 onion, peeled

2 to 3 celery stalks

1 bay leaf

¼ teaspoon dried thyme (optional)

2 to 3 peppercorns

Salt to taste

1 large carrot, peeled and chopped

1 cup cooked macaroni, such as elbows or bow ties

Put the chicken in a large pot and add the cold water, onion, celery, bay leaf, thyme, if using, peppercorns, and salt. Bring to a boil. Reduce the heat to low, cover, and cook for 1½ hours. Remove the chicken and set aside to cool slightly. Skim off any foam that rises.

Strain the broth through a cheesecloth-lined colander into a bowl and discard the solids. Rinse out the pot and return the broth to the pot. Skim off any fat that rises to the surface.

Add the carrot to the broth and bring to a boil. Reduce the heat and simmer for 5 minutes. Remove from the heat and set aside.

When the chicken is cool enough to handle, remove and discard the skin. Remove the meat from the bones and cut it into bite-sized pieces.

Add the chicken and macaroni to the soup and bring to a simmer over low heat. Cook just until the chicken and macaroni are heated through. Serve hot. Cover leftovers and refrigerate up to 2 days or freeze up to 3 months.

NUTRIENTS PER SERVING: 233 calories, 23 g protein, 11 g fat, 10 g carbohydrate, 1.8 mg iron, 487 RE vitamin A, 0.4 mg vitamin E, 4 mg vitamin C, 28 mg calcium.

Chicken Vegetable Soup: Add 1 cup sliced mushrooms, ½ cup chopped green beans, or ½ cup peas along with the carrot.

Chicken Rice Soup: Substitute 1 cup cooked white or brown rice for the macaroni.

Creamy Chicken Soup

MAKES 6 SERVINGS

This soup is thick and creamy because of the rice and eggs. Cooked carrots give it a warm golden color. I like to make this with a leftover roasted chicken. The addition of a jar of chicken baby food boosts the protein content. This soup freezes well and is great for times when you don't feel like cooking. If you don't have a leftover chicken carcass, make this with 2 pounds of chicken parts such as thighs and drumsticks.

1 meaty chicken carcass (enough to supply at least ¾ cup meat) or 3 pounds stewing chicken

3 celery stalks with leaves

1 onion, peeled

4 cups cold water

½ cup long-grain rice

2 carrots, chopped

1 jar pureed chicken baby food

One 13-ounce can evaporated milk

2 large eggs

In a large pot, combine the chicken carcass, celery, onion, and cold water. Bring to a boil, cover, reduce the heat to low, and simmer for 1 hour. Strain the broth through a cheesecloth-lined colander into a bowl. Set the carcass aside to cool slightly and rinse out the pot.

Return the stock to the pot, along with the rice and carrots. Bring to a boil, cover, reduce the heat, and simmer until the rice and carrots are very tender, about 20 minutes.

Meanwhile, remove all of the chicken from the carcass and discard the bones.

Add the cooked chicken, chicken baby food, and milk to the broth and simmer, uncovered, for 5 minutes.

In a small bowl, beat the eggs. Add ½ cup of the hot broth, stir well, then return the mixture to the soup and bring just to a boil. Reduce the heat to low, stir well, and simmer for 5 minutes more.

For a smoother consistency, puree the soup in a food processor. Serve hot. Cover leftovers and refrigerate up to 2 days or freeze up to 3 months.

NUTRIENTS PER SERVING: 263 calories, 17 g protein, 10 g fat, 25 g carbohydrate, 1.9 mg iron, 771 RE vitamin A, 0.7 mg vitamin E, 9 mg vitamin C, 217 mg calcium.

Healing Miso Soup

MAKES 4 SERVINGS

Miso, a paste made from fermented soybeans, is a staple of Japanese cooking. It adds an appealing salty flavor to many Asian dishes, along with about 2 grams of protein per table-spoon. I boost the protein content of this soup even more by adding tofu, which has 2 to 3 grams protein per ounce. Miso is available in health food stores.

1 tablespoon peanut oil

2 small carrots, peeled and cut into julienne strips

1/2 cup snow peas, cut into julienne strips

4 cups water

1/4 cup miso paste, or more to taste

8 ounces soft tofu, cut into 1/4-inch pieces

Heat the oil in a large saucepan over low heat, and add the carrots and snow peas. Cover and cook until the vegetables are tender but not mushy, about 5 minutes.

Add the water, and miso and stir to dissolve. Bring to a simmer and cook for 5 minutes. Add the tofu and simmer for 1 minute longer until hot. Serve warm. Although left-overs can be refrigerated up to 2 days, this soup tastes best the day it is made.

NUTRIENTS PER SERVING: 100 calories, 7 g protein, 6 g fat, 6 g carbohydrate, 1.5 mg iron, 1018 RE vitamin A, 1 mg vitamin E, 12 mg vitamin C, 88 mg calcium.

Creamy Carrot Soup

MAKES 4 SERVINGS

This calcium-rich soup is based on one my mother used to prepare for her dinner parties. Her recipe called for heavy cream, but I've replaced most of it with evaporated milk to boost the protein. If you need to reduce the fat content, use 2¹/₂ cups evaporated skim milk and omit the cream.

5 carrots, peeled and coarsely chopped

¹/₄ cup plus 1 tablespoon water

Pinch of salt

2 tablespoons salted butter

2 tablespoons all-purpose flour

2 cups evaporated milk

¹/₂ cup heavy cream

Sour cream for garnish

In a medium saucepan, combine the carrots, water, and salt and bring to a simmer over medium heat. Cook until tender, 5 to 6 minutes, covered. Remove from the heat and set aside.

Melt the butter in the top of a double boiler. Whisk in the flour until smooth. Gradually whisk in the milk, and cook, stirring, until the sauce is thickened, about 10 minutes.

Add the carrots with the cooking liquid and cook, stirring occasionally, for 45 minutes.

Puree the soup in a blender or food processor, in batches if necessary. Return it to the double boiler, add the cream, and cook just until heated through. Serve garnished with a dollop of sour cream. The soup can be covered and refrigerated up to 2 days; freezing is not recommended.

NUTRIENTS PER SERVING: 375 calories, 11 g protein, 26 g fat, 26 g carbohydrate, 0.9 mg iron, 2807 RE vitamin A, 10 mg vitamin E, 11 mg vitamin C, 374 mg calcium.

Buttermilk Vegetable Soup

MAKES 6 SERVINGS

Vegetables combined with buttermilk and cheese offer protein along with plenty of vitamins and minerals. Pumpkin is an exceptional source of vitamin A, beta carotene, and fiber. To make preparation easier, use canned pumpkin puree. Any pureed, cooked winter squash, such as butternut, acorn, or Hubbard, can be substituted for the pumpkin.

1 tablespoon salted butter

1 large potato, peeled and cubed

1 cup broccoli florets, cut into 1-inch pieces

1 small onion, finely chopped

2 cloves garlic, minced

2 cups canned chicken broth or Poultry Stock (page 248)

1 cup pumpkin puree, fresh or canned

³⁄₄ cup buttermilk

1 cup grated mild Cheddar or Muenster cheese

Melt the butter in a large heavy saucepan over low heat. Add the potato, broccoli, onion, and garlic and cook, covered, for 5 minutes until the onion is tender. Add the chicken broth and bring to a simmer. Cook uncovered until the potato is tender when pierced with a knife, 10 to 15 minutes.

Stir in the pumpkin puree and buttermilk and cook for 5 minutes longer. Transfer to a food processor and puree until smooth.

Return the soup to the pan and reheat over low heat. Add the cheese and stir until the cheese is melted. Serve immediately. Cover leftovers and refrigerate up to 2 days. If you want to freeze this soup, prepare it to the point where it is pureed until smooth, let cool, and freeze. Add the cheese to the hot soup just before serving.

NUTRIENTS PER SERVING: 189 calories, 9.7 g protein, 9 g fat, 18 g carbohydrate, 1.2 mg iron, 147 RE vitamin A, 0.34 mg vitamin E, 29 mg vitamin C, 200 mg calcium.

Vegetables

Vegetables carry the important nutrients vitamin A, beta carotene, and vitamin C. They also contain potassium, which is important for fluid balance, and fiber, which helps keep the digestive tract healthy. Although vegetables are an appealing part of many meals, they contain little protein and calories. One half cup of most vegetables yields only 2 grams of incomplete protein and only 25 calories. When combined with eggs, dairy, beans, nuts, poultry, fish, or meat, their protein value increases. Add butter or cheese to vegetables or bake them in a sauce to make the calorie count climb.

Most of the main dish recipes in this book incorporate vegetables because they taste good and are essential to proper nutrition. If your patient requests plain steamed vegetables, by all means serve them. But when extra protein and calories are needed, try the following recipes, all of which combine vegetables with high-protein ingredients. In some cases, the protein and calorie value of the dish is high enough to make it suitable for a main course or a one-dish meal.

Sautéed Squash, Potatoes, and Carrots

MAKES 4 SERVINGS

A combination of two or three root vegetables provides appealing flavor and keeps one from overpowering the others in this side dish. Toasting seeds or nuts brings out their flavor, and they add crunch and a little protein. Cut the potato and squash into pieces of the same size so that they cook evenly. For appearance, the peel is removed from the potato, but leave it for additional fiber if you like.

1 tablespoon salted butter

1 small onion, sliced into rings

1 carrot, peeled and sliced

1 small butternut squash, peeled and cut into thick matchsticks

1 large potato, peeled and cut into thick matchsticks

Grated nutmeg to taste

2 tablespoons toasted sunflower seeds, chopped cashews, or pine nuts

In a large skillet over low heat, melt the butter and sauté the onion until translucent, 2 to 3 minutes. Stir in the carrot, squash, and potato, and sprinkle with the nutmeg. Cover and cook until the vegetables are very tender, about 15 minutes. Sprinkle with the sunflower seeds and serve warm. Cover leftovers and refrigerate up to 3 days.

NUTRIENTS PER SERVING: 165 calories, 4 g protein, 6 g fat, 28 g carbohydrate, 1.6 mg iron, 1250 RE vitamin A, 0.27 mg vitamin E, 31 mg vitamin C, 63 mg calcium.

Variations: Substitute turnips, parsnips, or sweet potato for any of the vegetables. Experiment with different kinds of potatoes too: A sauté of three different types, such as new potatoes, Idaho, and russets, works well. Or try a combination of winter squashes, such as Hubbard, acorn, butternut, and even pumpkin.

Vegetable Croquettes

MAKES 16

This recipe is a good example of how you can fool the eye and meet nutritional needs. These silver dollar–size croquettes of rice, vegetables, and eggs are ideal for small appetites.

1 tablespoon canola oil

2 tablespoons minced onion

2 cloves garlic, minced

1 red bell pepper, cored, seeded, and diced

2 cups grated carrots

2 cups diced zucchini

2 ripe tomatoes, peeled, seeded, and chopped, or 2 canned tomatoes, drained, seeded, and chopped

1 bay leaf

1/2 teaspoon dried oregano

3 tablespoons salted butter

1/4 cup all-purpose flour, plus flour for shaping

1 cup canned chicken broth or Poultry Stock (page 248)

1/2 cup milk

2 large eggs, beaten

1 cup cooked rice

1/4 cup chopped fresh parsley

1 teaspoon grated lemon zest

2 cups seasoned bread crumbs

Preheat the oven to 350°F. Lightly oil a baking sheet. Heat the oil in a large saucepan over low heat. Add the onion, garlic, and red pepper and cook, stirring, until the pepper and onion are soft, 3 to 4 minutes. Add the carrots, zucchini, and tomatoes, stirring occasionally, until all the vegetables are soft and the liquid has evaporated. Stir in the bay leaf and oregano. Transfer to a large bowl and set aside.

Melt the butter in a medium saucepan over medium heat. Add the flour and stir until a smooth paste forms, then cook, stirring frequently, for 2 minutes. Gradually add the broth and milk, stirring with a wire whisk or wooden spoon until smooth, and cook, stirring frequently until thickened, for about 3 minutes. Reduce the heat to low, add the eggs, stirring constantly, and cook, stirring, until the sauce has thickened, about 3 minutes; do not boil.

Add the sauce to the sautéed vegetables, along with the rice, parsley, lemon zest, and 1 1/2 cups bread crumbs, and mix until well combined.

Shape the mixture into 16 small balls. Dust your hands with flour and form each ball into a cone shape.

Roll the croquettes in the remaining ¹/₂ cup bread crumbs and arrange on the baking sheet.

Bake for 45 minutes, or until lightly browned. Serve hot, with a cheese sauce if desired—or even catsup. Cover leftovers and refrigerate up to 2 days or freeze in individual portions for up to 3 months.

NUTRIENTS PER CROQUETTE: 152 calories, 5 g protein, 5 g fat, 21 g carbohydrate, 1.4 mg iron, 802 RE vitamin A, 0.4 mg vitamin E, 12 mg vitamin C, 48 mg calcium.

Slow-Baked Vegetables

MAKES 3 SERVINGS

If you or the person you are cooking for thinks of vegetables as boring, try this simple recipe. Brussels sprouts, peas, or green beans can be substituted for the broccoli and potatoes, and sweet potato can replace the carrots. The slow baking in milk really develops the flavor. If milk is not well tolerated, substitute an equal amount of soy milk or chicken or vegetable broth. (The protein value of the recipe will be lower if broth is used to replace the milk.)

1 cup chopped broccoli   **Salt and pepper to taste**

1 cup chopped carrots   **1 cup evaporated milk**

1 potato, peeled and sliced

Preheat the oven to 325°F. In a lightly oiled baking dish, combine all the vegetables. Season with salt and pepper and pour the milk over the top.

Cover and bake for 1 hour until very tender. Serve warm. Cover leftovers and refrigerate up to 2 days.

NUTRIENTS PER SERVING: 215 calories, 9 g protein, 6 g fat, 32 g carbohydrate, 1.3 mg iron, 2091 RE vitamin A, 0.86 mg vitamin E, 51 mg vitamin C, 258 mg calcium.

Apple Harvest Salad

MAKES 2 SERVINGS

This variation on classic Waldorf salad carries a protein-rich cooked salad dressing. The sunflower seeds add protein too.

2 apples, cut into small cubes

2 tablespoons finely chopped celery or ¼ cup bean sprouts

2 tablespoons toasted sunflower seeds

¾ cup Creamy Cooked Salad Dressing (recipe follows)

1 cup shredded Boston lettuce

Combine the apples, celery, and sunflower seeds in a bowl. Add the salad dressing and toss to coat. Arrange the lettuce in a salad plate, mound the salad on top, and serve. Keep leftovers refrigerated and use within 24 hours.

NUTRIENTS PER SERVING: 277 calories, 7 g protein, 14 g fat, 35 g carbohydrate, 1.9 mg iron, 167 RE vitamin A, 1.5 mg vitamin E, 15 mg vitamin C, 132 mg calcium.

Creamy Cooked Salad Dressing

MAKES 1 CUP

2 tablespoons all-purpose flour

1 teaspoon Dijon mustard

1 teaspoon sugar

⅛ teaspoon paprika

1 large egg, beaten

¾ cup milk

2 tablespoons red wine vinegar or balsamic vinegar

1 tablespoon salted butter, at room temperature

In the top of a double boiler, whisk together the flour, mustard, sugar, paprika, and egg. Whisk in the milk, then the vinegar. Set the double boiler over low heat and cook, stirring constantly, until the dressing is thickened and smooth, about 7 minutes.

Remove from the heat and stir in the butter. Serve at room temperature. Keep leftover dressing in a covered bowl in the refrigerator for up to 1 week.

NUTRIENTS PER ½ CUP: 185 calories, 7.5 g protein, 11 g fat, 14 g carbohydrate, 0.8 mg iron, 192 RE vitamin A, 0.6 mg vitamin E, 1 mg vitamin C, 126 mg calcium.

Baked Stuffed Sweet Potato

MAKES 1 SERVING

The addition of an egg binds the ingredients and boosts the nutritional value of the finished dish significantly. If a whole stuffed potato is too daunting for someone with a small appetite, cut it in half and serve at two meals. To prevent a crusty top from forming, wrap the prepared potato in aluminum foil before cooking.

1 large sweet potato	¼ teaspoon ground ginger
1 large egg	¼ teaspoon grated nutmeg
¼ cup sour cream	¼ to ½ cup seasoned
1 tablespoon brown sugar	bread crumbs

Preheat the oven to 350°F. Prick the sweet potato with a fork and bake for 1 hour or until tender when pierced with a fork. Or cook the potato in the microwave on high power for 5 minutes or until tender. Let rest for 2 minutes before proceeding.

Slice off the top of the potato and scoop the cooked pulp into a bowl, leaving a shell about ¼ inch thick. Add the egg, sour cream, brown sugar, ginger, and nutmeg to the potato pulp and mix until well blended. Add ¼ cup bread crumbs and mix well; if the mixture seems very moist, add up to ¼ cup more bread crumbs.

Stuff the mixture into the potato shell. (If there is too much potato filling, put the excess in a lightly oiled custard cup and bake it along with the potato.) Bake for 35 minutes, or until heated through and lightly browned on top. If using a microwave, cook the potato in a covered, microwave-safe dish for 5 minutes at full power. Keep covered and let rest for 3 minutes before serving. The potato should be hot and firm to the touch. Serve hot. Cover and refrigerate any leftovers and use within 2 days.

NUTRIENTS PER SERVING: 518 calories, 15 g protein, 19 g fat, 72 g carbohydrate, 3 mg iron, 2718 RE vitamin A, 5.9 mg vitamin E, 28 mg vitamin C, 183 mg calcium.

Scalloped Buttermilk Potatoes

MAKES 2 SERVINGS

While potatoes contain a healthy amount of vitamin C, they come up short as a protein source. Solve the problem by cooking potatoes with a buttermilk-based white sauce. I prefer buttermilk for flavor, but regular whole milk can be used if that is all you have on hand.

1 tablespoon vegetable oil

2 large russet potatoes, peeled and sliced

2 tablespoons salted butter

2 tablespoons all-purpose flour

1 cup warm buttermilk

Salt and pepper to taste

Preheat the oven to 325°F. Lightly oil a shallow baking dish or a glass pie plate. Bring a large pot of salted water to a boil. Add the potatoes and cook until barely tender for 5 minutes only. Drain, rinse with cold water, and set aside.

Melt the butter in a medium saucepan over low heat. Stir in the flour and cook, stirring, for 2 minutes until golden and well combined. Stir in the warm buttermilk and cook, stirring, until thickened, 4 to 5 minutes; do not boil.

Arrange the potato slices in a baking dish or pie plate, overlapping the edges slightly. Pour the sauce evenly over the potatoes. Bake for 1 hour, or until lightly browned on top. Serve hot. Cover leftovers and refrigerate up to 3 days.

NUTRIENTS PER SERVING: 415 calories, 11 g protein, 13 g fat, 66 g carbohydrate, 2.7 mg iron, 117 RE vitamin A, 0.7 mg vitamin E, 58 mg vitamin C, 168 mg calcium.

Turn a Fresh Salad into a Protein-Rich Meal

MAKES 1 SERVING

A salad can provide lots of protein if it contains ingredients such as cooked egg, sliced cheese, tuna, sliced meat, or nuts. Keep the ratio of vegetables to protein foods equal. For example, the following ingredients combined in a salad will yield at least 22 grams of protein.

1 hard-cooked egg, sliced into rings or cut into wedges

1 ounce Swiss cheese, cut into julienne strips

1 ounce lean ham, cut into julienne strips

¹⁄₂ tomato, diced

1 cup shredded lettuce

1 to 2 tablespoons Creamy Cooked Salad Dressing (page 107)

¹⁄₄ cup seasoned croutons

In a small bowl, toss together all of the ingredients and serve.

NUTRIENTS PER SERVING (WITH 1 TABLESPOON CREAMY COOKED SALAD DRESSING): 306 calories, 22 g protein, 18 g fat, 14 g carbohydrate, 2.4 mg iron, 317 RE vitamin A, 1.7 mg vitamin E, 30 mg vitamin C, 362 mg calcium.

Silky Smooth Vegetables

MAKES 1 SERVING

Pureed vegetables can be served as a side dish, used to garnish a dinner plate, or swirled into soups or casseroles. This is a great way for those with sore mouths or chewing problems to enjoy vegetables.

1 cup cooked cut-up vegetables, such as winter squash, carrots, sweet potatoes, or broccoli (peeled if skin is tough)

1 teaspoon salted butter

$\frac{1}{4}$ to $\frac{1}{2}$ cup milk, cream, cooking water, or stock or broth

Place the vegetables in a blender or food processor and puree with the butter, adding enough of the liquid to obtain the desired consistency. To use in soups or casseroles, make a thin puree, the consistency of gravy; to serve as a side dish, aim for the consistency of mashed potatoes. The puree keeps 3 days in the refrigerator and up to 5 months in the freezer.

Reheat in a saucepan over low heat before serving. Or, to serve as a side dish, scrape into a buttered custard cup and bake in a preheated 325°F. oven for 20 minutes.

NUTRIENTS PER SERVING (MADE WITH POTATOES): 270 calories, 6 g protein, 6 g fat, 49 g carbohydrate, 0.8 mg iron, 58 RE vitamin A, 0.5 mg vitamin E, 17 mg vitamin C, 92 mg calcium.

Pasta

Pasta and all types of noodles are a good choice when soft foods are desired. What's more, pasta is a great vehicle for carrying protein-rich foods like cheese, fish, and even peanut butter. Served plain, one half cup of pasta has only 2 to 3 grams of protein, but topped with cheese, nuts, fish, lean meats, or beans, the protein value jumps to 10 grams or more. While the traditional combination of spaghetti and meatballs is a good source of protein, and the tomato sauce is a superb source of vitamin C and fiber, don't limit the possibilities to traditional pasta and sauce combinations. Use pasta as a canvas, and incorporate foods that your patient finds appealing.

There is very little, if any, nutritional difference between vegetable-colored and plain pasta. Fresh pasta made with eggs, however, does contain more protein than dried pasta made with only flour and water. Whole wheat pasta is a good source of fiber. The following recipes combine pasta with protein-rich ingredients. Whenever possible, vegetables rich in essential nutrients like vitamins A and C are included.

Confetti Orzo

MAKES 4 SERVINGS

Orzo is a rice-shaped pasta, easy to eat because no fork twirling is required. Combined with carrots and flecks of parsley, it looks like a bowl of confetti. If the smell of rosemary is too overwhelming for your patient, leave it out. The cheese and milk provide high-quality protein.

½ **pound orzo, cooked**

½ **cup milk**

½ **cup canned chicken broth or Poultry Stock (page 248)**

½ **cup grated mild Cheddar cheese**

1 small carrot, finely chopped

2 tablespoons minced fresh parsley

1 tablespoon minced fresh rosemary

2 tablespoons seasoned bread crumbs

1 tablespoon olive oil

Preheat the oven to 325°F. Lightly butter a 2-quart baking dish. In a large bowl, combine the orzo, milk, broth, cheese, carrot, parsley, and rosemary and mix well. Pour the mixture into the baking dish.

Combine the bread crumbs with the oil and sprinkle over the top of the orzo. Bake for 1 hour, or until the crumbs are lightly browned. Serve hot. Cover leftovers and refrigerate up to 3 days.

NUTRIENTS PER SERVING: 340 calories, 12 g protein, 10 g fat, 50 g carbohydrate, 3 mg iron, 575 RE vitamin A, 0.12 mg vitamin E, 5 mg vitamin C, 171 mg calcium.

Rotini with Tuna and Eggplant

MAKES 3 SERVINGS

Canned tuna is an easy and inexpensive way to add protein to a dish. Use tuna packed in oil to add flavor and extra calories. The eggplant, red pepper, and tomatoes make for an enticing flavor combination. If the capers are a bit too adventurous, substitute ten coarsely chopped green olives.

**1 small eggplant, cut into
  ¹/₂-inch-thick slices (see Note)**

Salt

3 tablespoons olive oil

1 medium onion, chopped

2 cloves garlic, chopped

**1 red bell pepper, cored, seeded,
  and sliced**

One 6-ounce can tuna packed in oil

One 32-ounce can plum tomatoes

2 tablespoons capers

8 ounces rotini, cooked

**Freshly grated Parmesan
  cheese (optional)**

Sprinkle the eggplant slices with salt, place in a colander, and let drain for 20 minutes. Blot the slices with a paper towel, then cut into cubes.

In a large heavy skillet over low heat, heat the oil and sauté the onion and garlic until translucent; do not allow to brown. Add the eggplant and red pepper and cook until tender, about 5 minutes.

Add the tuna with its oil and the tomatoes to the pan, crushing the tomatoes with a spoon. Stir in the capers and eggplant mixture, cover, and simmer for 5 minutes until hot.

Pour the sauce over the rotini and serve immediately, topped with grated cheese if desired. Cover leftovers and refrigerate up to 3 days.

NOTE: Leaving the eggplant unpeeled increases the fiber content of the dish, but peel it if you prefer.

NUTRIENTS PER SERVING: 735 calories, 33 g protein, 26 g fat, 93 g carbohydrate, 6.7 mg iron, 343 RE vitamin A, 0.3 mg vitamin E, 71 mg vitamin C, 180 mg calcium.

Asian Noodles

MAKES 3 SERVINGS

Peanut butter on pasta might seem strange, but the combination can be appealing during illness and even a lifesaver if red meats and other traditional protein foods are refused. This sauce is traditionally prepared with hot chiles. Cream of coconut can be found in the cocktail mix section of most supermarkets. Cover and freeze the leftovers for later use.

²⁄₃ **cup smooth peanut butter**	**1 teaspoon rice wine vinegar**
¹⁄₃ **cup canned cream of coconut**	**1 teaspoon brown sugar**
1 cup hot water	**8 ounces spaghetti, cooked**
1 tablespoon soy sauce	**2 scallions, chopped, for garnish**

In a small saucepan over low heat, combine the peanut butter, cream of coconut, and water and heat, stirring frequently, until smooth, about 5 minutes. Add the soy sauce, rice vinegar, and brown sugar, reduce the heat to very low, and cook for 10 minutes, stirring occasionally.

Pour the sauce over the pasta, garnish with the scallions, and serve. Cover leftovers and refrigerate up to 3 days.

NUTRIENTS PER SERVING: 645 calories, 23 g protein, 40 g fat, 56 g carbohydrate, 2.7 mg iron, 17 RE vitamin A, 11.4 mg vitamin E, 2 mg vitamin C, 27 mg calcium.

Pasta Primavera

MAKES 3 SERVINGS

A traditional primavera sauce is made with cream, rich in calories but not in protein. This dish uses evaporated whole milk, a better protein source than cream. Diced vegetables provide important fiber and nutrients. They also add color, making the dish visually appealing—which is almost as important as taste when trying to encourage a patient to eat. Use seasonal vegetables if you like; substitute broccoli for the asparagus, red peppers for the carrot, or green beans for the peas.

¼ cup salted butter

1 medium onion, chopped

2 cloves garlic, chopped

½ pound asparagus, trimmed and cut into ¼-inch pieces

½ small head cauliflower, cut into small florets

1 cup fresh or thawed frozen peas

1 carrot, peeled and coarsely chopped

¼ cup canned chicken broth or Poultry Stock (page 248)

¾ cup evaporated milk

1 tablespoon chopped fresh basil or 1 teaspoon dried

½ cup freshly grated Parmesan cheese

½ cup ricotta cheese

8 ounces fettuccine, cooked

Pepper to taste

Melt the butter in a large skillet over medium heat. Add the onion and garlic and cook for 2 minutes, stirring occasionally until softened. Add the vegetables and broth, reduce the heat to low, and cook, covered, until the vegetables are tender but not mushy, 4 to 5 minutes.

Remove ½ cup vegetables and set aside. Add the evaporated milk and basil to the pan, stir, and bring to a boil. Reduce the heat to low and simmer until the liquid is reduced by one third, about 3 minutes. Stir in the cheeses.

Pour the sauce over the fettuccine and sprinkle with the reserved vegetables and pepper. Serve warm. Cover leftovers and refrigerate up to 3 days.

NUTRIENTS PER SERVING: 750 calories, 33 g protein, 34 g fat, 83 g carbohydrate, 4.8 mg iron, 1069 RE vitamin A, 5 mg vitamin E, 114 mg vitamin C, 680 mg calcium.

Classic Baked Macaroni and Cheese

MAKES 3 SERVINGS

Macaroni and cheese is often a favorite food during illness, perhaps because it is strongly associated with childhood comfort food. It is also soft, easy to chew, and simple to prepare. This version of macaroni and cheese is superior to the kind that comes in a box because it is made with real cheese and whole milk, providing more protein and better flavor. To boost the protein count even higher, add half a cup of chopped ham after the tomatoes.

8 ounces elbow macaroni, cooked

1 cup Robust White Sauce (page 174)

1 cup grated Cheddar cheese

1 large tomato, peeled, seeded, and chopped, or 1 cup canned crushed tomatoes (optional)

Topping (optional)

¼ cup seasoned bread crumbs

2 teaspoons olive oil

Preheat the oven to 400°F. Butter a baking dish. Put the macaroni into the dish, add the white sauce, cheese, and the tomatoes, if desired, and mix thoroughly.

For a crispy top, combine the bread crumbs and oil, sprinkle over the macaroni, and bake uncovered for 20 minutes. For a soft top, omit the bread crumb mixture and bake covered for 20 minutes. Serve warm. Cover leftovers and refrigerate up to 3 days.

NUTRIENTS PER SERVING: 697 calories, 27 g protein, 31 g fat, 77 g carbohydrate, 4 mg iron, 276 RE vitamin A, 0.5 mg vitamin E, 9 mg vitamin C, 298 mg calcium.

Beans and Grains

Beans and grains are a healthy food for those who are ill. Canned beans—white, baked, black, etc.—can be heated and ready to eat in no time. Rice, too, can be ready to eat in only twenty minutes. Many of my patients tell me that white rice served with a pat of butter and a sprinkle of salt, is just the right food when nothing else sounds appealing. Like pasta and noodles, beans and grains provide a substantial base for high-protein foods. Try kidney beans, navy beans, rice, barley, or cornmeal mixed with protein-rich ingredients such as cheese or bits of meat. I once had a patient who regularly prepared a lunch of white rice topped with a soft-cooked egg—an easy, economical, and nutritious way to use grains.

Beans are an unparalleled source of fiber as well as a good source of protein. They are often overlooked during illness because they are considered too hard to digest which isn't necessarily true. When served in small amounts, beans are not likely to cause digestive problems. To reduce the risk of gas, soak and rinse dried beans several times before cooking them. Canned beans seem to be less likely to cause gas than dried. Different types of beans have different effects on people—experiment with them to find which appeal to your patient.

Although rice and other grains included here, such as cornmeal and barley, are not nutrient-dense on their own (they do carry some protein and B vitamins), their biggest asset is the energy-yielding carbohydrates they contain and their ability to act as the foundation for flavorful, protein-rich ingredients.

To get the most protein when preparing grains or beans, combine them with other grains, beans, bits of meat, cheese, milk, or eggs. For extra calories and flavor, top them with butter or stir in a teaspoon of olive or canola oil. Choose dishes that cater to a patient's desires and help maintain an interest in eating. For example, the crunchiness of Herbed Wild Rice with Bulgur and Cashews (page 120) or the salty flavor of Mediterranean Chicken and Rice (page 122) might sound appealing to your patient. The smooth texture and mild flavor of Baked Cornmeal with Cheese (page 121) might soothe and comfort. Add protein-rich ingredients to familiar dishes or try one of the recipes that follow. The point is to experiment with different foods and flavors.

Chicken and Rice Casserole

MAKES 2 SERVINGS

White rice is an ideal food for an upset stomach because it is easily digested. By itself, rice is not a good source of protein or calories, but when tossed with chicken, the protein value improves significantly. I've made this recipe deliberately bland. To add some flavor, sprinkle with a tablespoon of grated Cheddar cheese before serving.

1 teaspoon salted butter

4 ounces boneless, skinless chicken breast or thigh, chopped

1 teaspoon chopped fresh chives

½ cup white rice

1 cup warm canned chicken broth or Poultry Stock (page 248)

Preheat the oven to 350°F. Melt the butter in a medium ovenproof saucepan. Add the chicken and chives and stir gently until the chives are wilted and the chicken is just turning opaque, about 1 minute. Add the rice and stir to coat each grain with butter.

Add the stock and bring to a boil. Stir once, cover, and bake for 25 minutes, or until the rice is tender. Fluff with a fork and serve. Cover leftovers and refrigerate up to 2 days.

NUTRIENTS PER SERVING: 255 calories, 16 g protein, 4 g fat, 37 g carbohydrate, 2 mg iron, 20 RE vitamin A, 0.5 mg vitamin E, 20 mg calcium.

Herbed Wild Rice with Bulgur and Cashews

MAKES 5 SERVINGS

Wild rice and bulgur tossed with cashews makes a complete protein combination almost equal to an equivalent amount of meat and poultry. The result is crunchy, a bit unusual, and a nice alternative to plain rice. Serve this when your patient is in need of a stimulating side dish. If you don't have wild rice, substitute brown rice. If your patient dislikes nuts, use eight ounces firm tofu cut into small cubes in place of the cashews.

½ cup wild rice

3 to 3½ cups canned chicken broth or Poultry Stock (page 248)

2 tablespoons salted butter or canola oil

½ cup bulgur

1 large carrot, peeled and chopped

1 celery stalk, diced

1 small onion, diced

1 teaspoon dried oregano

½ teaspoon dried marjoram

½ cup finely chopped fresh basil

½ cup toasted cashews, coarsely chopped

In a large saucepan, combine the wild rice with 2 cups broth. Bring to a boil, lower the heat, and simmer, covered, for 20 minutes.

While the rice simmers, melt the butter in a large saucepan over medium heat. Stir in the bulgur, coating the grains with butter. Add the carrot, celery, and onion and cook until the onion is tender, about 3 minutes. Remove from the heat and set aside.

When the rice has cooked for 20 minutes, add 1 cup broth, the vegetable-bulgur mixture, oregano, and marjoram. Bring to a boil, reduce the heat, cover, and simmer for 10 minutes. Cook until the rice and bulgur are tender. Remove the lid and cook for 5 minutes more; if the rice looks dry, add ½ cup broth or water.

Add the basil and cashews, toss with a fork, and serve immediately. Cover leftovers and refrigerate up to 3 days. (This can be frozen, but the cashews will get soggy.)

NUTRIENTS PER SERVING: 254 calories, 6 g protein, 12 g fat, 34 g carbohydrate, 2 mg iron, 48 RE vitamin A, 2 mg vitamin E, 11 mg vitamin C, 37 mg calcium.

Baked Cornmeal with Cheese

MAKES 4 SERVINGS

Its soft texture and soothing color make this dish very appealing. By itself, cornmeal has little flavor, but when combined with more flavorful ingredients like cheese, it becomes a delicious alternative to rice.

1 tablespoon salted butter

1 small onion, minced

3½ cups water

1 cup yellow cornmeal

1 cup grated Cheddar cheese

Preheat the oven to 325°F. Lightly butter a shallow 2-quart baking dish. Melt the butter in a large saucepan over low heat. Add the onion and cook until translucent, about 3 minutes. Add the water and bring to a boil. Slowly add the cornmeal, stirring constantly, and bring to a boil. Cover, reduce the heat to very low, and cook, stirring frequently, until thick and creamy, about 20 minutes.

Remove from the heat and add half the grated cheese to the cornmeal and stir until well combined. Pour the mixture into the baking dish. Sprinkle with the remaining cheese and bake for 10 minutes or until the cheese is melted. Cut into squares and serve immediately. Cover leftovers and refrigerate up to 2 days.

NUTRIENTS PER SERVING: 276 calories, 10 g protein, 13 g fat, 30 g carbohydrate, 3 mg iron, 130 RE vitamin A, 0.8 mg vitamin E, 2 mg vitamin C, 203 mg calcium.

Mediterranean Chicken and Rice

MAKES 3 SERVINGS

In this dish, rice is cooked with tomatoes and olives to give it a salty tang. Many people find their taste for salty flavors increases when ill.

2 tablespoons salted butter

3 tablespoons minced onion

1 clove garlic, minced

½ cup white rice

1 cup chopped, peeled ripe tomatoes or 1 cup crushed canned tomatoes

1¼ cups water

8 Greek or other black olives, pitted and chopped

½ cup cubed cooked chicken

Melt the butter in a medium heavy saucepan over low heat. Add the onion and garlic and sauté until the onion is translucent, 2 to 3 minutes. Add the rice and stir to coat each grain with butter. Add the tomatoes and water and bring to a boil. Stir, lower the heat, cover, and simmer until the rice is tender and the cooking liquid has been absorbed, about 20 minutes.

Using a fork, stir in the olives and chicken and cook until heated through, about 5 minutes. Serve immediately. Cover leftovers and refrigerate up to 2 days.

NUTRIENTS PER SERVING: 280 calories, 13 g protein, 12 g fat, 30 g carbohydrate, 2.5 mg iron, 128 RE vitamin A, 0.5 mg vitamin E, 13 mg vitamin C, 45 mg calcium.

Rice and Barley with Cashews

MAKES 2 SERVINGS

Serve this as a side dish instead of plain white rice. Barley has twice as much protein as white rice, and the nuts add even more. Substitute a quarter cup of toasted sunflower seeds for the cashews, if you like. This recipe can be doubled.

1 to 1¼ cups canned chicken broth or Poultry Stock (page 248)

½ cup water

1 tablespoon salted butter

¼ cup brown rice

¼ cup pearl barley

10 cashews, toasted and chopped

In a small saucepan, combine 1 cup broth, the water, and butter and bring to a boil. Add the rice and barley very slowly, so that the water continues to boil (this helps prevent clumping). Stir, reduce heat, cover, and cook until tender, about 35 minutes. If the grains seem dry, add ¼ cup additional broth or stock and stir until it is absorbed.

Sprinkle the rice and barley with the nuts and serve. Cover leftovers and refrigerate up to 2 days.

NUTRIENTS PER SERVING: 320 calories, 7 g protein, 15 g fat, 43 g carbohydrate, 2 mg iron, 53 RE vitamin A, 2 mg vitamin E, 22 mg calcium.

Winter Beans

MAKES 3 SERVINGS

Traditional New England baked beans made with molasses and brown sugar are a good source of protein. In this recipe sour cream adds important calories. While I prefer this homemade version, a can of ready-to-eat baked beans provides a quick, easy, and nutritious meal in a pinch.

2 cups cooked butter beans or white kidney beans, rinsed if canned

1 cup sour cream

¼ cup brown sugar

½ teaspoon dry mustard

Preheat the oven to 325°F. Lightly oil a small baking dish. Combine all the ingredients in a bowl, mix well, and spoon into the dish.

Bake, covered, for 2 hours, stirring once or twice. (There will still be some liquid even when done.) Serve hot. Cover leftovers and refrigerate up to 2 days.

NUTRIENTS PER SERVING: 400 calories, 13 g protein, 16 g fat, 53 g carbohydrate, 3 mg iron, 182 RE vitamin A, 2 mg vitamin C, 190 mg calcium.

Harvest Beans

MAKES 2 SERVINGS

The dense texture and bland flavor of beans is perfectly suited to the sweet combination of apples and cinnamon. Add yogurt to boost the calcium and protein content or sour cream to increase calories.

2 tablespoons unsalted butter

1 small onion, sliced into rings

4 large apples, peeled, quartered, and cored

1 teaspoon ground cinnamon

1 teaspoon fresh lemon juice

One 16-ounce can kidney beans, drained and rinsed

Sour cream or plain yogurt for garnish (optional)

Preheat the oven to 350°F. Melt the butter in a large ovenproof saucepan over medium heat.

Add the onion and cook until soft, about 2 minutes. Add the apples, cinnamon, and lemon juice, cover, reduce the heat to low, and cook for about 5 minutes until the apples are soft. Stir in the beans.

Cover and bake for 30 minutes until the liquid bubbles. Serve warm, garnished with a dollop of sour cream or yogurt, if desired. Cover leftovers and refrigerate up to 2 days.

NUTRIENTS PER SERVING: 500 calories, 16 g protein, 13 g fat, 85 g carbohydrate, 5 mg iron, 117 RE vitamin A, 2 mg vitamin E, 22 mg vitamin C, 100 mg calcium.

Marilyn's Farina Pie

MAKES ONE 10-INCH PIE (10 SLICES)

My college roommate and nutrition intern, Marilyn, would prepare this protein-rich, mild combination of farina, cheese, milk, and eggs whenever I was sick. It was the perfect sick day food. If fat digestion is a problem, use low-fat milk and part-skim ricotta cheese, and replace two of the whole eggs with four egg whites.

½ cup farina (cream of wheat)

2½ cups milk

¼ cup unsalted butter

1 pound whole-milk ricotta cheese

½ cup sugar

1 teaspoon vanilla

3 large eggs

Place an oven rack in the center of the oven and preheat the oven to 375°F. Lightly oil a 10-inch springform pan. In a large heavy saucepan over low heat, stir the farina into the milk and cook, stirring frequently to break up any lumps and prevent scorching, until the farina has thickened, about 15 minutes.

Remove from the heat, add the butter, and stir until it has melted. Stir in the ricotta, sugar, and vanilla until well combined. Add the eggs one at a time, beating until each is well blended.

Pour the mixture into the springform pan and bake for 45 to 50 minutes, or until the top is golden brown and a knife inserted in the center comes out clean. Let sit for 5 minutes, then remove the springform ring. Serve warm or cold. Cover leftovers and refrigerate up to 3 days.

NUTRIENTS PER SLICE: 255 calories, 10 g protein, 14 g fat, 21 g carbohydrate, 1 mg iron, 163 RE vitamin A, 175 mg calcium.

Chicken

Of all the protein sources I recommend to patients, chicken is one of the most appealing. If your patient has little appetite for anything else, take heart. Not only is chicken rich in protein (7 grams per ounce), it is low in fat, easily digested, and simple to prepare. What's more, leftover chicken makes delicious nourishing meals a snap. I cook chicken with vegetables or fruit to boost vitamin intake, and I increase the protein by serving it in a sauce made with milk, cheese, or yogurt. For a change in flavor, prepare chicken with a lightly seasoned sauce or gravy.

Careful handling is imperative whenever you cook chicken, but it is especially important when cooking for a patient whose immune system may be compromised. Cooking chicken thoroughly kills any bacteria that may be present. The meat should always reach an internal temperature of 180°F. for chicken on the bone, 170°F. for boneless chicken, at which point the juices run clear, with no trace of pink. Bacteria on raw poultry can contaminate whatever surfaces it touches. For example, if you use the same board to cut chicken and chop celery, the bacteria will be transferred to the uncooked vegetables and even to your hands and the knife. Be sure to thoroughly wash your hands and every utensil that comes into contact with raw chicken with very hot, soapy water immediately after using.

Roast Chicken with Vegetables

MAKES 4 SERVINGS

Marinating tenderizes and flavors food. I've removed the skin to reduce the fat in the gravy, but if fat and calories are needed, leave it on.

1 cup orange juice

2 tablespoons red wine vinegar

3 cloves garlic, coarsely chopped

1 tablespoon fresh rosemary leaves or ½ teaspoon dried, lightly crushed

One 3-pound roasting chicken, cut up, 2 whole chicken breasts, halved, or 6 chicken thighs, skin removed

2 small zucchini, cut lengthwise into 4 to 5 slices

2 carrots, peeled and cut diagonally into 1-inch pieces

Mix the orange juice, vinegar, garlic, and rosemary in a large glass bowl. Add the chicken and turn to coat with the marinade. Cover and refrigerate for at least 2 hours, turning the chicken in the marinade occasionally.

Preheat the oven to 325°F. Remove the chicken to a shallow baking dish, reserving the marinade. Cover and bake for 20 minutes.

Meanwhile, add the vegetables to the marinade and refrigerate. (Do not taste the marinade; it contains uncooked poultry juices.)

Add the vegetables to the baking dish and baste the chicken with the remaining marinade. Bake, uncovered, for 1 hour, basting the vegetables and chicken every 20 minutes with the pan juices. Serve hot. Cover leftovers and refrigerate up to 2 days or freeze in individual portions up to 6 months.

NUTRIENTS PER SERVING: 328 calories, 41 g protein, 11 g fat, 15 g carbohydrate, 2.4 mg iron, 1056 RE vitamin A, 0.3 mg vitamin E, 33 mg vitamin C, 59 mg calcium.

Chicken Dijon

MAKES 3 SERVINGS

When someone is ill, baked chicken in a rich sauce can be very comforting. This recipe gets most of its protein from the chicken, but the milk-based sauce gives it an extra protein boost. Boneless turkey can be used in place of the chicken.

¼ cup canola oil	**1 tablespoon finely chopped onion**
3 tablespoons fresh lemon juice	**2 tablespoons all-purpose flour**
1 cup seasoned bread crumbs	**1 cup warm milk**
2 teaspoons dry mustard	**1 tablespoon Dijon mustard**
1 pound boneless, skinless chicken breasts or thighs, cut into 6 pieces	**Pepper to taste**
	2 cups chopped broccoli
2 tablespoons salted butter	

Preheat the oven to 375°F. Lightly oil a square baking dish. In a small bowl, combine the oil and 2 tablespoons lemon juice. In a large flat dish, combine the bread crumbs with the dry mustard. Brush the chicken with the lemon-oil mixture, coat with the crumbs, and place in the baking dish. Bake, uncovered, for 40 minutes, or until the juices run clear when the chicken is pricked with a fork.

Meanwhile prepare the sauce. Melt the butter in a medium saucepan over low heat. Add the onion and cook until translucent. Stir in the flour and cook, stirring, for 2 minutes. With a wire whisk, beat in the warm milk, breaking up any lumps. Cook, stirring, until the sauce begins to thicken, about 3 minutes. Whisk in the mustard, the remaining 1 tablespoon lemon juice, and the pepper. Simmer for 2 minutes more. Set aside.

In a steamer, steam the broccoli over boiling water just until crisp-tender, about 2 minutes.

Arrange the broccoli around the cooked chicken. Pour the sauce evenly over the chicken and broccoli. (If the sauce has become too thick to pour, add 1 to 2 tablespoons milk, water, or chicken broth.) Bake, uncovered, until lightly browned and bubbling, about 10 minutes. Serve hot. Cover and refrigerate leftovers for up to 2 days or divide into individual portions, wrap in plastic, and freeze up to 6 months.

NUTRIENTS PER SERVING: 860 calories, 55 g protein, 35 g fat, 34 g carbohydrate, 3 mg iron, 114 RE vitamin A, 0.2 mg vitamin E, 8 mg vitamin C, 167 mg calcium.

Mediterranean Chicken Stew

MAKES 3 SERVINGS

Serve this when your patient needs a change from plain or cream-style chicken. The olives add a burst of Mediterranean flavor—and extra calories.

1 tablespoon olive oil

1 pound boneless, skinless chicken or turkey breasts or thighs cut into 12 pieces

1 onion, chopped

4 cloves garlic, chopped

One 32-ounce can crushed tomatoes

1 tablespoon fresh rosemary leaves or 1½ teaspoons dried, crushed

1 tablespoon chopped fresh basil or 1 teaspoon dried

1½ cups chopped broccoli

¼ cup chopped pitted Greek or other black olives

Heat the oil in a heavy skillet over high heat. Add the chicken, onion, and garlic and sauté until the chicken is lightly browned and the garlic and onion are soft, 3 to 5 minutes. Add the tomatoes, rosemary, and basil and bring to a simmer. Simmer, uncovered, for 40 minutes until it has reduced just a bit.

Add the broccoli, cover, and cook until tender, about 10 minutes. Stir in the olives and serve hot. Cover leftovers and refrigerate up to 2 days or divide into individual portions and freeze up to 6 months.

NUTRIENTS PER SERVING: 450 calories, 55 g protein, 15 g fat, 23 g carbohydrate, 4.6 mg iron, 411 RE vitamin A, 0.4 mg vitamin E, 96 mg vitamin C, 200 mg calcium.

Roast Chicken with Garlic Gravy

MAKES 4 SERVINGS

Don't be put off by the amount of garlic called for; once cooked, it becomes mild, creamy, and sweet.

One 4-pound chicken

Salt and pepper to taste

10 garlic cloves, coarsely chopped

1 onion, peeled

1 medium carrot, peeled and thinly sliced

2 tablespoons all-purpose flour

1 tablespoon salted butter, softened

1 to 1½ cups canned chicken broth or Poultry Stock (page 248)

Preheat the oven to 400°F. Sprinkle the cavity of the chicken with salt and pepper. Stuff the garlic, onion, and carrot into the chicken cavity. Place the bird in a roasting pan, add ¼ cup water, and roast for 20 minutes.

Baste the chicken with the pan juices, reduce the oven temperature to 350°F., and roast for 1 hour longer, or until the juices run clear when a thigh is pricked with a fork and a meat thermometer inserted halfway into the thickest part of the breast reads 185°F. Set the chicken on a warm platter and cover with foil. Remove and discard the onion, and set the carrots and garlic aside.

To make the gravy, using a soup spoon, skim the fat from the pan drippings. Add the carrots and garlic to the drippings and mash with a fork. In a small bowl, mix the flour and butter into a smooth paste. Whisk the paste into the drippings. Stir in 1 cup chicken broth, and cook over medium heat, stirring frequently, until the gravy starts to thicken, 4 to 5 minutes. Add up to ½ cup additional broth to thin the gravy to the desired consistency. Pour into a warm gravy boat.

Slice the chicken and serve with the gravy on the side. Cover and refrigerate leftover chicken up to 2 days or wrap in individual portions and freeze up to 6 months; leftover gravy can be refrigerated for up to 2 days or frozen for up to 6 months.

NUTRIENTS PER SERVING: 520 calories, 37 g protein, 32 g fat, 19 g carbohydrate, 2.5 mg iron, 594 RE vitamin A, 0.3 mg vitamin E, 8 mg vitamin C, 56 mg calcium.

Curried Chicken with Fruit

MAKES 4 SERVINGS

Curry powder gives chicken a smooth, satisfying flavor. Use less curry powder for more subtle taste. The yogurt melts and blends with the poultry juices and fruit to make a savory, protein-rich sauce.

1 teaspoon salted butter

1 clove garlic, minced

One 3-pound roasting chicken, cut up and skin removed

One 16-ounce can tomatoes

1 cup canned chicken broth or Poultry Stock (page 248)

1 tablespoon curry powder

1 large russet potato, peeled and cut into ½-inch pieces

2 small Cortland or other crispy apples, peeled, cored, and chopped

1 small banana, sliced

1 cup whole-milk plain yogurt

Melt the butter in a large skillet over low heat. Add the garlic and sauté until soft, about 2 minutes; don't let the garlic brown. Add the chicken and cook, turning frequently, until lightly browned on all sides, about 5 to 6 minutes.

Add the tomatoes, crushing them with a wooden spoon. Add the broth and bring to a boil. Sprinkle the curry powder over the chicken, reduce the heat to low, and stir in the potato. Cover and cook for 20 minutes.

Stir in the apples and banana. Cook, uncovered, until the juices run clear when the chicken is pricked with a fork and the sauce has reduced by one third, 10 to 15 minutes. Stir in the yogurt until blended and serve. Cover and refrigerate leftovers up to 2 days or divide into individual portions and freeze up to 6 months. (Add the yogurt after reheating.)

NUTRIENTS PER SERVING: 462 calories, 46 g protein, 15 g fat, 37 g carbohydrate, 3.5 mg iron, 124 RE vitamin A, 0.5 mg vitamin E, 34 mg vitamin C, 139 mg calcium.

Hungarian Chicken

MAKES 4 SERVINGS

Yogurt's tart flavor combines with the cooking juices to make a creamy calcium-rich gravy in this nutritious dish.

1 cup all-purpose flour

1 teaspoon dried thyme

1/2 teaspoon dried oregano

1 teaspoon salt

1 teaspoon pepper

One 3- to 4-pound chicken, cut up and skin removed

2 tablespoons salted butter

2 tablespoons olive oil

2 onions, cut into 1-inch pieces

1 clove garlic, chopped

3 carrots, peeled and sliced

1 cup canned chicken broth or Poultry Stock (page 248)

2 teaspoons Hungarian sweet paprika

1 cup fresh or thawed frozen peas

1/2 cup plain whole-milk yogurt

In a large plastic bag, combine the flour, thyme, oregano, salt, and pepper. Drop each piece of chicken into the seasoned flour and toss to coat. Shake excess flour from the chicken and set aside. Melt the butter and oil in a large deep skillet over medium heat. Add the chicken and cook until crisp. Remove from the pan and set aside.

Add the onions and garlic to the pan, cook until golden brown, reduce the heat to low, and cook until the onions are translucent, about 2 minutes. Add the chicken, carrots, broth, and paprika, stir, cover, and cook until the juices run clear when a chicken thigh is pierced with a fork, about 30 minutes. Add the peas and cook until tender, 3 to 5 minutes.

Remove the chicken to a warmed platter and cover with foil. Remove the pan from the heat and let cool for 1 to 2 minutes, then stir in the yogurt, scraping the sides and bottom of the pan to remove the browned bits. Pour the yogurt sauce over the chicken and serve hot. Cover and refrigerate leftovers up to 2 days, or divide into individual portions, without the sauce, and freeze up to 6 months.

NUTRIENTS PER SERVING: 610 calories, 48 g protein, 25 g fat, 46 g carbohydrate, 4.8 mg iron, 1691 RE vitamin A, 0.6 mg vitamin E, 25 mg vitamin C, 116 mg calcium.

Individual Chicken Pies with Dill

MAKES 4 PIES

There is something special about being served your very own pot pie. A homemade chicken pie, unlike the store-bought variety, allows for control over the ingredients it contains. This pie is thickened with chicken and nutrient-rich vegetables, rather than excessive flour or cornstarch.

Easy Pie Crust (recipe follows)

1 pound boneless, skinless chicken or turkey breasts or thighs

1 cup water

1 onion, quartered

Salt

1 tablespoon salted butter

1 tablespoon all-purpose flour

Pepper to taste

1 medium russet potato, peeled and grated

1 medium carrot, peeled and grated

$1/2$ cup diced green beans

1 tablespoon chopped fresh dill or 1 teaspoon dried

Preheat the oven to 350°F. Divide the dough into 8 equal portions. On a floured board, roll 4 portions of dough into 5-inch circles. Line four 1-cup custard cups or soufflé dishes with the circles and bake for about 6 minutes, until the crusts begin to brown. Let cool. Reduce the oven temperature to 325°F.

Meanwhile, roll the remaining 4 portions of dough into circles large enough to cover the dishes. Set aside.

In a heavy saucepan over medium-high heat, combine the chicken, water, onion, and a dash of salt and bring to a boil. Cover, reduce the heat, and simmer for 25 minutes. Remove the chicken from the broth with a slotted spoon and set aside to cool, then chop into $1/2$-inch cubes. Strain the broth. You should have $3/4$ cup; if necessary, add enough water to make $3/4$ cup. Set aside.

In a medium saucepan over low heat, melt the butter. Add the flour and cook, stirring, for 2 minutes. Stir in the ¾ cup strained broth and cook for 2 minutes, stirring frequently. Taste and add salt or pepper as needed. Add the potato, carrot, and green beans and bring to a boil. Reduce the heat to low and simmer, stirring frequently, until the sauce thickens and the vegetables are tender, about 10 minutes. Remove from the heat and add the chicken and dill.

Divide the prepared filling among the 4 baked pastry crusts. Top with the remaining pie crusts. Using a knife, make a slash in the top of each crust. Bake for 20 minutes, or until the crust is golden. Serve warm. Cover and refrigerate baked pies up to 2 days. To freeze, wrap the unbaked pies tightly in plastic wrap and freeze for up to 3 months. Defrost and bake as directed.

NUTRIENTS PER PIE: 723 calories, 34 g protein, 37 g fat, 66 g carbohydrate, 4.2 mg iron, 707 RE vitamin A, 0.6 mg vitamin E, 18 mg vitamin C, 61 mg calcium.

Easy Pie Crust

MAKES ONE 9-INCH DOUBLE PIE CRUST OR 4 INDIVIDUAL DOUBLE PIE CRUSTS

Using melted butter rather than solid butter or shortening makes fast work of this crust.

1½ cups all-purpose flour

½ teaspoon baking powder

½ teaspoon salt

⅓ cup salted butter, melted and cooled

3 to 4 tablespoons ice water

Preheat the oven to 350°F. In a medium bowl, combine the dry ingredients and stir in the butter. Add just enough of the water so that the dough holds its shape. Turn the dough out onto a floured board and knead until it's smooth. Divide the dough in half, or divide it into smaller portions for individual pies or tarts, and proceed as directed in the individual recipe.

For one 9-inch pie: Roll out half the dough to an 11- or 12-inch circle. Line a 9-inch pie plate with the crust and bake for 6 minutes, or until crisp. Let cool. Meanwhile, roll out the remaining dough to a 10-inch circle and set aside.

For four individual pies: Divide the dough into 8 equal portions. On a floured board, roll 4 of the portions into 5-inch circles. Line four 1-cup custard cups or soufflé dishes with the circles and bake for 6 minutes, or until the crusts begin to brown. Let cool. Meanwhile, roll out the remaining 4 portions of dough into 5-inch circles and set aside and refrigerate.

NUTRIENTS PER ONE QUARTER RECIPE: 302 calories, 5 g protein, 16 g fat, 36 g carbohydrate, 1.8 mg iron, 139 vitamin A, 11 mg calcium.

Fish and Shellfish

Fish is nearly equal to red meat in protein content, but it is lower in fat. The oilier (and stronger-flavored) fish, including tuna, halibut, and salmon, are rich sources of omega-3 fatty acids, which are thought to reduce the amount of cholesterol manufactured by the liver and to "thin" the blood, making clots less likely to form. While these "fishier"-tasting fish may not appeal to those with temperamental stomachs, they are an excellent source of nutrition for those whose illnesses have not dramatically robbed the appetite. Shellfish, too, are a good source of omega-3s. Among them, canned clams and fresh scallops are best suited for those who are ill, since fresh clams, mussels, oysters, and small shrimp still contain their digestive tracts, which can be a source of food poisoning.

Never purchase fish that smells "fishy." Not only is it unappealing, but it is old. When fresh fish is not available, use frozen or canned fish. Both are convenient and an economical way to incorporate protein into the diet.

Fish should always be cooked thoroughly, and this is especially important when it is being prepared for someone who is ill. As with meat and chicken, raw fish can carry harmful bacteria that can easily prey on the already weakened immune system of your patient. Follow the cooking instructions closely to ensure properly cooked fish.

This section features recipes that take advantage of the many beneficial qualities of fish and shellfish; they're protein-rich, low-fat, convenient, and appetizing.

Baked Fish Fillets

MAKES 2 SERVINGS

When it comes to fish, the most common question my clients ask is, "How do I cook it?"
Here is a very simple and good answer to that question. Use fresh or frozen fillets; freezing
has no effect on the protein. Use the leftovers to make a fish sandwich, topped with a slice
of cheese and spread with mayonnaise or tartar sauce.

2 teaspoons salted butter

**1 pound fish fillets, such as cod,
haddock, or red snapper**

¼ cup seasoned bread crumbs

Lemon wedges

Preheat the oven to 450°F. Using about 1 teaspoon of the butter, lightly butter a pie
plate. Place the fish in the pie plate, sprinkle with the bread crumbs, and dot with the
remaining butter. Bake for about 5 minutes if the fillets are thin, 10 minutes if they are
1 inch thick, or until opaque throughout.

To brown the crumbs, place the fish under the broiler for 1 minute. Serve hot with
lemon wedges. Cover leftovers and refrigerate up to 3 days.

NUTRIENTS PER SERVING: 270 calories, 42 g protein, 6 g fat, 9 g carbohydrate,
1.3 mg iron, 62 RE vitamin A, 0.7 mg vitamin E, 2.4 mg vitamin C, 51 mg calcium.

Fish Baked in Foil

MAKES 2 SERVINGS

Make fast work of this dish by assembling it early in the day. I use an ice cube instead of water because it doesn't spill during preparation and provides just the right amount of liquid for steaming the fish and vegetables. Try a variety of fresh or (defrosted) frozen fillets, such as salmon, cod, haddock, pollack, flounder, perch, or halibut.

1 teaspoon canola oil	**8 ounces fish fillets (see headnote)**
½ cup snow peas	**1 ice cube**
1 small tomato, quartered	**Salt and pepper to taste**
⅛ teaspoon dried tarragon or oregano	**Lemon slices**

Preheat the oven to 325°F. Lightly oil a 12-inch square of aluminum foil. Arrange the vegetables on the foil, sprinkle with the tarragon, and place the fish on top of the vegetables. Place the ice cube on top of the fish. Loosely wrap the foil around the fish, pinching the edges together, leaving about 3 inches of space between the top of the fish and the foil.

Bake for 25 minutes, or until the fish is firm and opaque and the snow peas are tender. Remove from the foil and serve hot. Sprinkle with salt and pepper and lemon slices. Cover leftovers and refrigerate up to 3 days.

NUTRIENTS PER SERVING: 256 calories, 24 g protein, 6.5 g fat, 5.5 g carbohydrate, 1.5 mg iron, 61 RE vitamin A, 0.3 mg vitamin E, 35 mg vitamin C, 21 mg calcium.

Haddock Poached in Wine

MAKES 3 SERVINGS

If wine is not recommended for your patient, replace it with two tablespoons water mixed with three tablespoons fresh lemon juice. Serve this over cooked noodles or with crusty bread.

1 small onion, finely chopped	**10 cherry tomatoes, halved**
1 clove garlic, finely chopped	**1 pound haddock fillets**
¼ cup chopped fresh parsley	**½ cup dry white wine**
½ teaspoon dried thyme	**2 teaspoons salted butter**

In a small bowl, combine the onion, garlic, parsley, thyme, and cherry tomatoes.

Place the fish in a cold heavy frying pan and sprinkle with the onion mixture. Add the wine and bring to a boil. Reduce the heat to low, cover, and simmer until the fish is firm and flakes when tested with a fork, 8 to 10 minutes.

Remove the fish to a warm platter and spoon the tomatoes on top. Bring the cooking liquid to a boil and simmer for 1 minute. Add the butter, stir to melt, and pour the sauce over the fish. Serve immediately. Cover leftovers and refrigerate up to 3 days.

NUTRIENTS PER SERVING: 220 calories, 30 g protein, 4 g fat, 9 g carbohydrate, 2.5 mg iron, 125 RE vitamin A, 0.6 mg vitamin E, 28 mg vitamin C, 77 mg calcium.

Clam Soufflé

MAKES 3 SERVINGS

My clients are often good sources of recipes. This is adapted from the favorite noon meal of a couple in their eighties. It's easy to make, rich in protein, and has a soft, creamy texture that can be very appealing on sick days.

One 10½-ounce can chopped clams

1 cup milk

½ cup grated mild Cheddar cheese

4 large eggs

4 slices bread, stale or lightly toasted

In a large bowl, combine the clams, milk, cheese, and eggs and mix thoroughly with a fork.

Preheat the oven to 350°F. Lightly oil a small baking dish. Tear the bread into bite-sized pieces and layer them in the dish. Pour the clam mixture over the bread and let sit for 30 minutes in the refrigerator.

Bake the soufflé for 40 minutes, or until puffed golden brown. Serve immediately. Cover leftovers and refrigerate up to 3 days.

NUTRIENTS PER SERVING: 352 calories, 26 g protein, 18 g fat, 22 g carbohydrate, 6 mg iron, 217 RE vitamin A, 1.3 mg vitamin E, 360 mg calcium.

Sea Scallops with Mushrooms and Cream

MAKES 3 SERVINGS

Scallops require no cleaning or trimming, which makes them easy to prepare. What's more, they have no bones, which makes them easy to eat. Replace the cream with evaporated skim milk if fat digestion is a problem.

1 tablespoon salted butter

½ pound mushrooms, sliced

2 tablespoons shallots, finely chopped

¼ cup dry white wine

1 pound sea scallops

½ cup heavy cream

1 cup cooked rice, mashed potatoes, or noodles

Melt the butter in a heavy skillet over low heat. Add the mushrooms and shallots, stir until they are coated with butter, and cook for 1 minute. Add the wine and cook until reduced by half, about 5 minutes.

Raise the heat to medium, add the scallops, and cook until they are firm and opaque, about 7 minutes. Remove from the heat and stir in the cream. Serve over rice, mashed potatoes, or noodles. Cover and refrigerate leftovers up to 2 days.

NUTRIENTS PER SERVING: 406 calories, 29 g protein, 20 g fat, 24 g carbohydrate, 2.2 mg iron, 243 RE vitamin A, 0.5 mg vitamin E, 3.3 mg vitamin C, 75 mg calcium.

Sole Florentine

MAKES 3 SERVINGS

This one-dish meal includes servings from the Protein, Vegetable, Calcium, and Bread/
Starch groups. Wrap individual portions in plastic wrap and freeze them for times when
you're in a pinch.

**¹⁄₂ pound spinach, trimmed and
stemmed, or frozen spinach,
thawed and drained**

¹⁄₄ cup seasoned bread crumbs

1 clove garlic, finely minced

¹⁄₄ teaspoon dried oregano

Pinch of dried tarragon

**1 tablespoon freshly grated
Parmesan cheese**

3 sole fillets, about 5 ounces each

¹⁄₂ cup Cheese Sauce (page 174)

Preheat the oven to 350°F. Lightly oil a small baking dish. In a medium bowl, combine the spinach, bread crumbs, garlic, herbs, and cheese and mix well. Spoon one
third of the spinach mixture onto each fillet. Roll up each fillet jelly roll–style, tucking
in any spinach that falls out.

Place the rolls seam-side down in the baking dish. (If cooking only 1 portion, bake in
a lightly oiled large custard cup.)

Pour the cheese sauce over the fish and bake for 20 minutes until the sauce bubbles.
Refrigerate leftovers and use within one day.

NOTE: To freeze, assemble individual portions, topped with the cheese sauce, wrap
in plastic, and freeze for up to 3 months. Freeze only fresh fish. Previously frozen fish
that is refrozen will be watery and may even develop harmful bacteria.

NUTRIENTS PER SERVING: 225 calories, 38 g protein, 3 g fat, 9 g carbohydrate,
2.9 mg iron, 529 RE vitamin A, 2.2 mg vitamin E, 26 mg vitamin C, 143 mg calcium.

Betty's Creamed Salt Cod

MAKES 2 SERVINGS

This once-popular dish is no longer a favorite because it's high in salt content. I include it here because its unique salty flavor and creamy texture can be appealing when someone is ill.

½ pound salt cod

2 tablespoons salted butter

1 tablespoon all-purpose flour

1 cup milk

1 large egg, beaten

2 large potatoes, mashed or boiled, for serving

1 cup cooked peas, for serving

In a heavy saucepan, cover the fish with cold water. Bring the water to a boil, pour it off, and cover the fish with cold water. Repeat 4 to 6 times, or until the fish is soft. Drain well, cut into 6 pieces and set aside.

Melt the butter in a medium saucepan over low heat. Stir in the flour until it makes a paste and cook for 1 to 2 minutes. Add the milk, stirring constantly, and cook, stirring, until the sauce begins to thicken, about 4 to 6 minutes.

Add about 2 tablespoons of the sauce to the beaten egg, mix well, and return the egg mixture to the pan. Cook, stirring, until the sauce thickens, about 5 minutes.

Add the salt cod to the sauce and cook until the fish is heated through, about 3 minutes. Serve over mashed or boiled potatoes, with peas if desired. Cover leftovers and refrigerate up to 3 days.

NUTRIENTS PER SERVING: 775 calories, 83 g protein, 21 g fat, 60 g carbohydrate, 4.2 mg iron, 247 RE vitamin A, 0.7 mg vitamin E, 38 mg vitamin C, 356 mg calcium.

Pan-Roasted Salmon

MAKES 2 SERVINGS

Roasting is the easiest way to cook fish, I think. If pepper is not tolerated, replace with half a teaspoon of dried herbs, such as tarragon, oregano, thyme, or crushed rosemary.

Pepper to taste

Lemon wedges for garnish

½ pound salmon steak, about 1 inch thick, cut in half

Sprinkle a small amount of pepper over the bottom of a small heavy skillet with a tightly fitting lid. Place the salmon on the pepper, cover, and cook over medium heat until the fish is firm to the touch and just flakes, about 10 minutes. Serve hot with lemon wedges. Cover leftovers and refrigerate up to 3 days.

NUTRIENTS PER SERVING: 206 calories, 24 g protein, 22 g fat, 0.4 mg iron, 17 RE vitamin A, 4.5 mg vitamin C.

Beef, Lamb, and Pork

Although we are constantly advised to reduce the amount of red meat we eat, beef, lamb, and pork are some of the best sources of protein and iron, and should be encouraged for those who are ill. Just a three-ounce serving (the size of a deck of cards) carries 21 to 28 grams of protein and 1 to 4 milligrams of iron. This section offers recipes for meat-based dishes that are manageable for a sick person, making it easier to attain the recommended intake of protein and iron, whatever the illness. For example, the Garden Meatballs (page 149), which provide 1 milligram of iron each, are perfect for those suffering from iron deficiency. They are small portions that can be eaten frequently throughout the day. Beef Pot Pie (page 147) offers an opportunity to combine bite-sized meat with vitamin-rich chopped vegetables for a nutrient-packed, one-dish meal.

Medications or treatments may temporarily inhibit the patient's appetite for red meat. During these times, offer poultry, fish, or eggs and then gradually reintroduce red meat in small amounts.

Beef Pot Pie

MAKES 8 SERVINGS

The soothing, aromatic cinnamon and clove in this dish may jump-start a waning appetite, and the moist texture makes the pie easy to chew and swallow.

8 ounces lean ground beef

1 small onion, chopped

1/2 cup canned beef broth or Beef Stock (page 249)

1 potato, peeled and diced

1 carrot, peeled and diced

1/4 teaspoon ground cinnamon

1/4 teaspoon ground cloves

1 tablespoon all-purpose flour

1 recipe Easy Pie Crust (page 136) or 1 ready-made refrigerated double pie crust

Preheat the oven to 375°F. In a large skillet over medium heat, combine the ground beef and onion and sauté until the meat is well browned and the onion is soft, 5 to 6 minutes. Drain off the excess fat, add the broth, potato, carrot, cinnamon, and cloves, and stir. Bring to a simmer, then cook for 1 to 2 minutes.

Gently stir in the flour and cook until the sauce is thickened, 1 to 2 minutes more. Remove from the heat and let cook slightly.

If using homemade pie dough, divide the dough in half. On a lightly floured board, roll out half the dough to a 12-inch circle and fit it into a 9-inch pie plate. Prick the bottom of the crust with a fork. Fill the shell with the meat filling, then roll out the remaining dough if necessary. Top the filling with the remaining crust. Pinch the edges together. Using a knife, make several small slashes in the top crust. Bake for 25 minutes, or until the crust is golden. Let cool slightly and serve. Cover and refrigerate leftovers up to 2 days or freeze up to 3 months.

NUTRIENTS PER SERVING: 257 calories, 9 g protein, 13 g fat, 27 g carbohydrate, 1.9 mg iron, 323 RE vitamin A, 0.25 mg vitamin E, 8 mg vitamin C, 19 mg calcium.

Individual Meat Tarts: Divide the pie dough into 6 equal portions. On a floured board, roll each into a 4-inch circle. Place one sixth of the meat mixture in the center of each circle. Fold in half and press the edges together to seal, making a half-moon shape. Prick each tart with a fork, place on a baking sheet, and bake for 20 minutes, or until the crust is golden. Serve hot.

Herbed Meat Loaf with Rosemary

MAKES 3 SERVINGS

Meat loaf is a classic comfort food for good reason; it is full-flavored, warm, and nutritious. Substitute ground turkey for the ground beef without changing the protein content.

1 small onion, minced

1 pound lean ground beef

2 large eggs, beaten

2 teaspoons finely chopped fresh rosemary

2 teaspoons finely chopped fresh parsley

1/4 teaspoon salt

1 1/3 to 1/2 cups seasoned bread crumbs

Preheat the oven to 350°F. Set aside 2 tablespoons of the onion. In a large bowl, combine the remaining onion and all the remaining ingredients except the bread crumbs. Mix with a wooden spoon until well blended. Add just enough bread crumbs to make the mixture stiff enough to hold its shape.

Shape the meat into a loaf and place in an 8- by 4-inch loaf pan or 8-inch square baking pan. (To reduce fat, cook on a rack in a roasting pan to allow the fat to drain from the meat.) Sprinkle the loaf with the reserved chopped onion and bake for 45 minutes. Serve hot. Cover and refrigerate leftovers up to 3 days or wrap in individual portions and freeze up to 3 months.

NUTRIENTS PER SERVING: 490 calories, 35 g protein, 30 g fat, 17 g carbohydrate, 4.3 mg iron, 70 RE vitamin A, 0.6 mg vitamin E, 69 mg calcium.

Garden Meatballs

MAKES 12

If your patient is iron-deficient, serve these as part of small, frequent meals to boost the iron count.

1 pound ground beef

2 carrots, grated (approximately 1 cup)

2 large eggs

1 to 1½ cups seasoned bread crumbs

1 to 2 cups canned beef or chicken or vegetable broth

Noodles, potatoes, or bread for serving

In a medium bowl, combine the meat, carrots, and eggs and mix well. Add enough bread crumbs so the mixture holds its shape.

Divide the mixture into 2 equal portions. Make 6 meatballs out of each portion.

Meanwhile, in a large saucepan, bring the broth to a simmer.

Add the meatballs to the broth, raise the heat to high, and bring to a boil. Reduce the heat to medium, cover, and cook until the meatballs are firm and no pink spots remain in the center, about 10 minutes. Serve over noodles or potatoes, or with bread. Cover leftovers and refrigerate up to 3 days or freeze up to 3 months. Thaw and reheat in the broth.

NUTRIENTS PER MEATBALL: 126 calories, 8.5 g protein, 7 g fat, 7 g carbohydrate, 1 mg iron, 274 RE vitamin A, 0.2 mg vitamin E, 20 mg calcium.

Sirloin Tips with Garlic

MAKES 3 SERVINGS

This dish can be on the table in just fifteen minutes. If wine is not tolerated, use an equal amount of beef broth.

1 tablespoon canola oil

2 tablespoons finely chopped shallots

1 clove garlic, chopped

1 pound sirloin tips, cut into 1-inch cubes

1 carrot, cut into julienne strips

¼ cup red wine

¼ cup water

8 ounces egg noodles, cooked (optional)

In a heavy skillet over high heat, heat the oil, sauté the shallots and garlic in the oil for 3 minutes until softened. Add the beef and brown it on all sides. Reduce the heat and cook for 3 minutes more.

Add the carrot and cook for 2 minutes. Add the red wine and water and simmer until the carrot is cooked, about 3 minutes more. Serve hot, over cooked noodles if desired. Cover leftovers and refrigerate up to 2 days or freeze up to 3 months.

NUTRIENTS PER SERVING (WITHOUT NOODLES): 366 calories, 45 g protein, 16 g fat, 4 g carbohydrate, 5 mg iron, 758 RE vitamin A, 3 mg vitamin C, 28 mg calcium.

Vegetable Beef Stew

MAKES 4 SERVINGS

Beef stew is a good source of concentrated calories, not to mention protein and iron. Serving this with Buttermilk Dumplings (page 152) is optional, but if you want to boost the calorie count, they're a great way to pack the calories on.

¼ cup all-purpose flour

Salt and pepper to taste

1 pound beef stew meat, cut into 1-inch cubes

2 tablespoons canola oil

2 tablespoons tomato paste

1 small bay leaf

1 medium potato, peeled and cut into 1-inch cubes

2 carrots, peeled and cut into coins

1 small turnip, peeled and cut into 1-inch cubes

Bring 2 cups of water to a boil. Meanwhile, in a medium bowl, combine the flour with salt and pepper to taste. Add the beef and toss to coat. Heat the oil in a large heavy saucepan over medium heat. Add the beef and brown on all sides.

Add boiling water to cover the beef, then add the tomato paste, bay leaf, and salt and pepper to taste. Cook, covered, for 1 hour.

Add the potato, carrots, and turnip and cook until all the vegetables are tender, about 20 to 25 minutes. Serve hot on its own or top with dumplings. Cover and refrigerate leftover stew up to 3 days or freeze up to 3 months.

NUTRIENTS PER SERVING: 544 calories, 34 g protein, 35 g fat, 24 g carbohydrate, 4.8 mg iron, 1032 RE vitamin A, 0.2 mg vitamin E, 22 mg vitamin C, 41 mg calcium.

Buttermilk Dumplings

MAKES 4 LARGE DUMPLINGS

1 cup sifted all-purpose flour

1 teaspoon baking powder

$\frac{1}{2}$ teaspoon salt

$\frac{1}{2}$ cup very cold milk

In a medium bowl, combine the dry ingredients and blend well. Add the milk and mix with a fork until all the ingredients are moistened. Do not overmix.

Bring the stew to a boil. Drop 4 large spoonfuls of batter into the boiling stew, cover, reduce the heat to low, and cook until the dumplings look dry and are firm and cooked through, about 10 minutes.

NUTRIENTS PER DUMPLING: 130 calories, 4 g protein, 1 g fat, 25 g carbohydrate, 1.1 mg iron, 12 RE vitamin A, 41 mg calcium.

Braised Lamb Shanks

MAKES 2 TO 3 SERVINGS

This dish is slow-baked—a good choice on days when you can't spend any time in the kitchen. If your patient likes potatoes, add two peeled large baking potatoes along with the lamb shanks in the last hour of cooking, spooning sauce over them.

1 tablespoon olive oil

1 tablespoon salted butter

Two 10-ounce lamb shanks

1 carrot, peeled and chopped

1 medium onion, chopped

2 cloves garlic, chopped

$\frac{1}{2}$ cup dry red or white wine

One 16-ounce can plum tomatoes

$\frac{1}{2}$ teaspoon finely chopped fresh rosemary or $\frac{3}{4}$ teaspoon dried, crumbled

1 small bay leaf

Salt and pepper to taste

Preheat the oven to 350°F. Heat the oil and butter in an oven-proof saucepan over medium heat. Add the shanks and brown on all sides. Remove the lamb to a plate and add the carrot, onion, and garlic to the pan. Reduce the heat to low and cook, covered, until the onion is translucent, about 3 minutes.

Add the wine, tomatoes, rosemary, bay leaf, and salt and pepper and stir. Return the lamb shanks to the pan and spoon some of the sauce over them. Cover and bake for 1 hour.

Turn the shanks to cover with the gravy and bake uncovered, for 1 hour more. Slice the meat from the bone and serve with the gravy on top. Cover leftovers and refrigerate up to 2 days or freeze the sliced meat up to 3 months.

NUTRIENTS PER SERVING: 886 calories, 72 g protein, 49 g fat, 23 g carbohydrate, 7.5 mg iron, 1154 RE vitamin A, 4.6 mg vitamin E, 32 mg vitamin C, 127 mg calcium.

Gingered Pork with Snow Peas

MAKES 3 SERVINGS

Several clients who suffer from nausea have told me that the salty flavor of this dish has helped reinvigorate their appetite. Serve this with white rice or noodles.

1 pound pork tenderloin, cut into ½-inch cubes

¼ cup soy sauce

¼ cup all-purpose flour

Salt and pepper to taste

1 tablespoon canola oil

2 scallions, chopped

2 cloves garlic, chopped

1 ounce fresh ginger, peeled and cut into 4 slices

1 cup canned beef broth or Beef Stock (page 249)

1 cup snow peas, trimmed

In a medium dish, combine the meat and the soy sauce and marinate for 20 minutes.

In a shallow bowl, combine the flour and salt and pepper. With a fork or slotted spoon, remove the pork from the soy sauce, shaking off excess sauce. Dredge the pork in the flour mixture and set aside.

Heat the oil in a medium sauté pan over low heat. Add the scallions, garlic, and ginger and cook until the scallions are soft, about 2 minutes. Raise the heat to medium-high. Push the scallions, garlic, and ginger to the side of the pan, add the pork, and cook until the meat is browned, about 3 minutes. With a wooden spoon, scrape up any flour that has stuck to the bottom of the pan. Add the beef broth, reduce the heat to low, and cook, covered for 7 minutes more. Add the snow peas and cook until tender, about 3 minutes. Remove the ginger and serve over noodles or rice. Cover leftovers and refrigerate up to 2 days or freeze up to 3 months.

NUTRIENTS PER SERVING: 296 calories, 36 g protein, 8 g fat, 16 g carbohydrate, 4 mg iron, 26 RE vitamin A, 1.5 mg vitamin E, 33 mg vitamin C, 49 mg calcium.

Sweets: Cakes, Cookies, Custards, and Puddings

Sugar-sweetened foods are a good source of calories and are often appealing to people with poor appetites. But, if eaten in excess, their sweet taste can become monotonous, leading to refusal of desserts altogether. If, on the other hand, sweets are the only foods the patient seems to be interested in, offer desserts made with protein-rich ingredients such as milk and eggs rather than nonnutritive foods like gelatin, sherbet, or candy.

Whether one is healthy or sick, sweet foods eaten between meals may diminish the appetite for meals. Small cookies such as the White Chocolate Oatmeal Cookies (page161) and Sweet Potato Cookies (page 163) are good snacks because they are high in calories and stimulate the appetite without causing a feeling of fullness. Protein-rich desserts such as Classic Baked Custard (page 159) and Banana Pudding (page 158) can replace meals entirely if the patient is uninterested in other foods.

Lemon Snack Cake

MAKES ONE 8-INCH SQUARE CAKE (12 SQUARES)

To boost the nutrient value of this protein-packed cake, slice a square in half, fill with chopped fresh fruits, and top with fruited yogurt or ice cream.

1½ cups all-purpose flour

1½ teaspoons baking powder

½ cup salted butter, softened

1 cup granulated sugar

4 large eggs, well beaten

½ teaspoon lemon extract

1 teaspoon grated lemon zest

¼ cup confectioners' sugar or 2 tablespoons cinnamon sugar (optional)

Preheat the oven to 325 F. Lightly oil an 8-inch square cake pan. In a small bowl, sift together the flour and baking powder and set aside.

In a medium bowl, cream the butter and granulated sugar. Add the flour mixture and eggs alternately, beating until well combined. Add the lemon extract and lemon zest.

Pour the batter into the pan and bake for 30 minutes, or until the top is golden and a cake tester inserted in the center comes out clean. Let cool for 5 minutes. Turn out onto a cake rack and sprinkle with the confectioners' sugar or cinnamon sugar if desired. Cut into squares and serve. Once the cake is cool, wrap leftovers in plastic and refrigerate up to 3 days or freeze up to 4 months.

NUTRIENTS PER SQUARE: 221 calories, 4 g protein, 9 g fat, 31 g carbohydrate, 0.9 mg iron, 101 RE vitamin A, 0.4 mg vitamin E, 13 mg calcium.

Tapioca Pudding

MAKES 5 SERVINGS

Unlike the old-fashioned method of folding raw egg whites into the cooked pudding, here the egg yolk and white are cooked to avoid any risk of food contamination.

1/3 cup sugar

3 tablespoons quick-cooking tapioca

2 cups milk

2 large eggs, beaten

1/2 teaspoon vanilla

1/2 cup crushed or chopped fruit such as pineapple or peaches (optional)

In a heavy saucepan, whisk together the sugar, tapioca, milk, and eggs and set aside for 5 minutes.

Bring the mixture to a boil, stirring, reduce the heat to low, and cook until thickened for 4 minutes, stirring occasionally. Remove from the heat and stir in the vanilla. Let cool briefly, but while warm, divide equally among 5 custard cups or dessert bowls. The tapioca will thicken as it cools. Top with fruit if desired and serve. Cover leftovers and refrigerate for up to 3 days.

NUTRIENTS PER SERVING: 162 calories, 5.6 g protein, 5 g fat, 23 g carbohydrate, 0.4 mg iron, 75 RE vitamin A, 1 mg vitamin E, 1 mg vitamin C, 128 mg calcium.

Banana Pudding

MAKES 5 SERVINGS

Bananas are not only a superb source of potassium but some people also find that they settle an upset stomach. Here a banana is used to make a creamy, high-calorie, protein-rich pudding.

½ cup all-purpose flour	3 large egg yolks
½ cup sugar	1 tablespoon salted butter, softened
Pinch of salt	1 teaspoon vanilla
2 cups warm milk	1 very ripe banana, sliced

In a heavy saucepan, combine the flour, sugar, and salt. Whisk in the milk, breaking up any lumps. Cook, stirring frequently, until the mixture starts to thicken, about 5 to 7 minutes. Do not let it boil. Remove from the heat.

In a medium bowl, beat the egg yolks. Gradually pour 1 cup of the hot milk mixture into the yolks, mixing well. Return the yolks to the remaining milk and cook over low heat, stirring constantly, until smooth and thick, about 3 minutes. Remove from the heat and stir in the butter and vanilla.

Stir the banana into the pudding and pour in a bowl or divide evenly among 5 custard cups. Serve warm or cold. Keep covered and refrigerated up to 3 days.

NUTRIENTS PER SERVING: 260 calories, 6 g protein, 9 g fat, 40 g carbohydrate, 1 mg iron, 253 RE vitamin A, 0.6 mg vitamin E, 3 mg vitamin C, 134 mg calcium.

Classic Baked Custard

MAKES 3 SERVINGS

This recipe is a staple in every American hospital for good reason; it is rich in protein and calories, and not overwhelming to the senses. Top it with fresh fruit to increase its nutritional value.

2 cups milk	**1 teaspoon vanilla**
½ cup sugar	**Pinch of salt**
2 large eggs	**Grated nutmeg**

Preheat the oven to 325° F. In a medium bowl, combine the milk and sugar. Add the eggs, vanilla, and salt and beat until well blended.

Divide equally among three 1-cup custard cups. Sprinkle with nutmeg and place the cups in a baking pan. Pour in enough hot water to reach halfway up the sides of the cups. Bake for 1 hour, or until the custard is set. The custard will keep, covered, up to 3 days in the refrigerator.

NUTRIENTS PER SERVING: 283 calories, 9 g protein, 9 g fat, 42 g carbohydrate, 0.5 mg iron, 125 RE vitamin A, 0.6 mg vitamin E, 1.6 mg vitamin C, 211 mg calcium.

Pumpkin Custard

MAKES 3 SERVINGS

Pumpkin contains beta carotene, a provitamin that is believed to reduce the risk of certain cancers and, perhaps, heart disease. Orange vegetables such as pumpkins, carrots, and winter squash are all rich in beta carotene.

2 large eggs

1 cup pumpkin puree, fresh or canned

¾ cup evaporated milk

⅓ cup packed brown sugar

¼ teaspoon ground cinnamon

¼ teaspoon grated nutmeg

Pinch of ground ginger

Pinch of ground cloves

Preheat the oven to 325°F. Combine all the ingredients in a bowl. Beat with an electric mixer until well blended and smooth. Divide equally among three 1-cup custard cups. Set the custard cups in a baking pan and add enough hot water to come halfway up the sides of the cups. Bake for 30 minutes, or until the custard is set. Serve warm or cold. The custard will keep, covered, up to 3 days in the refrigerator.

NUTRIENTS PER SERVING: 243 calories, 9 g protein, 8 g fat, 34 g carbohydrate, 1.6 mg iron, 198 RE vitamin A, 0.5 mg vitamin E, 5 mg vitamin C, 217 mg calcium.

White Chocolate Oatmeal Cookies

MAKES 2 DOZEN

The aroma of these nutritious cookies is subtle enough to appeal to the delicate senses of those who are ill. Serve with a glass of milk for dunking, for a calorie-rich snack.

2 cups all-purpose flour

1 teaspoon baking soda

½ cup (1 stick) salted butter, softened

¾ cup packed brown sugar

¼ cup granulated sugar

2 large eggs, lightly beaten

1 teaspoon vanilla

1 to 1½ cups rolled oats

6 ounces white chocolate, cut into ¼- to ½-inch chunks

Preheat the oven to 375°F. Lightly grease 2 baking sheets. Sift the flour and baking soda into a bowl. In a large bowl, cream the butter and the brown and granulated sugars. Beat in the eggs one at a time. With a wooden spoon, stir in the flour mixture. Stir in the vanilla. Stir in 1 cup oats and the white chocolate. The batter should be firm but not dry; add additional oatmeal if needed to make the dough hold its shape.

Using a tablespoon, drop small mounds of batter about 1 inch apart onto the baking sheets. Bake until lightly browned on the edges, 10 to 12 minutes. The cookies keep up to 1 week in the refrigerator.

NUTRIENTS PER COOKIE: 158 calories, 2 g protein, 7 g fat, 23 g carbohydrate, 1 mg iron, 43 RE vitamin A, 0.1 mg vitamin E, 15 mg calcium.

Oatmeal Cookies

MAKES 2½ DOZEN

These drop cookies can be prepared in less than thirty minutes. For chocolate chip oatmeal cookies, add half a cup of chips to the dough.

½ cup (1 stick) salted butter, softened

½ cup packed brown sugar

½ cup granulated sugar

2 large eggs

½ teaspoon vanilla

½ cup dry milk powder

1 cup whole wheat flour

½ teaspoon baking powder

½ teaspoon baking soda

1 cup rolled oats

Preheat the oven to 350°F. Grease 2 cookie sheets. In a large bowl, cream the butter and the brown and granulated sugars. Beat in the eggs one at a time. Add the vanilla, then add the all the remaining ingredients and stir with a wooden spoon until well combined.

Using a tablespoon, drop the dough about 2 inches apart onto the cookie sheets and bake for 12 minutes, or until the edges are slightly browned. The cookies keep for 1 week in the refrigerator or can be frozen for up to 9 months.

NUTRIENTS PER COOKIE: 86 calories, 2 g protein, 4 g fat, 12 g carbohydrate, 0.4 mg iron, 42 RE vitamin A, 0.3 mg vitamin E, 22 mg calcium.

Sweet Potato Cookies

MAKES 3 DOZEN

These soft, moist cookies are a good snack for those who have problems chewing. The sweet potatoes are a good source of beta carotene.

¹/₂ cup all-purpose flour	2 large eggs
¹/₂ cup whole wheat flour	1 teaspoon vanilla
1 teaspoon baking powder	1 cup mashed cooked sweet
¹/₂ teaspoon baking soda	potatoes
2 teaspoons ground cinnamon	¹/₂ cup rolled oats
¹/₂ cup (1 stick) salted butter, softened	¹/₄ cup raisins
	¹/₄ cup walnuts, chopped
³/₄ cup sugar	

Preheat the oven to 375°F. Lightly oil 2 cookie sheets. Sift together the white flour, whole wheat flour, baking powder, baking soda, and cinnamon. Set aside.

In a large bowl, cream the butter and sugar. Beat in the eggs, vanilla, and sweet potatoes. Gradually add the dry ingredients and mix until combined. Stir in the oats, raisins, and nuts until well combined.

Drop the dough by tablespoons onto the cookie sheets 2 inches apart. Bake for 8 to 10 minutes, until the edges are lightly browned. The cookies keep for a week in the refrigerator or can be frozen for up to 9 months.

NUTRIENTS PER COOKIE: 77 calories, 1.4 g protein, 3 g fat, 11 g carbohydrate, 0.4 mg iron, 184 RE vitamin A, 0.7 mg vitamin E, 1.6 mg vitamin C, 8 mg calcium.

when every
calorie counts

6

When unwanted weight loss caused by illness occurs, it is essential that your patient take advantage of every opportunity to consume calories. In these situations, even a balanced diet must take a back seat to providing large numbers of calories.

If the foods suggested in the Healing Food Guide and the recipes for high-protein, high-calorie foods in Chapter 5 do not apply because the person you are caring for is not eating much of anything, don't be discouraged. This chapter shows you how to make every calorie count by suggesting ways to add calories without increasing the amount of food served.

Knowing how to increase the calorie content of food is one of your best allies in helping a patient who is uninterested in food. For example, adding 100 calories to each breakfast, lunch, and dinner and providing two snacks each day adds up to 500 more calories daily, an amount that may stop weight loss and even produce a weight gain.

This chapter includes recipes that can be used to boost the calorie content of favorite foods or traditional meals. You might be surprised to see recipes for foods that usually

CALORIE BOOSTERS

- Melt any hard cheese over vegetables or toast, or stir it into sauces. Each ounce contains at least 100 calories.

- Add an extra egg to meat loaves, rice dishes, and casseroles, or whisk one into hot soup just before serving (make sure the egg is cooked before you remove the soup from the heat). One egg adds 70 to 80 calories.

- Mix nonfat dry milk powder into cooked cereals, rice, casseroles, cream sauces, and mashed potatoes. One tablespoon has 25 calories.

- Use evaporated milk rather than regular milk in soups, casseroles, puddings, or baked goods. The high protein content will give baked breads a tender cakelike consistency, and cakes will not rise as much, but evaporated milk adds twice the calories of regular milk.

- Spread peanut butter on toast, crackers, even slices of fresh pears or apples. At 90 calories per tablespoon, peanut butter is a calorie powerhouse. Almond and cashew butters, available in health food stores, are equally rich in calories.

- Spread butter and margarine liberally on toast, bread, pancakes, and other similar items that soak up fat like a sponge. Butter and margarine each contain 100 calories per tablespoon.

- Add baby food meats—pureed chicken, beef, and turkey—to soup, or stir into casseroles. Each small jar provides about 100 to 150 calories.

- Spoon sour cream onto baked potatoes, into soups, or over cold fruit. One heaping tablespoon adds almost 100 calories. Also see the recipe for Crème Fraîche on page 177.

- Top fruit, cakes, puddings, warm drinks, and ice cream with whipped heavy cream. Each generous spoonful adds 100 to 150 calories.

- Use commercially prepared nutrition products. For example, mix Polycose, a calorie supplement, into food and beverages to add calories without affecting taste. Read more about these products in Chapter 7.

APPETITE BOOSTERS

- Keep ready-to-eat food and snacks within arm's reach to capitalize on urges. Patients may eat out of stress and boredom. Place a bowl of peanuts or dried fruit within easy reach.

- Discourage skipping meals; it's very difficult for a sick person to compensate by eating twice as much at the next meal. Encourage your patient to take at least a bite of something—a slice of cheese, a hard-cooked egg, or even a piece of toast. Not eating can perpetuate a poor appetite. If solid food is not appealing, try a liquid meal (see Chapter 7).

- Encourage physical activity. Exercise can stimulate the appetite and improve our sense of well-being. A few paces around the living room may be enough to stimulate the digestive tract and senses and improve interest in eating. A car ride provides a bit of fresh air and change of scenery for the person who is not feeling well enough to take a walk.

- Avoid making a battle out of eating.

appear as appetizers such as Hummus (page 175) and Guacamole (page 176). These dips are packed with calorie-rich ingredients and are perfect for between-meal snacks. There are sauces, too, that not only add calories, but also make foods moister, which can increase their appeal during illness.

The 100-Calorie-an-Hour Meal Plan

Frequent small snacks are ideal for patients who need to maintain or gain weight. If a patient eats 100 calories' worth of food every waking hour, it adds up to 1600 calories a day. If a 400-calorie meal or drink is also consumed, the total climbs to a healthy 2000 calories. This approach may also appeal to people who become full quickly.

To make a 100-calorie-an-hour eating schedule work, cook in batches and freeze food in individual portions so that you're not spending every hour in the kitchen. For example, cook half a pound of pasta, toss it with a tablespoon of oil so it doesn't stick together, and store it in the refrigerator until needed. When it's time for your patient to eat, experiment with different toppings—butter one hour, salsa the next.

The 100-calorie-an-hour meal plan can be accomplished without any elaborate cooking. Keep on hand ready-to-eat foods such as peanut butter, individually wrapped cheese slices, cereal, canned soup, a variety of crackers, canned fruits, frozen or canned vegetables, yogurt, and juice. Stock the cupboard and refrigerator with bread, eggs, canned tuna, and canned beans.

Here's how a day's intake might look on the 100-calorie-an-hour meal plan. I've also indicated in parentheses the number of calories in a snack when it significantly exceeds 100. Encourage fluid intake to meet water requirements. Boost the calorie count higher by offering fruit juices.

7:00	1 poached egg on toast with butter, 2 ounces juice (200)
8:00	$^1/_2$ cup cereal with whole milk
9:00	1 slice whole wheat toast with butter
10:00	4 ounces fruit juice, 1 graham cracker
11:00	1 Square Lemon Snack Cake (200)
12:00	Half a sandwich: 2 ounces sliced turkey on 1 slice of bread (150)
1:00	$^1/_2$ cup cream of vegetable soup
2:00	1 small baked potato with butter
3:00	$^3/_4$ cup canned fruit in heavy syrup
4:00	4 Saltines and 1 tablespoon peanut butter
5:00	2 ounces sliced turkey and $^1/_2$ cup rice with butter (200)
6:00	$^3/_4$ cup vegetable juice and $^1/_2$ cup cottage cheese
7:00	1 Square Lemon Snack Cake (200)
8:00	4 saltines with 1 tablespoon peanut butter

The foods listed below contain 100 calories and can be served each hour to achieve at least 1600 calories a day. Although some are not nutrition powerhouses, steady calorie intake is a priority if unwanted weight loss or poor appetite is a problem. Indeed, it's easy to see that, for example, vitamin-rich fruits and vegetables generally must be eaten in greater quantities to meet the 100-calorie goal than a food like mayonnaise, which contains little other than fat. To provide nutrition as well as calories, offer foods from all food groups.

100-CALORIE PORTIONS OF FOODS

Protein Group

1½ ounces cooked beef, lamb, pork, liver, or poultry
1 large egg
2 ounces cooked fish
2 fish sticks
1 ounce hard cheese
½ cup soft cheese (such as cottage cheese or ricotta)
⅓ cup tuna with mayonnaise
5 ounces tofu
½ cup cooked beans
1 tablespoon peanut butter

Calcium Group

5 ounces tofu
6 ounces whole milk
7 ounces 2% milk
9 ounces buttermilk or skim milk
4 ounces fruited whole-milk yogurt
⅓ cup pudding or custard made with whole milk

Vegetable Group

2 cups cooked broccoli, carrots, or cauliflower
1 cup cooked parsnips, peas, potato, squash, or corn
3 to 4 cups raw leafy green vegetables

Fruit Group

8 ounces fruit juice
1½ cups fresh berries
1 large apple, pear, or peach
1 large banana
1½ cups fruit salad

Grain/Starch Group

1½ slices white, whole wheat, or raisin bread
1 biscuit
¾ cup cooked or ready-to-eat cereal
½ cup cooked pasta, rice, or bulgur
1 medium muffin or doughnut
1 pancake or waffle
1 unfrosted cupcake
8 saltine-type crackers

Fat/Oil Group

1 tablespoon butter or margarine
1½ tablespoons mayonnaise, salad dressing, or tartar sauce

Luscious Lemon Curd

MAKES 2 CUPS

Serve this instead of butter on muffins, scones, or toast. Use organic or unwaxed lemons if possible. Otherwise, scrub them with hot water to remove the wax coating.

¹⁄₂ cup sugar	**¹⁄₂ cup fresh lemon juice**
1 tablespoon cornstarch	**2 tablespoons unsalted butter**
1 tablespoon grated lemon zest	**3 large egg yolks**

In a stainless steel saucepan, combine the sugar, cornstarch, lemon zest, juice, and butter and cook over medium heat, stirring occasionally, until the mixture starts to thicken and bubble, about 3 minutes.

In a medium bowl, beat the egg yolks until smooth. Add about ¹⁄₄ cup of the hot lemon mixture, stirring constantly, then return the mixture to the saucepan. Bring to a boil, reduce the heat, and cook over low heat, stirring constantly, until the curd becomes the consistency of mayonnaise, 2 to 3 minutes.

Pour into a heatproof glass bowl. Place a piece of plastic wrap directly on the surface of the lemon curd to prevent a skin from forming. Serve warm or cold. Cover and refrigerate up to 3 days.

NUTRIENTS PER TABLESPOON: 27 calories, 0.2 g protein, 1 g fat, 21 g carbohydrate, 38 RE vitamin A, 0.7 mg vitamin E, 0.3 mg vitamin C, 2.7 mg calcium.

Creamy Yogurt Cheese

MAKES 2 CUPS

This is a wonderful supernutritious replacement for cream cheese. If you can find it, use whole-milk yogurt to increase the calorie content. Use the cheese to spread on bagels or as a topping for baked potatoes. Or try one of the variations.

1 quart yogurt, preferably whole-milk

Place a paper coffee filter in a sieve or small colander and set it over a bowl or plate. Pour in the yogurt, cover, and refrigerate overnight.

Scrape the thickened yogurt from the filter into a clean glass bowl. Cover, refrigerate, and use within 3 days.

NUTRIENTS PER ½ CUP: 140 calories, 8 g protein, 7 g fat, 11 g carbohydrate, 84 RE vitamin A, 274 mg calcium.

Fruited Yogurt Cheese: Stir ¼ cup mashed strawberries or bananas into 1 cup yogurt cheese.

Honey Yogurt Cheese: Add 1 tablespoon honey to 1 cup yogurt cheese.

Yogurt Herb Cheese: Mix 1 tablespoon each chopped fresh chives and basil and a pinch each of salt and pepper into 1 cup yogurt cheese.

Fortified Milk

MAKES 1 QUART

You can't tell by the taste, but adding powdered milk to whole milk boosts the protein, calcium, and calorie content. Keep a batch in the refrigerator and use it in milk shakes, on cereal, or in cooking.

1 quart whole milk   **1 cup dry milk powder**

Mix the whole milk and milk powder together in a clean container. Refrigerate for at least 6 hours, or overnight. Stir before using. Use within 3 to 4 days.

NUTRIENTS PER CUP: 211 calories, 14 g protein, 8 g fat, 20 g carbohydrate, 0.1 mg iron, 213 RE vitamin A, 0.2 mg vitamin E, 3 mg vitamin C, 500 mg calcium.

Milk-Free Sauce

MAKES 1 CUP

This sauce gets its protein from egg instead of the milk, traditionally used to make white sauce. Use this if your patient cannot tolerate milk but needs the calories or moisture that a smooth sauce provides. Serve it on top of vegetables, roasted potatoes, or even noodles.

2 tablespoons salted butter

2 tablespoons all-purpose flour

1 cup warm canned beef or chicken broth or Beef Stock (page 249) or Poultry Stock (page 248)

1 teaspoon fresh lemon juice

1 large egg

Melt the butter in a medium saucepan over low heat. Stir in the flour and cook, stirring, for 2 minutes. Stir in the stock and cook, stirring frequently, until the sauce starts to thicken, 5 to 8 minutes. Stir in the lemon juice.

In a small bowl, beat the egg. Stir in ¼ cup of the warm sauce, then return the mixture to the saucepan. Cook, stirring, until thick and smooth, about 3 minutes. Do not allow to boil. Serve warm. Cover and refrigerate leftovers up to 2 days.

NUTRIENTS PER ¼ CUP: 88 calories, 2.8 g protein, 7 g fat, 3.2 g carbohydrate, 0.5 mg iron, 76 RE vitamin A, 0.3 mg vitamin E, 0.3 mg vitamin C, 16 mg calcium.

Caper Sauce: Stir 2 tablespoons capers into the warm sauce. This is particularly good over fish.

Pepper Sauce: Add ¼ cup finely chopped red or green bell pepper to the hot sauce. Good on meat or vegetables.

Robust White Sauce

MAKES 1 CUP

For those who are ill, evaporated milk is a wonder. Eight ounces of canned evaporated milk has 17 grams of protein and 320 calories as compared to cow's milk, which has 8 grams of protein and 160 calories per eight ounces.

2 tablespoons salted butter   **1 cup warm evaporated milk**

2 tablespoons all-purpose flour

Melt the butter in a medium heavy saucepan over medium heat. Stir in the flour and cook, stirring, for 2 minutes. Add the warm milk, stirring constantly, and cook until the sauce comes to just under a boil. Reduce the heat to low and simmer, stirring until the sauce thickens, about 5 minutes. Serve warm. Cover and refrigerate leftovers up to 3 days.

NUTRIENTS PER ⅓ CUP: 129 calories, 5 g protein, 10 g fat, 9 g carbohydrate, 0.3 mg iron, 99 RE vitamin A, 0.2 mg vitamin E, 1.2 mg vitamin C, 167 mg calcium.

Cheese Sauce: When the sauce starts to thicken, gradually add ½ cup grated Cheddar (for a sharp sauce) or Muenster (for a milder sauce) cheese and 1 teaspoon Dijon mustard. Stir until it melts. Use as a topping on steamed broccoli, green beans, or Brussels sprouts.

Hummus

MAKES 1¼ CUPS

Smooth and creamy hummus is a refreshing change from cheese spreads. Adjust the amount of garlic and lemon to suit the desire of your patient.

One 19-ounce can chick peas, drained and rinsed

3 cloves garlic, minced

¼ cup fresh lemon juice, or more to taste

½ cup tahini

Combine all the ingredients in a food processor fitted with the metal blade. Process for 30 seconds. Scrape down the sides of the bowl and repeat until smooth. Taste and add more lemon juice if desired. Scrape into a glass bowl, cover, and refrigerate for 2 hours. Serve as a spread on crackers or bread. Hummus keeps up to 4 days in the refrigerator.

NUTRIENTS PER ¼ CUP: 398 calories, 16 g protein, 23 g fat, 36 g carbohydrate, 3 mg iron, 3.2 RE vitamin A, 5 mg vitamin E, 5 mg vitamin C, 61 mg calcium.

Guacamole

MAKES APPROXIMATELY ¾ CUP

Avocados are one of Mother Nature's only high-fat fruits (olives are the other). They are an ideal food to eat when sick because they are calorie-dense and mellow-flavored. Spoon this over cold shredded lettuce, or spread liberally on toast and crackers or warm soft tortillas.

1 ripe avocado, peeled and pitted   **1 tablespoon minced onion**

Juice of 1 lemon

Put the avocado in a glass bowl and mash it with a fork. Add the lemon juice and onion. Cover and refrigerate until ready to serve.

NUTRIENTS PER 2 TABLESPOONS: 50 calories, 0.8 g protein, 5 g fat, 0.8 g carbohydrate, 0.2 mg iron, 3 RE vitamin A, 0.7 mg vitamin E, 0.7 mg vitamin C, 5.6 mg calcium.

Smooth Peanut Spread

MAKES ABOUT ⅓ CUP

For an alternative to cheese dips, try this creamy peanut version.

¼ cup smooth peanut butter   **1 teaspoon fresh lemon juice**

1 tablespoon soy sauce

Combine all the ingredients in a glass bowl and stir until well blended. Serve as a dip with crackers, vegetables, or cut-up fruit. Keep covered and refrigerated and use within 3 days.

NUTRIENTS PER TABLESPOON: 74 calories, 3.4 g protein, 6.4 g fat, 3 g carbohydrate, 0.3 mg iron, 2.5 mg vitamin E, 5 mg calcium.

Tofu Dip

MAKES 1¼ CUPS

This dip is ideal for people who cannot tolerate dairy foods.

½ pound soft tofu

2 tablespoons mayonnaise

2 teaspoons dried dill

1 teaspoon fresh lemon juice

Pepper to taste

Combine all the ingredients in a blender. Puree until smooth, scraping down the sides with a spatula as necessary. Scrape into a glass bowl, cover, and refrigerate up to 3 days. Serve with crackers or with vegetables and fruit.

NUTRIENTS PER TABLESPOON: 10 calories, 0.5 g protein, 0.6 g fat, 2.5 g carbohydrate, 0.1 mg iron, 0.8 RE vitamin A, 0.4 mg vitamin E, 4.4 mg calcium.

Crème Fraîche

MAKES 2 CUPS

Crème fraîche is similar to sour cream, but with a smoother texture and less tang. Although not a good protein or vitamin source, it is a delicious way to add calories to cooked vegetables or cold fruit.

1 cup sour cream

1 cup heavy cream

Preheat the oven to 200°F. Then turn it off. Combine all the ingredients in a small heatproof bowl. Cover the bowl with plastic wrap and place it in the warm oven for 15 minutes.

Refrigerate the cream for 4 to 8 hours, or overnight, or until it has thickened. Serve cold. This keeps up to 4 days in the refrigerator.

NUTRIENTS PER ¼ CUP: 164 calories, 1.5 g protein, 17 g fat, 2 g carbohydrate, 199 RE vitamin A, 52.5 mg calcium.

Butter Crackers

MAKES ABOUT 2 DOZEN

Before butter was considered a no-no, my mother made these crackers to serve at her dinner parties. I resurrected the recipe, since it is a good way to add calories.

1 cup all-purpose flour

½ cup (1 stick) salted butter, softened and cut up

2 tablespoons grated Parmesan cheese

1 tablespoon cold water

Put the flour in a large bowl. Using 2 knives, cut in the butter and cheese until well distributed and the mixture resembles coarse cornmeal. Add the cold water and stir until the dough forms a ball and pulls away from the side of the bowl. (A food processor can be used for this task as well.)

On a lightly floured board, knead the dough into a soft, smooth ball. Roll the dough into a 1-inch-thick log and wrap in plastic. Refrigerate for 30 minutes.

Preheat the oven to 400°F. Remove the chilled dough and cut into ¼-inch-thick slices. Place the slices on ungreased cookie sheets 1 inch apart and bake for 5 to 7 minutes, until crisp. Transfer to a cookie rack and allow to cool. Store in an airtight plastic container for up to 7 days.

NUTRIENTS PER CRACKER: 55 calories, 0.8 g protein, 4 g fat, 4 g carbohydrate, 0.2 mg iron, 37 RE vitamin A, 9 mg calcium.

Better Butters

Butter contains very little water; it is almost pure fat, making it one of the densest sources of calories we consume. It is an ideal way to add calories without increasing volume. Butter, however, is not always appropriate for everyone during illness, because some people have difficulty digesting fat. If this pertains to your patient, read about fat and cooking in Chapter 15. Serve one of these butters when your patient has a craving for unusual flavors.

To make flavored butters:

Cream the softened butter with an electric mixer and beat in the flavoring ingredient. Spread on toast or crackers, or toss into pasta, rice, vegetables, or potatoes. Keep covered and refrigerated and use within 7 days.

Cheese Butter: Combine ½ cup (1 stick) soft salted butter and ¼ cup freshly grated Parmesan cheese.

Garlic Butter: Combine ½ cup (1 stick) soft salted butter and 2 cloves minced garlic. Cover and refrigerate overnight.

Sweet Lemon Butter: Combine ½ cup (1 stick) soft unsalted butter, 1 teaspoon grated lemon zest, and 1 tablespoon confectioners' sugar. Spread on warm toast, muffins, pancakes, French toast, or waffles.

Ginger Butter: Combine ½ cup (1 stick) soft unsalted butter and 2 teaspoons finely grated fresh ginger. Use for broiling fish or on cooked vegetables.

Olive Butter: Combine ½ cup (1 stick) soft salted butter and 2 tablespoons minced green olives. Spread on fresh Italian bread or crusty rolls.

when only
liquids will do

7

At some point during most long-term illnesses or following surgery, solid foods are physically difficult to eat or are simply not appealing. Fever, a sore mouth, confinement to bed, or pure lack of appetite makes liquid meals more appropriate. Indeed, offer liquid meals whenever solid food fails to interest your patient. This chapter provides recipes for a variety of great-tasting, nutritious beverages designed to stimulate the appetite.

About Liquid Diets

Liquids can be very nutritious. For example, one cup of Classic Cooked Eggnog (page 190) provides almost as much protein and as many calories as half a chicken sandwich. Even when liquids contain little more than calories, they are far better than no meal at all. Fruit and vegetable juices supply nutrition, some calories, but in general little protein.

A steady diet of liquids, however, can cause problems. A person drinking only liquids may fill up too easily, before enough nutrition and calories have been consumed. Or it can be difficult to supply enough necessary nutrition unless all the food groups suggested in the Healing Food Guide are served in liquid form. While it's easy to blend fruits and milk into a drink, it's more difficult to incorporate iron-rich meat such as beef or vitamin B–rich grains and starches. High-fiber foods, too, are not easy to liquefy, and a lack of fiber can lead to constipation.

As a result, in general, homemade liquid meals are best suited for use as snacks and the occasional meal. However, many very good commercial liquid supplements are available for patients who rely totally on liquid nourishment. These supplements are sold in convenient powders that require mixing or ready to drink in cans, and most offer complete nutrition when used as directed by a doctor or registered dietitian. Read more about these liquid supplements on page 185.

Making your own drinks, however, means you can select the ingredients. The beverage can be tailor-made to meet a sweet-tooth craving, to satisfy a desire for a particular flavor, or to make use of seasonal ingredients. Try exotic fruits such as vitamin A–rich papaya and mango. Or use a variety of flavorings such as maple syrup instead of honey, or try molasses for a less sweet taste.

Indeed, when liquids are necessary, milk shakes—the old standby—usually suffice only for a short time. The sweet taste quickly becomes monotonous and even undesirable. Fight boredom with unexpected combinations like frappes made from tofu (really—they're delicious!) or a Vegetable Shake (page 195).

When planning a liquid diet, don't overlook soup. Creamy Chicken Soup (page 98) and Creamy Carrot Soup (page 100) make good protein- and nutrient-rich liquids.

Keep in mind, too, the importance of adequate protein in the diet. Select ingredients from the Protein or Calcium groups, such as milk, yogurt, tofu, ice milk, and cooked eggs or egg substitutes. Also consider adding Carnation Instant Breakfast to milk or any of the recipes for sweet drinks that follow. One package supplies 25 percent of the RDA for many essential nutrients.

Finally, think about using the recipes in this chapter to make an occasional liquid meal or snack for yourself as well as for your patient. Too often the caregiver overlooks his or her own needs.

When Swallowing Is a Problem

If your patient frequently chokes or gags when eating, he or she probably has trouble swallowing. Although liquid meals may seem the ideal solution, this is not necessarily true. Strong gastrointestinal muscle coordination is needed to move liquids from the mouth to the stomach. If swallowing is affected by surgery, injury, obstruction, or nerve damage, it may be easier to swallow liquids that are the consistency of a thick milk shake rather than a thinner fluid like juice or broth. Add dry infant cereals, instant mashed potatoes, or even commercial thickeners, available from the pharmacy, to make drinks thicker and easier to swallow. Discuss swallowing difficulties with the health care provider; you may need to work with a trained occupational therapist to learn how to best cope with the problem (see Swallowing Difficulties, page 207).

Drinking liquids through a straw can help those patients with sore mouths, who are confined to bed, or who have difficulty holding a cup. Ordinary plastic straws may not be the right choice. Try an eighteen-inch flexible straw that allows the patient to drink without picking up the glass. Or look for straws designed to stay filled with liquid at all times so the patient never has to suck on an empty straw, wasting energy and filling the stomach with air in the process. See Resources (page 000) for ordering information.

Thirst Quenchers

Some medical treatments or medications lead to a constant dry mouth. Alleviate the problem temporarily with the following drinks. Don't rely on them, however, for complete nutrition; they satisfy thirst, but provide little protein. Serve them over ice, and your patient can suck on the ice after finishing the drink.

- Grapefruit Blush: Combine equal amounts of grapefruit juice with club soda; add honey to taste.

- Orange Sunrise: Combine equal amounts of orange juice, club soda, and cranberry juice.

- Mocha Soda: Combine 1 teaspoon instant coffee, 3/4 cup club soda, 2 tablespoons chocolate syrup, and 2 tablespoons milk or cream.

LAST-MINUTE LIQUID SNACKS

These drinks can be ready in minutes. Keep the ingredients on hand so you can prepare a meal or snack on a moment's notice. The drinks marked with an asterisk are a good source of protein. As always, use whole-milk dairy products because they contain more calories—but switch to low-fat alternatives if fat digestion is a problem.

To prepare, simply blend all ingredients in a blender for 1 to 2 minutes, until smooth. Serve immediately.

- ³/₄ cup fruit juice and 1 cup plain yogurt*
- 1 banana and 1 cup yogurt*
- 1 cup sherbet and ¹/₂ cup milk*
- 1 cup lemon yogurt and ¹/₂ cup lemon sherbet*
- ¹/₂ cup grapefruit juice, ¹/₂ cup lime sherbet, and ¹/₂ cup club soda
- 1 cup light cream, 1 ripe peach, peeled and cut up, and 1 tablespoon honey
- ¹/₂ cup cottage cheese, 1 cup cooked, canned, or cut-up very ripe fresh fruit, and 1 tablespoon honey*
- ¹/₂ cup ice cream and ¹/₂ cup light cream

Clear- and Full-Liquid Diets

Clear- or full-liquid diets are frequently prescribed prior to or following various medical procedures or when digestive problems occur. A *clear-liquid diet* consists of "clear" foods—those composed primarily of water and carbohydrates, such as apple juice and Jell-O. The diet supplies essential fluids while allowing the bowel to rest, which is particularly important when the patient is suffering from diarrhea or vomiting. However, a clear-liquid diet is deficient in all nutrients. If a clear-liquid diet is necessary for an extended period of time, your patient will need a clear-liquid commercial nutrition supplement, ordered by the physician, to meet his or her nutrient needs.

Offer the following foods to the patient on a clear-liquid diet: clear broth or bouillon, clear juices such as apple, cranberry, or grape, strained juices such as orange or lemonade, plain or flavored gelatin, frozen pops or fruit ices made from clear fruit juice, plain tea, black coffee, clear carbonated beverages such as ginger ale, 7-Up, or Sprite, sugar and honey if dissolved in a beverage, and hard candy.

The *full-liquid diet* includes foods that are liquid at room temperature. Such foods may be useful when the patient is going from a clear-liquid diet to solid foods, when chewing or swallowing are difficult, or right after surgery. In addition to the foods listed in the clear-liquid diet, the following foods are allowed on a full-liquid diet. Try to offer foods from all food groups.

- *Protein Group:* Eggs in custard
- *Calcium Group:* All forms of milk, including lactose-reduced; strained cream soup made with milk, such as cream of chicken or vegetable; plain or flavored yogurt without seeds or whole fruit pieces; pudding and custard made with milk; milk shakes; eggnog; ice cream
- *Vegetable Group:* Vegetable juice
- *Fruit Group:* Fruit juice
- *Grain/Starch Group:* Refined and strained cooked cereals, such as farina
- *Fats/Oil Group:* Butter, margarine, oils, and cream
- *Other Foods:* Sugar, honey, syrup, and any type of tea or coffee

Medical Nutrition Supplements

When patients are losing weight too quickly and find it difficult to eat (or cook), I steer them toward what I call canned fortified milk shakes—more properly known as medical nutrition drink supplements. Manufactured by pharmaceutical companies, these drinks are complete meal replacements containing 250 to 350 calories per serving and up to 25 percent of the RDA for all nutrients. They often require no preparation at all, and they come in a variety of flavors. While they cost more than homemade liquid drinks, they can supply 100 percent of an adult's nutritional needs when consumed in prescribed amounts, eliminating the need for additional liquid or solid food. Many of these drinks are also lactose-free, ideal for lactose-intolerant patients.

Medical nutrition drinks should be considered whenever food intake is poor. Look at how Ensure, a popular supplement, compares to milk.

	Ensure (8 ounces)	Cow's Milk (8 ounces)
Calories	240	150
Protein (g)	14.5	8.1
Fat (g)	5.5	8.1
Calcium (mg)	240	291
Iron (mg)	5.9	0.1
Vitamin C (mg)	6.9	2

Cow's milk is the most nutritionally dense liquid we can consume, yet, as you can see, it does not offer as much nutrition as a medical nutrition supplement. Although milk does a bit better on the calcium and fat content, overall the calories and essential nutrients such as vi-tamin C and iron are significantly lower.

These drinks are not without problems. They can become boring because they tend to be very sweet, and taste and texture is always the same. To reduce sweetness, dilute them with whole milk. If lactose intolerance is a problem, try soy milk or lactose-reduced milk such as Lactaid. The flavoring suggestions on page 187 may also be useful. Change the texture by freezing the drinks. Serve partially frozen ice cream, or freeze in ice cube trays with Popsicle sticks and serve like frozen pops.

Some patients complain that medical nutrition drinks have a medicinal smell. Drinking through a straw from a covered cup can help alleviate this drawback.

SPECIALIZED MEDICAL NUTRITION SUPPLEMENTS

- Polycose (made by Ross Laboratories) has almost no taste but adds needed calories to beverages or cooked foods. It comes in powder or liquid form: One tablespoon of powder contains 23 calories; one ounce of liquid contains 60 calories. It contains no protein, fat, or milk sugar, making it well tolerated by most patients.

- MCT oil (Mead Johnson Nutritionals) is a calorie supplement derived from coconut oil. Easier to digest than other oils, it is useful when fat absorption is a problem. One tablespoon contains 14 grams of fat and 110 calories. It is not used as a cooking oil, but instead is mixed into foods before serving.

- ProMod (Ross Laboratories) adds protein. It comes in powder form. One tablespoon provides 3 grams of protein and only 0.5 grams of fat. It is sprinkled on food.

For those who need extra calories and protein but cannot eat or drink extra food, specialized medical nutrition supplements can help. They may also be useful for those who have an intolerance to extra calories in the form of fat. Polycose, MCT oil, and ProMod are three such products. Ask the health care provider or registered dietitian if these products are right for your patient.

CHOOSING MEDICAL NUTRITION SUPPLEMENTS

There are many different medical nutrition supplements on the market. Some of the most common of those that provide complete nutrition are listed below, with their manufacturers identified in parentheses. If you want more information, ask the physician, a registered dietitian, or a pharmacist for assistance.

CITROTEIN: A clear-liquid supplement available in fruit flavors (Sandoz Nutrition)

ENRICH: Lactose-free drink; contains fiber (Ross Laboratories)

ENSURE, ENSURE PLUS, ENSURE HN, ENSURE PLUS HN: Lactose-free drinks; "plus" varieties have extra calories; "HN" varieties are higher in protein (Ross Laboratories)

INSTANT BREAKFAST: A complete drink when mixed with milk (Carnation Company)

MERITENE: A milk-based powder (Sandoz Nutrition)

RESOURCE: Lactose-free drink (Sandoz Nutrition)

SUSTACAL, SUSTACAL HC, SUSTACAL PUDDING: Lactose-free products; "HC" means high-calorie (Mead Johnson Nutritionals)

SUSTAGEN: Milk-based powder drink (Mead Johnson Nutritionals)

If the flavor of the supplements you use becomes boring, try these suggestions.

- Add 1 teaspoon lime or lemon fruit drink powder, or lemon or almond extract, to 1 cup vanilla-flavored supplement.

- Add 2 teaspoons smooth peanut butter to 1 cup supplement; mix in a blender.

- Add 1 teaspoon instant coffee to 1 cup supplement; mix in a blender.

Banana Smoothie

MAKES 2 CUPS

Because of the high potassium content of bananas, physicians often recommend them to patients on diuretics. They are also an excellent source of fiber. Nutrition aside, bananas make the creamiest soothing smoothies ever.

½ cup milk

1 cup ice cream

1 ripe banana

2 tablespoons dry milk powder

½ cup orange juice

Combine all the ingredients in a blender and puree until smooth. Serve immediately. Cover leftovers and refrigerate up to 2 days. Pulse once or twice in the blender to add volume.

NUTRIENTS PER CUP: 262 calories, 7 g protein, 40 g carbohydrate, 10 g fat, 0.3 mg iron, 139 RE vitamin A, 0.3 mg vitamin E, 28 mg vitamin C, 218 mg calcium.

Ice Cream Frappé

MAKES 1½ CUPS

This is a winner every time; it is a fortified version of the popular soda fountain favorite. Select whichever flavor of ice cream is appealing. Add fresh peaches or berries for extra fiber and flavor.

½ cup ice cream

1 cup Fortified Milk (page 172) or 1 cup whole milk plus 2 table-spoons dry milk powder

1 teaspoon vanilla

Combine all the ingredients in a blender and puree until smooth. Serve immediately. Leftovers can be covered and refrigerated up to 2 days, but the frappé will lose much of its volume and become a bit watery. Blend before serving.

NUTRIENTS PER CUP: 280 calories, 10 g protein, 29 g carbohydrate, 14 g fat, 0.2 mg iron, 190 RE vitamin A, 0.1 mg vitamin E, 2.3 mg vitamin C, 361 mg calcium.

Classic Cooked Eggnog

MAKES 2½ CUPS

This is a variation of the cooked eggnog recipe developed by the American Egg Board.

3 large eggs	**2 cups milk**
2 tablespoons sugar	**½ teaspoon vanilla**

In a medium saucepan, beat together the eggs and sugar. Stir in 1 cup of the milk and cook over low heat, stirring frequently, until the mixture starts to thicken, about 4 minutes.

Remove from the heat and stir in the remaining 1 cup milk and the vanilla. Pour into a clean glass container, cover, and refrigerate for several hours, or until chilled. Use within 2 days.

NUTRIENTS PER CUP: 250 calories, 14 g protein, 20 g carbohydrate, 12 g fat, 0.9 mg iron, 188 RE vitamin A, 1 mg vitamin E, 1.9 mg vitamin C, 263 mg calcium.

Eggnog Substitute

MAKES 1½ CUPS

Although I'm not usually a fan of food substitutes, here is another safe way to make eggnog, using egg substitute.

¼ cup egg substitute	**2 teaspoons sugar**
1 cup milk	**½ teaspoon vanilla**

Combine all the ingredients in a blender and puree until smooth. Serve immediately. Cover leftovers and refrigerate up to 2 days. Pulse once or twice in the blender to add volume.

NUTRIENTS PER SERVING: 160 calories, 10 g protein, 13 g carbohydrate, 7 g fat, 0.9 mg iron, 151 RE vitamin A, 0.1 vitamin E, 1.5 mg vitamin C, 216 mg calcium.

Cold Caffè Latte

MAKES 1 CUP

Though black coffee has no nutritive qualities, it often appeals to sick people. Use it to your advantage by combining coffee with fortified milk for a nutritious coffee shake that carries 12 grams of protein per cup. For the hot version, replace the ice with ¼ cup hot water. Heat for one minute in the microwave and serve in a mug.

1 tablespoon instant coffee

1 cup cold Fortified Milk (page 172) or 1 cup whole milk plus 2 tablespoons dry milk powder

½ teaspoon sugar, or more to taste

¼ teaspoon vanilla

¼ cup crushed ice

Combine all the ingredients in a blender and puree until smooth. Serve immediately.

NUTRIENTS PER CUP: 205 calories, 12 g protein, 20 g carbohydrate, 8 g fat, 0.4 mg iron, 153 RE vitamin A, 0.2 mg vitamin E, 2 mg vitamin C, 405 mg calcium.

Creamy Coconut Milk

MAKES 1½ CUPS

Cream of coconut is very high in fat and calories. Find presweetened cream of coconut in the drink mix section of the supermarket. Store it in a covered container in the freezer and scoop out by the tablespoon as needed. To make a piña colada shake, substitute for pineapple juice the fortified milk.

2 tablespoons cream of coconut

½ cup cut-up fresh fruit, such as strawberries or papaya

1 cup Fortified Milk (page 172) or 1 cup whole milk plus 2 tablespoons dry milk powder

Combine all the ingredients in a blender and puree until smooth. Serve immediately.

NUTRIENTS PER CUP: 181 calories, 8 g protein, 15 g carbohydrate, 10 g fat, 0.6 mg iron, 103 RE vitamin A, 0.3 mg vitamin E, 31 mg vitamin C, 274 mg calcium.

Yogurt Smoothie

MAKES 2 CUPS

Yogurt is believed to aid digestion and assist in the fight against infection. When blended with fresh fruit, it makes a refreshing cool drink. Use any soft fruit that can be easily pureed.

1 cup whole-milk yogurt, plain or with fruit

1 cup cut-up fresh fruit, such as peaches, bananas, strawberries, pineapple, or papaya

Combine the yogurt and fruit in a blender and puree until smooth. Serve as is or over ice. Cover leftovers and refrigerate up to 2 days. Pulse once or twice in the blender to add volume.

NUTRIENTS PER CUP: 106 calories, 5 g protein, 15 g carbohydrate, 3 g fat, 0.1 mg iron, 88 RE vitamin A, 6 mg vitamin C, 141 mg calcium.

TAILOR-MADE DRINKS FOR SPECIAL NEEDS

- If milk is called for in liquid meals but is not well tolerated, substitute soy milk or Lactaid milk.

- To increase calorie intake, use whole-milk, not low-fat, dairy products.

- To boost protein content, add two tablespoons dry milk powder for every cup of milk or liquid called for in a recipe.

- If fat is not well tolerated, use low-fat dairy products (Lactaid milk is low in fat). Substitute non fat milk or evaporated skim milk for cream. Use low-fat frozen yogurt or ice milk to replace ice cream. Use low-fat products such as low-fat milk fortified with skim milk powder.

- To increase fiber content, add one tablespoon wheat germ to beverages and do not peel fruit whenever possible. Do wash fruit thoroughly.

Peanut Butter Smoothie

MAKES 2 CUPS

A Reese's Cup in a glass.

3 tablespoons smooth peanut butter

1 cup vanilla ice cream

¼ cup dry milk powder

½ cup milk

1 tablespoon chocolate syrup

Combine all the ingredients in a blender and puree until smooth. Serve immediately.

NUTRIENTS PER CUP: 340 calories, 13 g protein, 28 g carbohydrate, 22 g fat, 0.5 mg iron, 160 RE vitamin A, 5 mg vitamin E, 1.5 mg vitamin C, 270 mg calcium.

Curry Smoothie

MAKES 2 CUPS

Think of this as chilled curry soup. The yogurt or buttermilk provides essential protein. Serve this when sweet-tasting drinks become monotonous.

1 apple, peeled and chopped

1 clove garlic, minced

1 tablespoon apple juice

¼ teaspoon curry powder

1 cup buttermilk or 1 cup plain whole-milk yogurt

In a medium saucepan over low heat, combine apple, garlic, and apple juice and cook until the apples and garlic are soft, about 5 minutes. Stir in the curry powder.

Transfer into a blender, add the buttermilk, and puree until smooth. To reheat, stir over low heat in the saucepan or in the microwave if desired. Do not let it boil. Serve in a mug. Cover leftovers and refrigerate up to 2 days. Reheat before serving.

NUTRIENTS PER CUP: 93 calories, 4 g protein, 17 g carbohydrate, 1 g fat, 0.2 mg iron, 15 RE vitamin A, 0.9 mg vitamin E, 4 mg vitamin C, 150 mg calcium.

Cantaloupe Cooler

MAKES 1½ CUPS

Select a ripe melon for this drink and adjust the flavorings to suit your patient's tastes.

½ cup cubed ripe cantaloupe

½ cup orange juice, preferably fresh

1 teaspoon fresh lime juice, or more to taste

Pinch of ground ginger, or more to taste

½ cup plain whole-milk yogurt

Put all the ingredients in a blender and puree until smooth. Taste for seasoning and add more lime juice or ginger if desired. Serve over ice, or refrigerate until very cold. For the best taste, drink within 24 hours, puree leftovers before serving.

NUTRIENTS PER CUP: 103 calories, 4 g protein, 16 g carbohydrate, 3 g fat, 0.3 mg iron, 217 RE vitamin A, 0.3 mg vitamin E, 64 mg vitamin C, 107 mg calcium.

Breakfast Shake

MAKES 1 CUP

This ready-in-minutes breakfast is nutritionally equivalent to a bowl of cereal and two eggs. The wheat germ gives it a pleasant, nutty taste.

1 small ripe banana

½ cup egg substitute

2 tablespoons frozen orange juice concentrate

1 tablespoon wheat germ

1 tablespoon honey

Combine all the ingredients in a blender and puree until smooth. Serve over crushed ice.

NUTRIENTS PER CUP: 358 calories, 18 g protein, 62 g carbohydrate, 5 g fat, 3.7 mg iron, 290 RE vitamin A, 0.4 mg vitamin E, 64 mg vitamin C, 88 mg calcium.

Vegetable Shake

MAKES 1½ CUPS

Believe it or not, sweet potatoes and frozen yogurt are a very appealing combination. For the best flavor, make sure the potatoes are thoroughly cooked.

½ small cooked sweet potato, peeled

¼ cup egg substitute

½ cup vanilla frozen yogurt

1 tablespoon honey, light corn syrup, or molasses

Combine all the ingredients in a blender and puree until smooth. Serve over ice, or refrigerate for 1 hour, or until chilled. Cover leftovers, and refrigerate up to 2 days.

NUTRIENTS PER CUP: 370 calories, 3 g protein, 25 g carbohydrate, 30 g fat, 0.5 mg iron, 836 RE vitamin A, 0.5 vitamin E, 13 mg vitamin C, 71 mg calcium.

but i'm just
not hungry

8

fatigue, sore mouth, food aversions, diarrhea, nausea, vomiting, and pain—potential side effects of many illnesses—can all affect the desire to eat. When poor appetite develops, knowing how to prepare and serve food to make it more appealing is crucial.

A balanced diet is always the ideal, but for the person who has little or no interest in food, it may be an impossible goal. In this instance, the focus shifts from a balanced diet to calories in any form. Any food that contains calories can be considered nutritious for the person who is eating very little. Candy bars, pickle sandwiches, or other unusual combinations will fill the bill, as long as your patient desires them. I once had a client who liked to mix equal portions of cola and milk. While it was certainly not a nutritionist's ideal food, he liked it, and it did supply protein and calories.

This chapter looks at common obstacles to eating during a serious illness and provides a variety of tips and new directions to take to help overcome them.

Certainly, overcoming the challenge of feeding someone who just doesn't feel like eating is not easy. It can be frustrating when a thoughtfully prepared meal is refused. Symptoms can wax and wane, and the appetite follows these rhythms. Take advantage of the good days by offering high-calorie food. On days food is refused, don't be alarmed. Encourage small servings and wait for the good days to come around again.

When Appetite Is Poor

Our sense of hunger is triggered by a remarkable balance of chemicals that includes the nutrients we eat and the hormones our bodies make. Fluctuations of nutrients such as sodium and potassium in the blood level can signal thirst; a change in blood glucose can stimulate hunger. The sight and taste of food stimulates the flow of saliva, to aid digestion. The hypothalamus, located in the brain, coordinates all these signals to stimulate hunger.

During illness, food intake generally decreases if the disease or its treatment affects an area that regulates appetite or hunger. Some drug treatments and radiation therapy for cancer, for example, can do this. Further, not eating can in itself contribute to a diminished appetite.

When a person stops eating, the body uses the energy it has stored as glycogen to supply glucose, the basic fuel for the body. Our glycogen reserves are small, however, and when they are depleted, the body begins to break down fat to meet energy needs. It also may use muscle tissue, taking protein from it to turn into glucose. This mechanism is useful only in the short term, and prolonged use of muscle tissue for energy creates several drawbacks, not the least of which is that it produces ketones, toxic compounds that appear in the blood when fatty acids are not fully oxidized. Ketones may further suppress appetite. Indeed, some experts theorize that ketones signal the body that food is not available, and hunger sensations then diminish as a survival mechanism. In essence, the less eaten, the less desire there may be to eat. The goal, then, is to help your patient eat despite lack of appetite.

To encourage appetite, try these tips:

- *Serve six small meals a day.* Resist the urge to offer large portions, which may overwhelm your patient. Serve second helpings on request rather than run the risk of killing an already frail appetite with just the sight of a large meal.

- *Serve 100 calories of food every hour.* A 100-calorie portion of food is so small it may be tolerated by even those with the weakest appetites. One slice of American cheese, one quarter-cup whole-milk custard, or one graham cracker with two teaspoons peanut butter all provide 100 calories. See page 167 for information on the 100-calorie-an-hour meal plan and a list of 100-calorie portions of foods.

- *Serve food when appetite is at its peak.* If your patient is hungriest in the morning, serve the largest meal of the day then.

- *Cook with calorie-rich foods.* Many people continue serving low-calorie, low-fat foods and beverages when someone is ill in the mistaken belief that these foods are better for the patient. While such foods may be best for those who are overweight or a well-nourished person trying to lead a healthy lifestyle, low-calorie, low-fat foods are the worst possible choices for someone who is struggling to make every bite count. Not only do these foods provide only minimal calories, they replace foods that provide needed calories!

- *Encourage your patient to drink liquid meal replacements.* When solid foods are refused, replace lost calories and other nutrients with drinks such as flavored whole milk, eggnog, milk shakes, cream soups made with milk, and/or medical nutrition drink supplements. See Chapter 7 for more details.

- *Serve small meals on attractive plates.* Some of my clients say that food is more appealing when the plate size is proportional to the size of the meal; dessert or bread plates are just the right size for a mini-meal. Others report just the opposite. They find small portions served on large dinner platters less intimidating. Whether you use large or small plates, take advantage of the effect color may have. Studies have shown that bright-colored plates, such as red, yellow, or orange ones or those with bright floral patterns, stimulate appetite better than those in dark or subdued colors like blue, green, black, or white.

- *Fortify every dish.* Pack every bite with as many calories as possible. Try, for example, adding dry milk powder when appropriate or doubling the butter on a slice of toast. See page 166 for more information about adding calories without adding more food.

- *Limit liquids at meals.* Fluids can fill people up before they've eaten adequately. Indeed, drinking lots of fluid before eating is a technique used by dieters to limit the amount they eat. Try to hold off liquids completely, even water, until after all the solid foods in a meal are eaten.

- *Keep snack food nearby.* Place small bowls of nutritious nibbles such as dried fruits and peanuts within easy reach, particularly while the patient is watching television or reading.

- *Create pleasant surroundings.* Most people don't like eating alone. If you or someone else can't be around, turn on the television or radio. Obviously, clean up medicine bottles, dirty cups, and so forth before serving meals. The sight of an unappealing item can destroy a fragile appetite.

- *Limit coffee and cigarettes at meals or snack time.* A cup of coffee and a cigarette takes the place of breakfast for many people. Both the nicotine in cigarettes and the caffeine in coffee can decrease appetite. Of course, quitting smoking is the best choice; if your patient can't do that, at least help him or her avoid smoking—and drinking coffee—before meals.

- *Involve the health care provider.* Discuss any changes in appetite with the health care provider. Sometimes medications may be at the root of the problem, and a simple adjustment can correct it. Also ask about the use of alcohol, which can interfere with medications or be otherwise unadvisable in some illnesses. For some people, however, a glass of wine or sherry improves appetite.

Coping with Changes in Taste and Smell

Together, the senses of taste and smell produce the sensation of flavor. Thus, the proper functioning of these senses is intimately linked to the desire for food. During serious illness, however, many things can decrease these senses. Indeed, changes in taste or smell may lie at the root of a person's loss of appetite.

For example, the taste buds are critical to the sense of taste, yet treatments such as radiation and chemotherapy, and some medications, negatively affect taste bud reproduction. Furthermore, in order for the taste buds to experience the sensation of taste, food must be mixed with saliva. These same treatments and medications, however, can decrease saliva production, leading to the common symptom of dry mouth. Saliva also keeps mouth bacteria under control. When saliva is not present in adequate amounts, bacteria can increase and damage mouth cells, causing additional taste changes.

To help your patient cope with changes in taste and smell, consider the following suggestions.

- *Substitute different foods from within the same food group.* If red meat is intolerable, try poultry, fish, or eggs, all of which are equal to beef in protein value. Consult the Healing Food Guide, but don't sacrifice calories for the sake of a balanced diet. When a person isn't eating much, anything he or she will eat is nutritious, no matter how strange the combination.

- *Experiment with salty and sweet tastes.* During illness, sweet tastes may be more difficult to perceive than salty tastes. As a result, a savory stew or hearty soup may be more appealing than a sweet pudding. Serve fewer sweets, or cut the sugar in recipes in half to produce a cookie, cake, or pudding that may be more acceptable.

- *Experiment with flavors.* Tart foods may enhance taste; try adding lemon juice or zest to meats and vegetables. Unusual flavors, such as chopped pickles, capers, olives, and bacon bits sprinkled over main dishes, may also appeal.

- *Experiment with bland foods.* If your patient complains of bitter-tasting food, serve bland dishes like plain rice, boiled potatoes, hot or cold cereal, or chunks of cold tofu.

- *Control odors.* If the smell of food causes nausea, cook in the microwave. Cooking times are shorter and less aroma is generated. Cook outdoors on the grill, or turn on the kitchen fan if cooking inside. Frozen dinners require shorter cooking times, producing less odor, than baked or roasted fresh foods, and they can also be covered while cooking to reduce smells. If liquids smell unpleasant, serve them in a covered cup with a straw.

- *Vary food temperatures.* The peak flavor in food is reached when it's served between 72°F. and 105°F., or just warm to the touch. If your patient better tolerates foods with less flavor, serve food hot or cold. Keep the temperature in the middle range if more flavor is desired.

- *Encourage the patient to drink fluids.* Fluids can help eliminate strange taste sensations. Experiment with a variety of juices or flavored waters to reduce unpleasant tastes. A mouthwash of lemon juice and water before meals may also help.

Overcoming Fatigue

Low energy may be one reason for lack of interest in eating. Medical treatments, frequent medical appointments, anxiety, and nutrient deficiencies can all contribute to fatigue. What's more, as the caregiver, you may need to consider the potential for fatigue in yourself. Your own lack of energy will certainly interfere with your ability to shop, cook, and otherwise care for your patient.

Here are some suggestions for dealing with fatigue, both your patient's and your own.

- *Keep plenty of ready-to-eat foods on hand.* Make up a list of your patient's favorite foods and check it each time you go to the grocery store. Some good choices are: canned vegetables, cream soups, chili, tuna or salmon, frozen pastas, burritos, fish sticks, vegetables, TV dinners, pizzas, ice cream, and frozen pops; cheese, yogurt, prepared milk shakes, chocolate milk, eggnog, and milk; fresh fruits and vegetables such as carrots and celery, prepared fruit and vegetable salads; and peanut butter, crackers, and cookies.

- *Discuss the problem with the health care provider.* Improved medical management may eliminate fatigue. I once had a patient who was certain he was gravely ill because he no longer had the energy to pursue his passion for fishing. A few simple blood tests showed his diabetes was poorly controlled. A change in medication and diet restored his energy so quickly he was fishing by the weekend. Explore medical reasons for fatigue before trying to live with the problem.

- *Ask for help.* If friends and family offer to help, ask them to make individual portions of foods that can be frozen.

- *Use community services.* Many organizations can help with meals: Meals-on-Wheels, the Visiting Nurses Association, the American Cancer Society, churches, and other local groups. See Resources, page 340, for more ideas.

Soothing a Sore or Dry Mouth

The mouth is the gateway to the body. When it hurts, eating is no longer pleasant. While mouth sores and dryness may not be avoidable—they are not uncommon in patients undergoing radiation therapy—there are foods and techniques that are soothing to a sensitive mouth.

- *Serve moist foods.* Cream soups, meat with gravy, and vegetables with sauces are easier to chew and/or and swallow than thinner soups and plain meat or vegetables. High-fat gravy and sauces that are made with butter and whole milk can also act as lubricants. The liquid drinks in Chapter 7 may help.

- *Avoid irritating foods.* Spicy, acidic, or rough-edged foods, such as tomato sauce or lettuce, can irritate a tender mouth. Serve cooked eggs, baked vegetables (see page 105), soft casseroles, or plain fish. Read more about a soft diet on page 212.

- *Use straws.* Liquids and tepid strained soups can be sipped through a straw positioned to avoid painful areas (see Resources, page 340).

- *Serve liquids with meals.* Serve calorie-rich liquids such as mild fruit juice, fruit drinks, or milk, with every meal.

- *Use a spray bottle.* "Mist" the mouth frequently to help soothe a constant dry mouth. Artificial saliva is also available (see Resources, page 340). Some users find it helpful, although others complain it is too sticky and doesn't last long enough.

- *Use tart flavors to cut mucus.* Some medications and treatments can cause excessive mucus production. Eating citrus or lemon foods with meals or sucking on sour candy before or after eating, may help, as may a tart drink, such as club soda and grapefruit juice.

LEARNED FOOD AVERSIONS

Learned food aversions (LFAs) are unique taste changes linked to unpleasant experiences. They may develop when a food is consumed simultaneously with an anxiety-provoking experience. When the food is served again, distasteful memories are evoked, and the food cannot be tolerated.

Chemotherapy agents frequently produce nausea and vomiting. To reduce the risk of developing an LFA to favorite, healthy foods, avoid serving those foods for twenty-four hours before and after treatment. Instead, encourage less-nutritious foods before treatment. The choice is highly individual, but try, for example, a bacon sandwich or chocolate doughnut. If the treatment creates an LFA, it will be to the planned item, not to a favorite nutritious food.

Diarrhea

Short-term bouts of diarrhea are not likely to be harmful, but when diarrhea persists, the body loses considerable amounts of fluid and salt, both of which are necessary for proper functioning. It also diminishes appetite and can interfere with nutrient absorption. When battling diarrhea, the goal is to give the body the substances it needs without aggravating the condition. To deal with diarrhea, try the following:

- *Replace fluids.* Offer about one half-cup of clear liquids (see page 184) every thirty to sixty minutes, or serve a cup of ice chips.

- *Avoid caffeine.* Coffee, black tea, and cola drinks all contain caffeine, a diuretic, which draws water out of the body.

- *Avoid lactose.* Milk products contain lactose (milk sugar). When diarrhea is chronic, the intestines may lose the ability to digest lactose. Read more about lactose intolerance in Chapter 16.

- *Limit fat.* Foods high in fat may not be easily digested during bouts of diarrhea. Avoid fried foods and foods served or prepared with lots of butter or cream. Read more about fat in Chapter 15.

- *Serve foods rich in soluble fiber.* Foods such as oatmeal, pears, and potatoes may help control diarrhea. They contain the soluble form of fiber that has been found to reduce diarrhea symptoms. Metamucil, a soluble-fiber product made from psyllium seeds, can help too. Ask the health care provider before using any fiber products. Foods containing insoluble fiber, such as raw fruits, vegetables, and bran, are not good choices; they can make diarrhea worse. Read more about fiber in Chapter 10.

- *Avoid gas-producing foods.* Foods commonly not well tolerated include strong-flavored vegetables such as onions, cabbage, broccoli, and garlic. Likewise, carbonated beverages promote gas formation and may add to discomfort.

- *Serve potassium-rich foods.* Fruits and vegetables are good potassium sources. Try to get the patient to eat the recommended amounts of these foods (at least five servings a day). Choose peeled and cooked versions to reduce fiber, or try juices.

- *Try the BRAT diet.* A diet of bananas, rice, apples, and tea or toast (BRAT) has been a pediatric standby for the treatment of diarrhea in children for decades.

- *Serve tepid foods.* Cook foods thoroughly, but cool to room temperature before serving. Very hot or cold foods stimulate the gastrointestinal tract and can aggravate diarrhea.

- *Use magnesium-containing antacids and supplements cautiously.* A study conducted at Baylor University in Texas discovered that chronic diarrhea occurs in some people as a result of too much magnesium in the form of supplements or magnesium-containing antacids. Discuss the use of antacids with the doctor; the patient should not take supplements of magnesium that exceed the RDA.

Managing Nausea and Vomiting

Nausea and vomiting can occur as a result of an illness or as a side effect of its treatment. Radiation therapy, gastroparesis (paralysis of the stomach muscles), high blood levels of calcium caused by disease, or the high levels of urea that accompany some forms of kidney disease, among many other conditions, can produce nausea and vomiting.

Prolonged vomiting leads to dehydration and reduced food intake. Let the health care provider know if your patient frequently suffers nausea and vomiting. In many cases, medications can control the problem. When nervousness, anxiety, and tension cause nausea and vomiting, relaxation therapies such as hypnosis or guided imagery, and even prayer, can help. You and your patient can also try the following strategies.

- *Have the patient avoid eating or drinking for at least one to two hours after vomiting.* Then he or she can try sips of clear liquids, progressing to solid foods as tolerated. Read about clear-liquid diets on page 184.

- *Avoid high-fat foods.* Foods high in fat can be difficult to digest and can aggravate nausea. Serve a low-fat menu, at least temporarily. Read more about fats in Chapter 15.

- *Control odors.* In some cases, food odors trigger nausea. See page 201 for information about how to minimize odors.

- *Advise the patient to eat slowly.* This may stimulate the intestines less and help prevent nausea and vomiting.

- *Advise him or her not to lie down after meals.* Have the patient stay in an upright position for at least one hour; gravity may help keep food down. At the least, keep the head above the stomach.

- *Serve foods of similar temperatures.* For example, eating a cold fruit and a hot soup can trigger vomiting. Instead, serve both at room temperature.

- *Serve plain foods.* Simple starchy foods, such as plain crisp crackers, a boiled potato, or a bowl of white rice, are often better tolerated than seasoned foods or combinations of foods.

- *Try salty foods.* Salty foods often taste good after vomiting; they also help replace lost salts. Try canned soups, pretzels, or salted crackers. Many people find salted potato chips appealing.

- *Use straws.* Sipping liquids through a straw can reduce odors and slow intake to a trickle, which may stimulate the intestines less.

- *Serve meals when nausea subsides.* Many people try to stay on a regular meal schedule even when ill. But if nausea is a problem at regularly scheduled mealtimes, serve meals at unusual times.

- *Drink liquids after meals.* To limit the volume of food in the stomach; offer liquids about thirty minutes after eating.

- *Consider antinausea medication.* Explore this option with the health care provider. If it is prescribed, the patient should take it thirty minutes before eating for best results.

- *Take any medications that cause nausea only after meals.* Ask the pharmacist if nausea is a side effect of the medicine(s) your patient takes.

- *Make sure the patient wears comfortable clothes.* Generally, this means those that do not restrict the stomach.

- *Try the White Diet.*

THE WHITE DIET

Generally, good cooks enhance the eye appeal and aroma of food to pique the senses and stimulate the digestive tract. But such stimulation may be detrimental when someone is ill. A recent study published in the *Journal of the American Dietetic Association* found that bland, colorless, odorless foods may reduce the nausea and vomiting that commonly accompanies cancer treatments.

The study included nineteen patients receiving the chemotherapy agent cisplatin: Ten ate a "white diet" of cottage cheese, unsweetened applesauce, hot cream soup, vanilla ice cream, gelatin, and cola; the nine others selected a varied diet from the hospital menu. Those following the white diet vomited less and ate more than people who selected freely from the menu.

To modify the white diet for a lactose-intolerant patient, serve soup made with a nondairy product and nondairy frozen desserts instead of ice cream. Most people, except those who are severely intolerant, can tolerate the small amounts of lactose in cottage cheese.

The white diet is not balanced, but it is sufficient in the short term. It is also rich in potassium, which may cause problems for some patients with kidney disease. Ask the health care provider or registered dietitian about the usefulness of this diet for your patient.

Controlling Excess Gas

Intestinal gas can be both uncomfortable and embarrassing. Baked beans and vegetables from the cabbage family, such as cabbage, broccoli, Brussels sprouts, cauliflower, onions, and garlic, are common culprits, but it's actually a highly individual matter. Test whether a specific food causes problems for your patient by avoiding suspected foods for three or four days. Then reintroduce them one at a time, allowing several days between the reintroduction of each one. If problems with gas stop, but recur when a particular food is eaten again, you've found the offender.

Also try the following strategies for reducing gas.

- *Encourage the patient to correct habits or problems that lead to swallowing air.* People who suffer excess gas often eat fast or talk while eating and swallow a lot of air as a result. Carbonated beverages, chewing gum, and ill-fitting dentures also contribute to the problem.

- *Talk to the health care provider.* He or she may recommend or prescribe antacids or medications that can help.

- *Try Beano.* Beano is an over-the-counter digestive enzyme that helps break down complex sugars in gassy foods into more easily digestible simple sugars. It is available in tablet and liquid form in many pharmacies and grocery stores. For more information about Beano, see Resources, page 340.

Managing Swallowing Difficulties

The person who has difficulty swallowing risks dehydration, constipation, and depression. What's more, eating can become very frightening to the person with such difficulty, ultimately leading to malnutrition. It can even lead to choking and death.

The following suggestions do not take the place of the help of an occupational therapist trained in treating swallowing disorders. Indeed, do not try to treat such a disorder without professional help; it is a very serious problem.

- *Be aware of symptoms that indicate swallowing difficulties.* Several basic symptoms include reluctance to eat, marked slowness in eating, excessive chewing or fatigue at meals, frequent throat clearing, complaints of food sticking in the throat, or painful swallowing.

- *Serve soft foods.* Serve baked vegetables instead of raw, pot-roasted meats instead of grilled.

- *Serve moist foods.* Gravy and stocks act as lubricants and ease difficulties in swallowing.

- *Alter food consistency.* Finely chop food or puree it in a blender.

- *Thicken liquids.* Thin liquids are often more difficult to swallow than thicker fluids. Under the advice of a doctor or occupational therapist, add infant cereal as a thickener.

- *Make sure the patient eats in an upright position.* Let gravity help. He or she should keep the head elevated above the stomach, not eat slumped in a bed or on a couch.

Managing Pain and Stress That Affects Appetite

While alleviating the pain and stress that frequently shuts down appetite during illness may not be easy to do, managing the environment in which the patient eats is much simpler. For example, food is tastiest and best digested when a person feels calm and tranquil. And, a person is likely to eat more if eating in a pleasant environment. The company of good friends or comfortable, familiar surroundings can also help distract your patient from his or her illness and promote better eating.

Staying in the hospital often means eating unfamiliar foods, usually alone, while sitting in bed. Even eating in one's own bed at home instead of at the table can diminish interest in food. The following suggestions may help.

- *Create diversions.* Turn on the radio or TV to reduce feelings of isolation. If the patient is in the hospital, ask if a VCR can be brought in for entertainment.

- *Familiarize the surroundings.* If the patient is staying in the hospital, bring in a favorite coffee mug from home, a photo album, or other family pictures to share with staff and visitors.

- *Encourage your patient to wear street clothes whenever possible.* It may help promote a sense of well-being and have a positive effect on appetite.

- *Manage stress.* Both you and your patient will benefit. Consult a psychologist and consider medication if indicated. Join support groups and talk to family and friends about the illness and the changes it has brought. Discuss your problems with people who are dealing with or have dealt with similar illnesses.

- *Manage pain.* Discuss the use of pain medications with the doctor. They may help improve the patient's appetite if taken before meals.

FOOD CRAVINGS

It is commonly thought that the body develops food cravings to get what it wants. Feelings of thirst signal a need for liquids. A craving for salty foods may signal the need for sodium. A meat craving may signal the body's need for iron. Nevertheless, food cravings are not reliable indicators of nutritional needs. For example, cancer patients who undergo certain treatments crave fruit, but fruit is not a good source of calories or protein, both of which are in demand by the body during cancer therapy. If the person you care for craves certain foods, satisfy the desire, but then try to balance the day's intake with a variety of foods from the Healing Food Guide.

Use the Microwave to Make Fast, Healthy Meals

A microwave oven works with small, invisible waves similar to radio waves. They vibrate the molecules in food to create heat and cook the food. Salt and fat molecules heat up the fastest, so foods high in salt or fat cook the most quickly. Food with a high water content cooks more slowly. For example, a stick of butter is almost pure fat; it melts completely within sixty to ninety seconds in a microwave. A small potato approximately the same size as the stick of butter contains lots of water and little fat; it takes three to four minutes to cook.

- One half cup of fruits or vegetables cooks in about two minutes on high, if covered.

- To cook meats, poultry and fish evenly, cut into pieces about half an inch thick—the depth microwaves penetrate. Large cuts of meat are best cooked in conventional ovens.

- Stir and rotate foods for even cooking.

- Follow cooking and "resting" times in recipes to avoid food poisoning. The food finishes cooking during the rest time.

- To defrost frozen foods, cook on medium for two to four minutes.

- To reheat refrigerated foods, cover with microwave-safe plastic wrap and cook in one-minute increments until warm enough to eat.

- When purchasing a microwave oven, choose one with at least 650 to 700 watts, enough space to hold a full-size dinner plate, and an automatic turntable.

soft, mechanical-soft, and low-fiber diets

9

by modifying the texture or consistency of food, or how it is seasoned, sometimes appetite can be revived. At the very least, mildly flavored, soft foods often have a psychological advantage—they appear to be more digestible and easier to tolerate than raw or spicy foods.

Keep three food characteristics in mind when the mouth, stomach, or intestinal tract is inflamed or tender: texture, spiciness, and fiber content. If your patient experiences difficulty in eating due to pain in any of these areas, a soft, mechanical-soft, or low-fiber diet may make eating less of a challenge.

The Soft Diet

Fluids and solid foods are lightly seasoned and moderately low in fiber on a soft diet. Individualize the diet based on your patient's appetite, chewing and swallowing ability, and food tolerances. For example, a person who has undergone surgery may not tolerate highly seasoned foods, but they may be well tolerated by the person who must follow a soft diet because of dental problems.

Who Should Eat a Soft Diet?

Those who are progressing from liquids to solid foods, have mild gastrointestinal problems, are too weak to chew well, or have dental problems that interfere with eating can benefit from a soft diet. A soft diet can be nutritionally balanced, and therefore can be used indefinitely by anyone who finds it appealing.

What to Eat on a Soft Diet

- *Protein Group:* All lean, tender cuts of meat, poultry, and fish and shellfish; eggs; mild-flavored cheeses; creamy peanut butter; tofu. Avoid strong-smelling or highly seasoned meats and cheeses. Beans may cause distress for some people.

- *Calcium Group:* All milk and milk products; soups made with milk; custards; pudding; ice cream; tofu, cooked green leafy vegetables. Avoid yogurt with nuts or dried fruits.

- *Vegetable Group:* Cooked vegetables and lettuce, as tolerated. Avoid raw and fried vegetables, corn, and gas-producing vegetables (e.g., broccoli, Brussels sprouts, cabbage, onions, etc.).

- *Fruit Group:* Cooked or canned fruits and juices; grapefruit and orange sections without membranes; and soft fruits such as avocados, bananas, strawberries, and melons. Avoid other fresh and dried fruits.

- *Grain/Starch Group:* White, refined-wheat, or light-rye enriched breads, soft rolls, and crackers; cooked and ready-to-eat cereals. Avoid bran cereals, whole-grain breads or crackers with seeds, and items with nuts or dried fruits.

- *Fat/Oil Group:* Butter or margarine; salad dressings; all cooking oils. Avoid highly seasoned salad dressings.

- *Other Foods:* Seasonings and Condiments: Salt, flavorings, jams, jelly, syrup, and honey. Pepper, herbs, spices, catsup, mustard, and vinegar in moderation. Avoid strongly flavored items such as garlic, chili sauce, and horseradish.

- *Beverages:* Most beverages. Carbonated drinks may be bothersome for some individuals. Avoid alcoholic beverages.

The Mechanical-Soft Diet

The **mechanical-soft** diet is the traditional name of the diet recommended for the person who has difficulty chewing and swallowing.

Who Should Eat a Mechanical-Soft Diet?

Patients who have dental or esophageal problems, or who have recently had surgery on the head, neck, or mouth. The diet presents no nutritional risks, since all food groups are included.

What to Eat on a Mechanical-Soft Diet

- *Protein Group:* Ground or finely chopped beef, chicken, turkey, lamb, or pork, served with gravy or a sauce; soft casseroles or soups made with these ingredients; chopped egg, tuna, or chicken mixed with mayonnaise or salad dressing; cheese and cheese dishes.

- *Calcium Group:* All types of milk, yogurt, custards, pudding, and ice cream; cream soup made with soft ingredients; tofu; chopped cooked green leafy vegetables.

- *Vegetable Group:* Chopped, mashed, or pureed cooked vegetables without skin or seeds; boiled, baked, or mashed potatoes; vegetable soups made with soft ingredients. Avoid raw or fried vegetables and corn.

- *Fruit Group:* All juices and canned or cooked fruit without skin or seeds. Avoid coconut, fresh pineapple, and dried fruits.

- *Grain/Starch Group:* Cooked cereals without added fruit or nuts; plain dry cereals softened in milk; soft breads, pancakes, muffins, and soft waffles; breads and plain crackers softened in soup or beverage; soft cookies without fruit or nuts. Avoid any grain food that contains seeds, dried fruits, or nuts.

- *Fat/Oil Group:* Butter, margarine, cooking oils, salad dressings, and creams. Avoid nuts.
- *Other Foods:* Seasonings and Condiments: All herbs and spices, jam, jelly, syrup, honey, catsup, and mustard.
- *Beverages:* Coffee, tea, and carbonated beverages may be bothersome for some individuals. Use as tolerated.

The Low-Fiber Diet

The low-fiber diet is often used when the gastrointestinal tract is inflamed and irritated or when it is desirable to minimize fecal volume.

Who Should Eat a Low-Fiber Diet?

A low-fiber diet is frequently used when ulcerative colitis, Crohn's disease, or diverticulosis inflames the intestines, when the gastrointestinal tract is narrow or constricted at any point, or following abdominal surgery.

Once symptoms are relieved, however, patients should progress to a higher-fiber diet as recommended by the health care provider. Long-term use of this diet is associated with constipation and diverticulosis.

What to Eat on a Low-Fiber Diet

- *Protein Group:* Ground or well-cooked tender beef, lamb, ham, veal, pork, poultry, and fish; eggs and cheese. Avoid tough fibrous meats with gristle, dried beans, peas, lentils, legumes, and peanut butter.
- *Calcium Group:* No more than 2 cups per day of milk and foods containing milk. Milk is not high in fiber, but may increase fecal volume.
- *Vegetable Group:* No more than two servings per day. Most well-cooked and canned vegetables without seeds; lettuce if tolerated. Avoid sauerkraut, winter squash, peas, most raw vegetables and vegetables with seeds, and juice with pulp.
- *Fruit Group:* No more than two servings per day. Most canned and cooked fruits; applesauce; fruit cocktail; and ripe bananas. Avoid dried fruits, all berries, and most raw fruits. Avoid prune juice and any juice that contains pulp.

- *Grain/Starch Group:* Refined breads, rolls, biscuits, muffins, and crackers; pancakes or waffles, plain pastries; refined cooked cereals such as grits and farina; refined cereals including puffed rice and puffed wheat. Avoid any items made with whole-grain flour, bran, seeds, nuts, coconut, or raw or dried fruits; cornbread; graham crackers; oatmeal; granolas; popcorn.

- *Fat/Oil Group:* Margarine, butter, cooking oils, and salad dressings; bacon; plain gravies. Avoid nuts.

- *Other Foods:* Seasonings and Condiments: Salt, pepper, sugar, spices, herbs, vinegar, catsup, and mustard. Avoid seeds.

- *Beverages:* Coffee, tea, and carbonated beverages; strained fruit drinks. (Limit milk as discussed.)

The recipes that follow are appropriate for anyone on a soft diet. Several recipes include soft cooked fruits and vegetables. When on a low-fiber diet, select recipes with a lower-fiber content.

Scalloped Shrimp with Egg Noodles

MAKES 2 SERVINGS

Shrimp is an excellent way to get protein on a soft diet. It does contain cholesterol, but can be part of a healthy diet if eaten in moderation.

2 teaspoons salted butter

8 ounces shrimp, peeled and deveined

³⁄₄ cup milk

2 tablespoons dry sherry

1 teaspoon paprika

1 large egg yolk

2 cups cooked egg noodles

¹⁄₄ cup seasoned bread crumbs

2 teaspoons olive oil

Preheat the oven to 350°F. Lightly butter a 1-quart baking dish. Melt the butter in a sauté pan over medium heat. Add the shrimp and cook until pink and opaque, 2 to 3 minutes. Remove the shrimp and set aside.

Add ¹⁄₂ cup of the milk, the sherry, and paprika to the pan and simmer until slightly reduced for 3 minutes, stirring occasionally. In a small bowl, beat the egg yolk with the remaining ¹⁄₄ cup milk. Beat about 3 tablespoons of the hot milk mixture into the egg yolk, then return the mixture to the pan, stirring constantly. Cook, stirring until the sauce thickens, 3 to 5 minutes. Stir in the shrimp and remove from the heat.

Spread the cooked noodles over the bottom of the baking dish. Pour the shrimp and sauce over the noodles.

Toss the bread crumbs with the olive oil and sprinkle over the shrimp mixture. Bake for 15 minutes, or until the crumbs are golden. Serve hot. Cover leftovers and refrigerate up to 2 days.

NUTRIENTS PER SERVING: 543 calories, 37 g protein, 18 g fat, 52 g carbohydrate, 6 mg iron, 380 RE vitamin A, 0.5 mg vitamin E, 4 mg vitamin C, 200 mg calcium, 4 g fiber.

Baked Couscous with Vegetables

MAKES 5 SERVINGS

Couscous is granular semolina, a staple of North African cooking. Like other pastas, couscous is very versatile and provides a backdrop for all kinds of flavors and seasonings.

1 medium carrot, peeled and chopped

½ cup chopped green beans

2 tablespoons olive oil

2 to 2½ cups canned chicken broth or Poultry Stock (page 248)

1 cup couscous

1 teaspoon fresh rosemary leaves, crushed

½ cup grated Muenster cheese

Preheat the oven to 325°F. In an ovenproof saucepan, sauté the vegetables in the olive oil just until they soften, about 3 minutes.

Add 2 cups broth and bring to a boil. Gradually add the couscous, reduce the heat to low, stir, and cook, covered, for 5 minutes.

Fluff the couscous with a fork and add the rosemary. If the couscous looks dry, stir in ½ cup additional broth. Sprinkle with the cheese and bake, covered, for about 3 minutes, until the cheese melts. Serve immediately. Cover leftovers and refrigerate up to 2 days.

NUTRIENTS PER SERVING: 232 calories, 11 g protein, 10 g fat, 25 g carbohydrate, 1 mg iron, 451 RE vitamin A, 3 mg vitamin C, 103 mg calcium, 3 g fiber.

Tricolor Vegetable Sauté

MAKES 3 SERVINGS

Vegetables provide essential healing nutrients and can be prepared so that they are appetizing to patients with upset stomachs. Here the vegetables are slow-cooked in their own juices, making them tender and easily digestible. One serving of this counts as one of the two recommended vegetable servings on the low-fiber diet.

2 teaspoons salted butter

1 small sweet potato, peeled and thinly sliced

1 small potato, peeled and thinly sliced

½ cup thinly sliced green beans

Melt the butter in a heavy saucepan or skillet over very low heat. Add the vegetables, toss them in the melted butter, cover, and simmer until tender, about 20 minutes. Check the vegetables after 5 minutes and add 2 tablespoons water if they seem dry. Serve hot. Cover leftovers and refrigerate up to 3 days.

NUTRIENTS PER SERVING: 98 calories, 2 g protein, 3 g fat, 17 g carbohydrate, 0.7 mg iron, 865 RE vitamin A, 1.8 mg vitamin E, 20 mg vitamin C, 21 mg calcium, 2 g fiber.

Vegetable Upside-Down Cake

MAKES 8 SERVINGS

This meal-in-a-dish is packed with nutrients. The vegetables are topped with a biscuit-like batter, then inverted to reveal a pretty arrangement of vegetables. Those on a low-fiber menu should limit themselves to two servings per day.

1¹⁄₂ cups all-purpose flour

¹⁄₂ cup cornmeal

2 teaspoons baking powder

¹⁄₄ cup salted butter, softened

1 cup milk

1 large egg, beaten

1 tablespoon honey

4 cups cooked vegetables, such as peas, chopped carrots, and chopped broccoli (defrosted frozen vegetables can be substituted)

Cheese Sauce (page 174; optional)

Preheat oven to 400°F. Butter a heavy ovenproof 9-inch skillet. Combine all the dry ingredients in a large bowl. Using 2 knives, cut in the butter until the butter is the size of small peas. In a small bowl, mix the milk, egg, and honey together. Stir into the flour mixture to make a thick, smooth batter.

Arrange the vegetables in an attractive pattern in the skillet. Pour the batter over the vegetables and bake for 20 to 25 minutes, or until a knife inserted into the cake comes out clean.

To serve, invert the cake onto a platter. Cut into wedges and serve plain or with Cheese Sauce. Cover leftovers and refrigerate up to 3 days.

NUTRIENTS PER SERVING: 252 calories, 8 g protein, 8 g fat, 38 g carbohydrate, 2 mg iron, 1230 RE vitamin A, 19 mg vitamin C, 75 mg calcium, 4 g fiber.

Butternut Squash Gratin

MAKES 3 SERVINGS

I have found that this dish appeals to die-hard vegetable haters. Substitute broccoli, carrots, parsnips, turnips, or even rutabagas for the squash if you like.

**2 cups cubed peeled
    butternut squash**

1 tablespoon salted butter

2 tablespoons all-purpose flour

1 cup buttermilk, warmed

¼ cup bread crumbs

2 teaspoons olive oil

Preheat the oven to 325°F. Lightly butter a glass pie plate or a gratin dish. In a steamer, steam the squash over boiling water until tender but not mushy, 5 to 8 minutes. Set aside.

Melt the butter in a medium saucepan over low heat. Stir in the flour and cook for 1 to 2 minutes. Stir in the buttermilk and cook, stirring until the sauce thickens, 4 to 5 minutes.

Arrange the squash evenly in the pie plate or dish. Pour the buttermilk sauce over the squash. Toss the bread crumbs with the oil and sprinkle over the top. Bake for 40 to 45 minutes, until the sauce is bubbly and the top is golden. Serve warm. Cover leftovers and refrigerate up to 3 days.

NUTRIENTS PER SERVING: 198 calories, 5 g protein, 9 g fat, 26 g carbohydrate, 1 mg iron, 530 RE vitamin A, 14 mg vitamin C, 126 mg calcium, 4 g fiber.

Creamy Rice Pudding

MAKES 3 SERVINGS

This combination of rice, milk, and eggs makes an excellent replacement for a traditional meal. Serve this for breakfast, lunch, or dinner or as a snack.

½ cup white rice	**¼ teaspoon grated nutmeg**
4 cups milk	**½ cup packed brown sugar**
½ teaspoon ground cinnamon	**2 large eggs, beaten**

Preheat the oven to 300°F. Lightly oil a 1½ quart baking dish. In a large bowl, combine the rice, milk, cinnamon, nutmeg, and brown sugar and mix thoroughly with a fork. Pour into the baking dish.

Bake for 1 hour, stirring every 15 minutes. Then bake for 1 hour without stirring.

Stir the beaten eggs into the pudding, making sure they are evenly distributed. Bake for 30 minutes more until all the liquid is absorbed. Stir before serving. Serve warm or cold topped with ice cream, whipped cream, or frozen yogurt if desired. Cover leftovers and refrigerate up to 2 days.

NUTRIENTS PER SERVING: 460 calories, 15 g protein, 11 g fat, 75 g carbohydrate, 3 mg iron, 140 RE vitamin A, 2 mg vitamin C, 344 mg calcium, 0.5 g fiber.

Pear Bread Pudding

MAKES 4 SERVINGS

This is a nice way to slide fresh fruit into a soft diet.

¼ **cup packed brown sugar**

½ **teaspoon ground cinnamon**

1 **teaspoon vanilla extract**

2 **large eggs, beaten**

2 **cups milk**

6 **slices stale or lightly toasted white bread, torn into small pieces**

2 **ripe pears, peeled, cored, and chopped**

Preheat the oven to 325°F. Butter a 1-quart baking dish.

In a medium bowl, combine the brown sugar, cinnamon, vanilla, eggs, and milk and mix thoroughly with a whisk or a fork.

Put the bread and pears in the baking dish and pour the egg mixture over the top. Toss the pears and bread together, and spread out in the dish.

Bake for 50 minutes, or until all the liquid is absorbed and the top is lightly browned. Serve warm or chilled. Cover leftovers and refrigerate up to 3 days.

NUTRIENTS PER SERVING: 287 calories, 10 g protein, 8 g fat, 44 g carbohydrate, 1 mg iron, 94 RE vitamin A, 2 mg vitamin C, 220 mg calcium, 2.5 g fiber.

Lemon-Orange Muffins

MAKES 18

These sugar-glazed muffins are especially easy to chew and swallow and are most appetizing when served warm.

2 cups all-purpose flour

2 teaspoons baking powder

½ teaspoon baking soda

¼ teaspoon salt

1 large egg

3 tablespoons sugar

3 tablespoons honey

2 tablespoons canola or vegetable oil

1 cup plain whole-milk yogurt

1 tablespoon grated lemon zest

½ teaspoon lemon extract

Glaze

4 to 7 tablespoons confectioners' sugar

1 teaspoon grated orange zest

¼ cup orange juice

Preheat the oven to 350°F. Lightly oil 18 muffin cups. Sift together the flour, baking powder, soda, and salt.

In a medium bowl, beat the egg with a fork. Add the sugar, honey, and oil and blend with the fork. Add the yogurt, lemon zest, and extract and stir to combine. Add the dry ingredients and mix with the fork until moistened. Spoon into the muffin cups and bake for 20 minutes until golden on top.

Meanwhile, prepare the glaze. In a small bowl, combine ¼ cup confectioners' sugar and the orange zest. Gradually add the orange juice. Add additional sugar if a thicker glaze is desired.

Drizzle or spread the glaze over the warm muffins. Cover and refrigerate up to 7 days or freeze up to 3 months.

NUTRIENTS PER MUFFIN: 102 calories, 2 g protein, 2 g fat, 18 g carbohydrate, 10 RE vitamin A, 2 mg vitamin C, 20 mg calcium, 0.4 g fiber.

Poached Fruit

MAKES 2 SERVINGS

Warm, cooked fruit is usually more appealing than raw to a sick person. Top it with yogurt for a balanced snack. Serve this as a side dish or spoon onto puddings or cake.

2 pears, apples, or peaches, peeled, halved, and cored or pitted

1 cup water

¼ cup packed brown sugar

¼ teaspoon ground cloves

Preheat the oven to 325°F. Lightly butter a baking dish or 2 custard cups. Arrange the fruit in the dish or cups.

In a small saucepan, combine the water, brown sugar, and cloves. Cook over medium heat, stirring frequently, until the sugar is dissolved, 3 to 4 minutes.

Pour the poaching liquid over the fruit and bake, uncovered, for 45 to 50 minutes, or until the fruit is tender when pricked with a fork. Serve hot, topped with ice cream, whipped cream, or vanilla yogurt if desired.

NUTRIENTS PER SERVING (MADE WITH PEARS): 158 calories, 0.5 g protein, trace fat, 41 g carbohydrate, 0.9 mg iron, 2 mg vitamin C, 32 mg calcium, 3 g fiber.

No-Bake Fruit Pie

MAKES 8 SERVINGS

Layers of ladyfingers, delicate custard, sweet fruit, and honey make an enticing dessert that is soft enough for even the sorest mouth.

12 ladyfingers

2 large eggs plus 1 large egg yolk, beaten

2 cups cold milk

¼ cup honey

2 tablespoons unsalted butter, at room temperature

1½ teaspoons vanilla extract

1½ cups mixed fruit, raw or cooked, such as blueberries, mandarin oranges, strawberries, raspberries, and/or cut-up peaches, pears, and kiwi.

Glaze

1 tablespoon sugar

¼ cup honey

1 tablespoon unsalted butter

Split the ladyfingers and arrange them to cover the bottom of a 9-inch pie plate.

In a heavy saucepan over low heat, combine the eggs and egg yolk, milk, and honey and cook, stirring constantly with a wooden spoon, until the mixture thickens enough to coat the spoon, about 5 to 6 minutes. Do not let it boil, or it will curdle. Remove from the heat and stir in the butter and vanilla. Stir until the butter melts.

Pour the hot custard over the ladyfingers. (The custard will thicken as it cools.) Arrange the fruit over the custard. Set aside.

To make the glaze, in a saucepan over low heat, combine the sugar, honey, and butter and cook, stirring, until the sugar dissolves. Pour the glaze over the fruit. Serve warm or refrigerate for 1½ hours, or until completely cooled. Cover leftovers and refrigerate up to 3 days.

NUTRIENTS PER SERVING: 328 calories, 8 g protein, 10 g fat, 52 g carbohydrate, 1.2 mg iron, 172 RE vitamin A, 2 mg vitamin C, 106 mg calcium, 0.6 g fiber.

the high-
fiber diet

fiber—the undigestible part of fruits, vegetables, and grains—is commonly referred to as roughage or bulk. There are two types of fiber, and most foods contain both, especially whole or minimally refined foods.

Soluble fiber, found in particularly large quantities in oat bran, beans, and some fruits, such as apricots and blackberries, forms a gel when mixed with water. Research shows that it may help control blood sugar and cholesterol levels.

Insoluble fiber does not dissolve in water. On the contrary, it works like a sponge, absorbing water in the intestine, thereby adding to the bulk and pushing waste through more quickly. This movement helps fight constipation and may even help protect against colon cancer. Insoluble fiber is found in plentiful amounts in foods you may already recognize as high in fiber: wheat bran, whole grains, and many fruits and vegetables.

On average, Americans consume only one third of the 20 to 35 grams of fiber recommended every day for good health. To get enough fiber in your patient's diet, serve plenty of fruit and vegetables each day. Choose whole-grain cereals, breads, pasta, and brown rice. A serving of high-fiber cereal such as Fiber One starts the day with 13 grams of fiber.

Who Should Eat a High-Fiber Diet?

A high-fiber diet is an essential part of the treatment for constipation, diverticulosis, hemorrhoids, colitis, and irritable bowel disease. It can also help control blood sugar and cholesterol levels. High-fiber diets are essential to a lifetime of good health for most people and should not be recognized as a short-term approach to eating. There are exceptions, however. With some illnesses you must limit fiber, in which case the low-fiber diet (see Chapter 9) is appropriate. What's more, people accustomed to a low-fiber diet should gradually work fiber into the diet. See "Adding Fiber to the Diet," page 246.

What to Eat on a High-Fiber Diet

Serve the recommended number of servings from each food group in the Healing Food Guide. But choose foods as directed below to get 25 to 30 grams of fiber each day.

- *Protein Group:* At least one serving of beans, lentils, or dried peas each day; offer nuts as snacks or garnishes for vegetables and other dishes.

- *Calcium Group:* Green leafy vegetables. Count them as servings from the Vegetable Group.

- *Vegetable Group:* At least three servings daily of raw or cooked vegetables such as asparagus, celery, green beans, broccoli, cabbage, carrots, cauliflower, leafy greens, onion, snow peas, squash, and/or canned tomatoes.

- *Fruit Group:* At least two servings of fruits such as apples, nectarines, oranges, peaches, banana, grapefruit, pears, and/or berries.

- *Grain/Starch Group:* Five servings of whole-grain breads, cereals, muffins, crackers, pasta, popcorn, brown rice, sweet potatoes, and/or potatoes with skin. Choose fiber-rich cereals such as Fiber One, All-Bran, Bran Buds, and raisin bran.

- *Fat/Oil Group:* Nuts as desired.

- *Other Foods:* Plenty of fluids, at least eight to ten glasses a day. Remember that some of this requirement is fulfilled with soups and vegetables and fruits such as cucumbers and watermelon.

ADDING FIBER TO THE DIET

If your patient is accustomed to a low-fiber intake, a large dose of fiber eaten all at once or even over the course of a day will leave him or her feeling bloated and gassy. Even worse, extreme fiber overload can block the intestinal tract.

Start by switching to whole-grain cereals, breads and pasta, and brown rice as tolerated. Increase fruit and vegetable intake to recommended amounts. Add beans next.

If you use unprocessed bran, start with only one teaspoon. Gradually increase the amount over a period of several days, limiting intake to a total of one to two tablespoons a day. Encourage your patient to drink plenty of liquids. Keep a pitcher of water at the bedside.

Here is a sample High Fiber menu.

Fiber-rich cereal, whole wheat, and generous portions of squash contribute the most fiber in this menu.

Food	Fiber (g)
Breakfast	
3/4 cup orange juice	0.2
1/2 cup Fiber One cereal	13
1 slice whole wheat toast	3
2 teaspoons margarine	0
1 cup milk	0
Coffee/tea	0
Lunch	
Turkey sandwich made with	
2 slices whole wheat bread,	6
lettuce, and tomato	0.5
1/2 cup coleslaw	2.5
1 medium apple (with peel)	3
Dinner	
Baked fish	0
1 baked potato with skin	5
1/2 cup mashed peeled	
winter squash	2.5
1/2 cup cooked spinach	2
2 teaspoons butter	0
1 cup cubed cantaloupe	1
Water	
Snack	
1 medium orange	3
Total Fiber Content	41.7

About the Recipes

The high-fiber recipes that follow feature plenty of beans, whole grains, and vegetables.

Whole wheat flour is heavier than white flour and gives food a denser texture. If this is undesirable, use a combination of white and whole wheat flour in recipes. See the recipes for Whole Wheat English Muffins (page 237) and Everyday Bread (page 240). King Arthur Flour makes a white-whole-wheat flour with cooking properties similar to white flour but the fiber value of whole wheat.

If your patient is troubled by gas or intestinal discomfort after eating beans, see page 206 for tips to overcome such problems.

Spinach Lentil Soup

MAKES 4 SERVINGS

Here is a quick, simple soup, rich in beta carotene, calcium, iron, and, of course, fiber.

4 scallions, chopped

2 cloves garlic, chopped

2 tablespoons olive oil

1 cup brown lentils, rinsed and picked over

4 cups canned chicken broth or Poultry Stock (page 248)

1 pound spinach, washed and trimmed

1/2 teaspoon ground cumin

In a large saucepan, sauté the scallions and garlic in the olive oil for 2 minutes, until soft. Add the lentils and broth, bring to a boil, reduce the heat, and simmer until the lentils are soft, about 20 minutes.

Add the spinach and cumin. Cover and cook for 5 minutes more until the spinach is tender. Serve hot. Cover leftovers and refrigerate up to 2 days or freeze up to 3 months.

NUTRIENTS PER SERVING: 242 calories, 18 g protein, 9 g fat, 25 g carbohydrate, 7 mg iron, 782 RE vitamin A, 2.2 mg vitamin E, 18 mg vitamin C, 145 mg calcium, 8 g fiber.

Six-Bean Soup

MAKES 4 SERVINGS

I came up with this recipe when I did not have enough of any one type of dried bean. The result was much more interesting and flavorful than one-bean soup.

¼ cup each of any 6 different dried beans, such as kidney, navy, red lentil, green lentil, black-eyed pea, green split pea, and/or yellow split pea, rinsed and picked over

1 onion, chopped

2 cloves garlic, chopped

1 tablespoon olive oil

One 16-ounce can tomatoes, chopped

1 cup canned chicken or vegetable broth or Poultry Stock (page 248)

1 bay leaf

Salt and pepper to taste

Put all the beans in a large container, cover with cold water, and soak 8 hours or overnight. Drain and rinse.

In a large heavy pot, sauté the onion and garlic in the oil until just tender, 2 to 3 minutes. Add the beans and all the remaining ingredients. Add enough water to cover the beans by 2 inches. Bring to a boil, cover, and simmer, stirring occasionally, until the beans are tender, about 2 hours. Serve hot. Cover leftovers and refrigerate up to 2 days or freeze in individual portions up to 6 months.

NUTRIENTS PER SERVING: 216 calories, 12 g protein, 5 g fat, 33 g carbohydrate, 4.3 mg iron, 146 RE vitamin A, 1.6 mg vitamin E, 28 mg vitamin C, 96 mg calcium, 9 g fiber.

Crunchy Brown Rice Pilaf

MAKES 2 SERVINGS

Brown rice is the entire grain with only the inedible outer husk removed. The high-fiber bran coating gives it a nutlike flavor and chewy texture. For a one-dish meal, add half a cup chopped leftover meat, tofu, or toasted nuts with the bean sprouts and water chestnuts.

2 scallions, chopped

1 tablespoon olive oil

1/2 cup brown rice

1 1/2 cups canned chicken broth or
   1 1/2 cups Poultry Stock
   (page 248)

1/4 teaspoon dried thyme

1 cup canned sliced water chestnuts

1/2 cup bean sprouts

Reserve 1 tablespoon of the scallions for garnish. Heat the oil in a medium saucepan over medium-low heat. Add the rice and the remaining scallions and sauté just until the scallions soften, 2 to 3 minutes. Add the chicken broth and thyme, cover, and simmer for 30 minutes over low heat. Stir to coat rice.

Add the water chestnuts and bean sprouts, toss with a fork, and cook until the rice is tender, about 5 minutes more. If the rice appears dry, add 1/2 cup water. Serve warm, garnished with the reserved scallions. Cover leftovers and refrigerate up to 3 days.

NUTRIENTS PER SERVING: 307 calories, 9 g protein, 9 g fat, 47 g carbohydrate, 2.3 mg iron, 27 RE vitamin A, 0.5 mg vitamin E, 7 mg vitamin C, 30 mg calcium, 3 g fiber.

Black-Eyed Pea Salad

MAKES 3 SERVINGS

Serve this hearty salad as a side dish or stuff it into a pita pocket for a meatless yet protein- and iron-rich sandwich.

1 cup black-eyed peas, rinsed and picked over

1 cup peeled chopped canned or fresh tomatoes

10 Greek or other black olives, pitted and sliced

½ small red onion, chopped

¼ teaspoon pepper

1 tablespoon orange juice

1 tablespoon rice vinegar

1 tablespoon packed brown sugar

1 tablespoon olive oil

¼ cup chopped fresh parsley

In a large heavy pot, combine the beans and 3 cups cold water, bring to a boil, and simmer until tender, about 30 minutes. Remove from the heat, drain, and rinse.

Transfer the beans to a glass bowl, add the tomatoes, olives, onion, and pepper, and toss.

In a small saucepan, combine the orange juice, rice vinegar, and brown sugar and heat, stirring until the sugar is dissolved, about 2 to 3 minutes. Pour the warm dressing over the beans, add the oil, and toss. Sprinkle with the parsley and serve warm or chilled. Cover leftovers and refrigerate up to 2 days.

NUTRIENTS PER SERVING: 153 calories, 3 g protein, 6 g fat, 22 g carbohydrate, 2 mg iron, 155 RE vitamin A, 1.5 mg vitamin E, 23 mg vitamin C, 127 mg calcium, 4 g fiber.

Red Lentils and Sausage

MAKES 4 SERVINGS

Red lentils give this dish a beautiful, appetizing look, but yellow or European lentils taste just as good.

1 cup red lentils, rinsed and picked over

1 small onion, chopped

1 clove garlic, chopped

1 tablespoon olive oil

2 Italian sweet sausages, cut into ½-inch slices

1 cup chopped broccoli

2 medium carrots, peeled and chopped

In a medium saucepan, combine the lentils and 2 cups water and bring to a boil. Cook until tender, about 15 minutes. Drain and set aside.

In a large saucepan, sauté the onion and garlic in the oil over medium heat until the onion is translucent, about 2 minutes. Add the sausage and cook until no longer pink, about 4 minutes. Drain off the fat.

Add the broccoli, carrots, lentils, and ¼ cup water and simmer until the vegetables are tender but not mushy, 8 to 10 minutes. Serve hot over rice or noodles. Cover leftovers and refrigerate up to 2 days or freeze up to 3 months.

NUTRIENTS PER SERVING: 283 calories, 17 g protein, 13 g fat, 27 g carbohydrate, 4 mg iron, 1048 RE vitamin A, 1.65 mg vitamin E, 28 mg vitamin C, 52 mg calcium, 7 g fiber.

Lamb and Bean Cassoulet

MAKES 4 TO 6 SERVINGS

This is a much simplified version of the traditional French cassoulet. Serve it with a green salad and crusty bread.

1 pound Great Northern beans, rinsed and picked over

1 tablespoon salted butter

1 lamb shank, 10 ounces

8 ounces Italian sweet sausage, coarsely chopped

4 cloves garlic, chopped

1 tablespoon dried parsley or ¼ cup fresh, chopped parsley

1 teaspoon dried thyme

1 bay leaf

2 cups bottled tomato sauce or Meatless Tomato Sauce (page 277)

4 small yellow onions, peeled

Put the beans in a large bowl, cover with water, and soak for at least 8 hours, or overnight. Drain.

Preheat the oven to 350°F. Melt the butter in a large heavy ovenproof pot over medium heat. Add the lamb shank and brown on all sides. Add the sausage, reduce the heat to low, and brown until it is no longer pink, about 10 minutes. Add the beans and enough water to cover the beans and meat. Add the garlic and herbs and bring to a boil, skimming off any foam. Cover, place in the oven, and cook for 1½ hours.

While the beans cook, put the tomato sauce in a heavy saucepan and bring to a boil. Reduce the heat and simmer until reduced by half, about 30 minutes.

Add the onions to the beans, cover, and cook for 1 hour more, or until the beans are tender. If the beans appear dry, add 1 cup water.

Stir the thickened tomato sauce into the beans and cook, uncovered, for 20 minutes, or until the meat is falling off the bone and the beans are very tender. Serve hot. Cover leftovers and refrigerate up to 3 days or freeze up to 2 to 3 months.

NUTRIENTS PER SERVING: 566 calories, 42 g protein, 27 g fat, 40 g carbohydrate, 6.5 mg iron, 153 RE vitamin A, 3 mg vitamin E, 24 mg vitamin C, 143 mg calcium, 9 g fiber.

Sweet Bran Muffins

MAKES 12

Home-baked bran muffins are a far better source of bran than those from the grocery store, which typically contain very little bran. To make fruit muffins, stir half a cup of mashed bananas or fresh or frozen blueberries into the batter.

1 cup whole wheat flour	**2 cups bran flakes**
1 cup all-purpose flour	**1 large egg, beaten**
1 tablespoon baking powder	**1 cup milk**
½ teaspoon ground cinnamon	**¼ cup packed brown sugar**
½ teaspoon salt	**¼ cup salted butter, melted**

Preheat the oven to 350°F. Lightly oil 12 muffin cups. Combine the flours, baking powder, cinnamon, and salt in a large bowl.

In a medium bowl, combine the bran flakes with the egg, milk, and brown sugar and mix well. Add to the dry ingredients, along with the melted butter, and stir until the dry ingredients are moistened. Do not overmix.

Spoon the batter into the muffin cups, filling them two-thirds full. Bake for 25 minutes until the tops are brown and crusty. Serve warm or wrap in plastic and refrigerate up to 4 days or freeze up to 3 months.

NUTRIENTS PER MUFFIN: 168 calories, 5 g protein, 5 g fat, 27 g carbohydrate, 2.3 mg iron, 159 RE vitamin A, 0.7 mg vitamin E, 4.6 mg vitamin C, 42 mg calcium, 2.5 g fiber.

Whole Wheat English Muffins

MAKES 12

These muffins are a bit more dense than traditional English muffins. Toast them and top with anything from jam and butter to bean puree and roasted vegetables.

½ cup warm water (105°F. to 115°F.)

1 package active dry yeast

1 tablespoon sugar

1¾ cups whole wheat flour

1½ cups all-purpose flour

1 teaspoon salt

¾ cup warm milk

1 large egg, beaten

¼ teaspoon baking soda

1 tablespoon water

½ cup yellow cornmeal

Combine the water, yeast, and sugar in a small bowl. Set aside in a warm spot for 5 minutes, or until foamy.

Combine the whole wheat flour, all-purpose flour, and salt in a large bowl. Add the milk, egg, and the yeast mixture and beat with a wooden spoon until thoroughly mixed.

Turn the dough out onto a floured board and gently knead until smooth and elastic, 4 to 5 minutes. Place the dough in a lightly buttered bowl, turn to coat, and cover with a dish towel. Allow to rise in a warm spot until doubled in size, about 45 minutes.

In a small cup, dissolve the baking soda in the water. Add to the risen dough and knead until thoroughly incorporated. Turn the dough out onto the lightly floured board and roll out ½ inch thick. Using a 3-inch round cookie cutter or biscuit cutter, cut out muffins and place on a baking sheet dusted with cornmeal, about 1 inch apart. Cover with a clean dish towel and allow to rise until doubled in size, about 1 hour.

Heat a large cast-iron skillet or a griddle over medium heat. Place the muffins in the skillet and cook, turning once, until lightly browned on both sides, about 15 minutes. Serve hot or let cool, split, and toast. Wrap in plastic and refrigerate up to 1 week or freeze up to 6 months.

NUTRIENTS PER MUFFIN: 159 calories, 8 g protein, 2 g fat, 31 g carbohydrate, 1.7 mg iron, 16 RE vitamin A, 0.8 mg vitamin E, 29 mg calcium, 3 g fiber.

Best Biscuit Sticks

MAKES 10

A great high-fiber snack any time of day.

2 cups whole wheat flour

**1 tablespoon plus ½ teaspoon
     baking powder**

1 tablespoon brown sugar

1 cup milk

⅓ cup salted butter, melted

Preheat the oven to 400°F. In a large bowl, combine the flour, baking powder, and brown sugar. Add the milk and mix with a fork until the dough holds together. Turn the dough out onto a floured board and knead for 1 minute.

Roll the dough into a rectangle about 7 inches by 10 inches. Cut the rectangle crosswise into 10 strips.

Pour the melted butter onto a dinner plate or in a shallow bowl. Roll each stick in the butter to coat all over and place on an ungreased cookie sheet: For crisp sticks, place them 1 inch apart; for softer sticks, place them so they just touch each other.

Bake for 15 to 18 minutes, until golden. These taste best hot out of the oven. Refrigerate up to 4 days or freeze up to 3 months. Wrap in foil and reheat in the oven before serving.

NUTRIENTS PER STICK: 129 calories, 4 g protein, 4.5 g fat, 20 g carbohydrate, 1 mg iron, 65 RE vitamin A, 1 mg vitamin E, 40 mg calcium, 3 g fiber.

Butter Bran Cookies

MAKES 3½ DOZEN

These are as good as any Christmas butter cookie. What's more, they have more fiber than store-bought fig bars. Of course, those on a low-fat diet should eat these in moderation since they contain a fair amount of butter.

¾ cup whole wheat flour

½ cup all-purpose flour

2 teaspoons baking powder

½ cup (1 stick) salted butter, softened

½ cup sugar

1 large egg, beaten

1 tablespoon canola oil

½ teaspoon vanilla

1 cup bran flakes

Preheat the oven to 400°F. Lightly grease 2 cookie sheets. Sift both flours and the baking powder together and set aside.

In a large bowl, cream the butter and sugar until fluffy. Add the egg, oil, and vanilla and mix well. Add the dry ingredients and the bran flakes and stir until well blended.

Drop the dough by spoonfuls onto the cookie sheets, 1 inch apart.

Bake for 8 minutes, or until crisp and the edges are browned. Refrigerate up to 1 week or freeze up to 9 months.

NUTRIENTS PER COOKIE: 50 calories, 1 g protein, 3 g fat, 6 g carbohydrate, 0.3 mg iron, 38 RE vitamin A, 0.2 mg vitamin E, 2.8 mg calcium, 0.5 g fiber.

Everyday Bread

MAKES 1 LOAF (12 SLICES)

This makes wonderful breakfast toast and delicious sandwich bread. For even more fiber, use all whole wheat flour.

1 package active or dry yeast

1 cup warm water (105°F. to 115°F.)

2 teaspoons sugar, 1 tablespoon molasses, or 1 tablespoon honey

3 to 4 cups whole wheat flour

1 cup all-purpose flour

1 teaspoon salt

2 tablespoons canola oil

In a small bowl, dissolve the yeast in the warm water. Add the sugar and set aside in a warm spot for 5 minutes, or until foamy.

In a large bowl, combine 2 cups whole wheat flour, the all-purpose flour, and salt. Add the yeast mixture and oil and mix with a wooden spoon until well combined. Add 1 cup more whole wheat flour, then add enough additional flour to make a dough, and using your hands mix until a soft dough forms.

Turn the dough out onto a floured board and knead until smooth, about 5 minutes. Put it in a buttered bowl, turn to coat, cover with a dish towel, and let rise in a warm, draft-free spot until doubled in size, about 1 hour.

Lightly oil a 9- by 5-inch loaf pan. Punch down the dough, shape it into a loaf, and place in the pan. Cover with a dish towel, let rise in a warm draft-free spot until doubled in size, about 1 hour.

Preheat the oven to 400°F. as the dough rises. Bake the bread for 25 minutes, or until it is brown on top and sounds hollow when tapped. Let cool on a rack before slicing. Refrigerate up to 1 week or freeze up to 6 months.

NUTRIENTS PER SLICE: 164 calories, 5 g protein, 3 g fat, 30 g carbohydrate, 1.7 mg iron, 1.2 mg vitamin E, 12 mg calcium, 4 g fiber.

Oatmeal Molasses Pudding

MAKES 3 SERVINGS

Serve this warm, topped with cool yogurt or ice cream for a sweet high-fiber treat.

3 cups milk

½ cup rolled oats

⅔ cup molasses

¼ cup bran flakes

¼ cup cornmeal

1 teaspoon salt

Preheat the oven to 325°F. Lightly grease a 1-quart baking dish. In a large saucepan, bring 2 cups of the milk just to a simmer. Add the oatmeal and cook, stirring, until it thickens. Remove from heat, stir in the remaining 1 cup milk, the molasses, bran flakes, cornmeal, and salt.

Pour the mixture into the baking dish and bake for 1 hour, stirring every 30 minutes. Then bake without stirring for 1 hour more. Bake until the pudding is firm. Serve warm with ice cream or yogurt. Cover leftovers and refrigerate up to 3 days.

NUTRIENTS PER SERVING: 416 calories, 12 g protein, 9 g fat, 72 g carbohydrate, 13 mg iron, 151 RE vitamin A, 0.5 mg vitamin E, 790 mg calcium, 1 g fiber.

the low-sodium diet

11

Sodium is a natural and essential mineral found in food and water. It helps maintain proper water balance in the body, conduct nerve impulses and contract muscles. All bodily fluids and every cell contain sodium. Yet many people get far more of it than they need. This becomes a problem if a person is diagnosed with high blood pressure or another disease that requires a reduced sodium intake.

Table salt is often regarded as the culprit in a diet that contains too much sodium. Indeed, one teaspoon of salt contains about 2400 milligrams of sodium—the daily limit recommended by some health experts for all healthy people! (On average, however, we eat about 4000 to 6000 milligrams of sodium daily.) Yet table salt provides only about 15 percent of the sodium in the typical American diet. The largest portion comes from processed foods.

Cutting back on sodium can be difficult. Studies show it takes about six months for a person to adjust to a low-sodium diet. But this is a small trade-off for the health benefits it achieves. For example, a low-sodium diet can help control high blood pressure—a much better prescription than a lifetime of medication.

For the cook who has always relied on salt to bring out flavor, the transition can also be a challenge. Cooking without salt means experimenting with herbs and spices and searching for flavor replacements for high-salt ingredients. In this chapter, I give you plenty of recipes to help you in your quest for tasty low-sodium dishes.

Who Should Eat a Low-Sodium Diet?

A low-sodium diet can help when the body retains fluids, as in the instance of high blood pressure, congestive heart failure, or liver disease. Ask the health care provider about the right amount of sodium for your patient. Some people require a very low sodium intake (500 to 1000 milligrams a day), whereas many people with the above conditions may consume more sodium.

If your patient eats poorly, a low-sodium diet may be inappropriate. Just a few bites at meals or snacks will not add up to much sodium. It may be perfectly acceptable to satisfy your patient's strong desire for salty pretzels or pepperoni since the amount consumed will likely be small. Discuss this situation with the health care provider.

What to Eat on a Low-Sodium Diet

Modify the basic plan outlined in the Healing Food Guide as described below, considering any food that contains over 400 milligrams of sodium as high in sodium. All processed foods list their sodium content on the Nutrition Facts panel of the label. Increasing Your Sodium Savvy, on page 245, gives you a quick start in identifying high-sodium foods.

- *For a 3000-milligram-sodium diet:* Eliminate high-sodium processed foods and beverages such as those from fast food restaurants; salad dressings; smoked, salted, and koshered meats; regular canned foods; pickled vegetables; luncheon meats; commercially softened water. Up to ¼ teaspoon table salt can be used in cooking or at the table.

- *For a 2000-milligram-sodium diet:* Eliminate processed and prepared foods and beverages high in sodium. Limit milk and milk products to 2 cups daily. Do not use any salt in cooking or at the table.

- *For a 1000-milligram-sodium diet:* Eliminate processed and prepared foods and beverages high in sodium. Omit regular canned foods, many frozen foods, most deli foods, fast foods, cheeses, margarine, and regular salad dressings. Limit regular breads to 2 servings a day and milk and milk products to 2 cups a day. Do not use any salt in cooking or at the table.

- *For a 500-milligram-sodium diet:* Eliminate canned or processed foods that contain salt. Eliminate vegetables naturally high in sodium, such as celery. Limit meat to 6 ounces a day and milk to 1 cup a day. Use low-sodium breads. Use distilled water for cooking and drinking. Do not use any salt in cooking or at the table.

- *For a 250-milligram-sodium diet:* Follow the 500-milligram-sodium diet but use only low-sodium milk.

Increasing Your Sodium Savvy

Most foods contain some sodium. If they are processed, it's likely they contain a lot. The sodium content of processed foods is listed on the nutrition label. The following tips can also help you control the amount of sodium your patient eats.

- Canned foods such as water-packed tuna or beans should be rinsed before serving.

- Avoid smoked foods such as ham, hot dogs, sausage, bacon, and corned beef—sodium plays an essential role in the smoking process.

- Most cheeses are loaded with sodium; offer low-sodium varieties instead.

- Foods made with salty brine, such as sauerkraut and pickles, rank high on the list of salty foods.

- Most breads contain about 125 milligrams of sodium per slice, since salt is used to help activate the yeast.

- Sodium is a principal ingredient in baking powder and baking soda. Any food that contains them most likely contains a fair amount of sodium too.

- Commercial salad dressings, particularly the low-fat varieties, may be full of sodium. Make your own with vinegar or lemon juice and olive oil.

- Most water contains some sodium. If a very low-sodium diet is recommended, distilled water may be the only alternative. Check with the water department to find out the amount of sodium in the water supply.

- Regular canned soups, bouillon cubes, frozen dinners, pot pies, potato chips, salted snacks, and fast-food meals generally feature hefty amounts of sodium. Eye before you buy. Read the nutrition information on the labels of all these foods. Many are available in low-sodium variations.

Sodium Content of Selected Cheeses

American cheese, 1 ounce	406 mg
Cheddar cheese, 1 ounce	176 mg
Cottage cheese, 1/2 cup	456 mg
Cream cheese, 1 ounce	85 mg
Parmesan cheese, 1 ounce	528 mg
Swiss cheese, 1 ounce	74 mg
Processed cheese spread, 1 ounce	381 mg

USING HERBS AND SPICES

Try the following herb combinations in stews, soups, casseroles, and vegetable dishes. Dried herbs are stronger than fresh; one teaspoon of a dried herb equals two teaspoons of fresh.

Fish—tarragon, dill, and fennel
Poultry—sage, rosemary, and oregano
Beef—cumin, garlic, and marjoram
Lamb—cinnamon, rosemary, and thyme
Pork—ginger, coriander, and cumin
Vegetables—chives, dill, and parsley
Soups—bay leaf, rosemary, and peppercorns

Using Salt

Salt enhances the flavor of many foods. For this reason, it is often essential, especially if appetite is frail. Fortunately, small amounts can be used on many sodium-controlled diets. For example, in a beef stew that serves ten, one teaspoon of salt called for in the recipe translates into just 240 milligrams of sodium per serving from the added salt. That's an amount that fits well within diets that allow 2000 or more milligrams of sodium a day.

Adding salt after the food is cooked, however, provides for more intense flavor—and less control over the amount added. Encourage the patient on a low-sodium diet to shake the salt into the palm of his or her hand, then sprinkle the amount judged appropriate on the food. (Remember, one teaspoon of salt contains about 2400 milligrams of sodium.)

The recipes for Poultry Stock and Beef Stock can serve as the foundation for many different types of soup. The Coconut Crust Lemon Tartlet (page 256) and Beaten Biscuits (page 257) use no baking powder or baking soda.

Salt-Free "Salt"

MAKES 2 TABLESPOONS

Holly Shimizu, curator of the herb garden at the U.S. National Arboretum in Washington, D.C., shared this recipe for a salt substitute.

2 teaspoons garlic powder	**1 teaspoon powdered lemon zest or dehydrated lemon juice**
1 teaspoon dried basil	
1 teaspoon dried oregano	**1 tablespoon white rice**

Put all the ingredients except the rice in a blender and blend until the herbs are finely chopped. Store in a glass jar with the rice to prevent caking. Use to replace salt when cooking meat, fish, poultry, or vegetables.

Low-Sodium Stocks

Making a good soup stock without salt is a challenge. The key is in the slow cooking and generous portions of the best ingredients. These compare far more favorably to canned versions, which contain approximately 900 milligrams of sodium per cup. Freeze this in two-cup portions.

Poultry Stock

MAKES 5 TO 6 CUPS

1 onion, quartered

3 cloves garlic, crushed

1 tablespoon canola oil

3 to 4 pounds chicken, cut up, including neck, or 1 turkey carcass (from a 12-pound turkey)

3 carrots, peeled and chopped

3 stalks celery, chopped, with leaves

2 tablespoons chopped fresh parsley

2 teaspoons fresh chopped dill or 1 teaspoon dried

2 teaspoons fresh thyme leaves or 1 teaspoon dried

8 peppercorns

1 bay leaf

1 tablespoon red wine vinegar

In a large stockpot over medium heat, cook the onion and garlic in the oil until translucent. Add the remaining ingredients except the vinegar. Add enough cold water to cover the chicken and bring to a boil. Cover and simmer for 4 hours, skimming off any surface foam that develops in the first 20 minutes.

Strain the stock. Return it to the pot, add the vinegar and stir. Bring to a boil, reduce the heat to low, and simmer for about 1 hour. Cool and freeze in 2-cup portions for up to 2 months.

NUTRIENTS PER CUP: 74 calories, 2 g protein, 3 g fat, 10 g carbohydrate, 1.6 mg iron, 1229 RE vitamin A, 0.5 mg vitamin E, 10 mg vitamin C, 58 mg calcium, 65 mg sodium.

Beef Stock

MAKES 5 TO 6 CUPS

1 tablespoon unsalted butter

3 pounds beef bones (ask the butcher)

1 onion quartered

2 cloves garlic, crushed

3 stalks celery, cut up, with leaves

1 bay leaf

6 peppercorns

8 cups cold water

¼ cup red wine (optional)

In a heavy stockpot over low heat, melt the butter and brown the bones, onion, and garlic in the butter. Cover and cook for 5 minutes.

Add the remaining ingredients and bring to a boil. Reduce the heat and simmer, covered, for 3 hours. Skim any foam that rises to the top.

Strain the stock and return to the pot. Cook, uncovered, over low heat at a simmer for 1 hour more. Cool and freeze in 2-cup portions for up to 6 months.

NUTRIENTS PER CUP: 48 calories, 2 g protein, 3 g fat, 3 g carbohydrate, 0.5 mg iron, 25 RE vitamin A, 0.3 mg vitamin E, 4 mg vitamin C, 26 mg calcium, 48 mg sodium.

Confetti Pepper Soup

MAKES 3 SERVINGS

Tofu is a good source of protein and it absorbs the flavor of the broth in this cheerful tri-color soup.

1 clove garlic, minced

1 tablespoon canola oil

2 cups Poultry Stock (page 248)

½ red bell pepper, cored, seeded, and chopped

½ green bell pepper, cored, seeded, and chopped

½ yellow or orange bell pepper, cored, seeded, and chopped

4 ounces firm tofu, cut into ¼-inch cubes

In a small pot over medium-high heat, cook the garlic in the oil until golden, about 2 minutes. Add the stock and peppers and simmer over low heat until the peppers are tender, about 8 minutes.

Add the tofu cubes and cook until heated through, about 5 minutes. Serve hot. Cover and refrigerate leftovers up to 2 days.

NUTRIENTS PER CUP: 240 calories, 16 g protein, 12 g fat, 17 g carbohydrate, 6 mg iron, 436 RE vitamin A, 0.5 mg vitamin E, 32 mg vitamin C, 128 mg calcium, 247 mg sodium.

Split Pea Soup

MAKES 6 SERVINGS

Most pea soups call for salt pork or a ham bone. This version uses turkey bones, which contain far less sodium yet are full of flavor.

6 carrots, peeled and quartered

1 small onion, chopped

3 cloves garlic, crushed

1 tablespoon canola oil

1 pound split peas, rinsed and picked over

1 turkey carcass

1 bay leaf

6 cups water

1 cup whole-milk plain yogurt or sour cream, for garnish

In a large heavy pot over low heat, sauté half the carrots, the onion, and garlic in the oil until the onion is translucent, about 3 minutes. Add the peas and stir to coat with the oil. Add the turkey carcass, bay leaf, and water. Bring to a boil, reduce the heat to low, and simmer until the peas are soft, about 3 hours or check every hour or so, adding water if the soup has thickened too much.

Strain the soup through a colander. Discard the bones and press the peas through the colander. Pour the strained soup back into the pot, add the reserved carrots, and cook until the carrots are fork-tender, 10 to 15 minutes.

Serve with a dollop of the yogurt or the sour cream. Cover and refrigerate leftovers and use within 2 days or freeze up to 6 months.

NUTRIENTS PER SERVING: 368 calories, 9 g protein, 4 g fat, 28 g carbohydrate, 2 mg iron, 2043 RE vitamin A, 2 mg vitamin E, 9 mg vitamin C, 87 mg calcium, 68 mg sodium.

Hearty Beef Vegetable Soup

MAKES 2 SERVINGS

Make extra batches of this soup and freeze it; it will then be as convenient to use as the high-sodium canned version.

1 small onion, chopped

2 teaspoons unsalted butter

¼ pound lean beef chuck, cut into small cubes

1 tablespoon pearl barley

2 cups Beef Stock (page 249)

1 carrot, peeled and quartered

1 tablespoon tomato paste or 1 ripe tomato, peeled and quartered

¼ cup peas or chopped green beans

In a large saucepan over low heat, cook the onion in the butter until translucent, for 2 minutes. Add the beef and cook until lightly browned on all sides. Add the barley and beef stock, bring to a simmer, and cook for 20 minutes. Add the carrot, tomato paste, and peas and cook until all the vegetables and the barley are tender, about 10 minutes more. Serve warm. Cover leftovers and refrigerate up to 2 days.

NUTRIENTS PER SERVING: 245 calories, 22 g protein, 15 g fat, 17 g carbohydrate, 3.4 mg iron, 1086 RE vitamin A, 1 mg vitamin E, 22 mg vitamin C, 13 mg calcium, 85 mg sodium.

Summer Salsa

MAKES 1½ CUPS

This recipe is rich in fiber, potassium, and vitamin C from the tomatoes and chiles. The olives provide just enough salty flavor without raising the sodium level too high.

1 cup ripe tomatoes, diced

2 ounces canned, mild Mexican chiles, chopped and rinsed

3 scallions, chopped

5 green olives, pitted and chopped

2 tablespoons olive oil

Pepper to taste

In a glass bowl, combine the tomatoes, chiles, scallions, olives, 2 tablespoons of the olive oil, and the pepper. Stir, cover, and refrigerate for at least 1 hour before serving. Serve on salt-free crisp crackers. Cover and refrigerate leftovers up to 2 days.

NUTRIENTS PER 2 TABLESPOONS: 30 calories, 1 g protein, 2 g fat, 1 g carbohydrate, 0.2 mg iron, 44 RE vitamin A, 6.4 mg vitamin C, 10 mg calcium, 128 mg sodium.

Basil Salsa

MAKES ¾ CUP

Our family is always experimenting with low-sodium, low-fat recipes. We developed this as an alternative to the traditional pesto made with olive oil, nuts, and cheese.

2 tablespoons minced fresh parsley or coriander

2 tablespoons minced garlic

2 tablespoons minced fresh basil

2 tablespoons minced fresh chives

2 slices Italian bread, soaked in water and squeezed dry

1 tablespoon olive oil

Pepper to taste

About 18 melba toast rounds, for serving

Preheat the broiler. Combine all the ingredients in a glass bowl. With a wooden spoon, mash the bread and stir until well blended.

Put a tablespoonful of the mixture on each melba toast round and broil for 5 minutes, or until the top is crusty and lightly browned. Serve warm.

NUTRIENTS PER SERVING (1 MELBA TOAST AND 1 TABLESPOON SALSA): 13 calories, 1 g protein, trace fat, 3 g carbohydrate, 0.8 mg iron, 142 RE vitamin A, 22 mg vitamin C, 36 mg calcium, 23 mg sodium.

Lemon-Glazed Carrots

MAKES 2 SERVINGS

Any fresh vegetable can be served on a low-sodium diet; just don't add salt. To add flavor to any vegetable, add lemon juice.

3 carrots, peeled, sliced into ¼-inch coins

Juice of 1 small lemon

1 tablespoon water

1 teaspoon unsalted butter

2 teaspoons sugar

In a large skillet, combine the carrots, half the lemon juice, and water. Cover and cook over medium heat until the carrots are just tender, about 3 minutes.

Stir in the butter, sugar, and the remaining lemon juice, reduce the heat to low, and cook until all of the liquid evaporates and the carrots are glossy. Serve immediately. Cover leftovers and refrigerate up to 3 days.

NUTRIENTS PER SERVING: 88 calories, 1 g protein, 2 g fat, 18 g carbohydrate, 0.5 mg iron, 3056 RE vitamin A, 0.5 mg vitamin E, 24 mg vitamin C, 31 mg calcium, 38 mg sodium.

Sweet Potato Fries

MAKES 2 TO 3 SERVINGS

A small amount of Parmesan goes a long way, flavor-wise, without boosting the sodium content. To reduce the fat content, use only one tablespoon of olive oil.

**2 large sweet potatoes, cut length-
wise into ¼-inch slices**

2 tablespoons olive oil

**1 tablespoon freshly grated
Parmesan cheese**

½ cup sour cream (optional)

**¼ cup chopped fresh chives
(optional)**

Preheat the oven to 350°F. Place the potatoes in a bowl, drizzle the oil over them, and toss with a wooden spoon so they are evenly coated.

Arrange the slices on a cookie sheet and sprinkle with the Parmesan cheese. Bake, turning once, for 20 minutes, or until browned on both sides.

If desired, combine the sour cream and chives in a small bowl to serve as a dip.

Transfer the potatoes to a platter and serve immediately, plain or with the sour cream dip. These are best eaten hot out of the oven.

NUTRIENTS PER SERVING: 250 calories, 3 g protein, 15 g fat, 28 g carbohydrate, 0.5 mg iron, 2493 RE vitamin A, 5 mg vitamin E, 28 mg vitamin C, 75 mg calcium, 70 mg sodium.

Coconut Crust Lemon Tartlets

MAKES 2 INDIVIDUAL TARTS

Not only does this tart use no added salt, but it is easier to make than a pie with a traditional crust because it requires no rolling of the dough.

Crust

1 cup unsweetened flaked coconut, available at health food stores (if the flakes are large, finely chop them)

1 tablespoon sugar

1 large egg white

Filling

2 large eggs

½ cup sugar

2 teaspoons grated lemon zest

Juice of 1 lemon (about ⅓ cup)

1 tablespoon unsalted butter

Kiwi slices or strawberries for garnish

Preheat the oven to 350°F. To make the crust, combine the coconut and sugar in a small bowl. In a separate bowl, beat the egg white until foamy. Fold it into the coconut mixture. Butter two 1-cup custard cups, divide the mixture between two cups, and press it evenly over the bottom and up the sides of each cup. Bake for about 6 to 8 minutes, or until the coconut has turned golden brown. Set aside to cool.

To make the filling, in a small bowl, beat the eggs with the sugar until light and slightly thickened, about 4 minutes.

In a medium saucepan over low heat, combine the egg mixture, lemon zest, and lemon juice and cook, stirring constantly, until the filling thickens to the consistency of mayonnaise. Add the butter and stir until it melts. Pour the filling into the individual crusts. Refrigerate until cold. Serve with a garnish of fresh fruit. These keep covered in the refrigerator up to 3 days.

NUTRIENTS PER TARTLET: 555 calories, 10 g protein, 23 g fat, 82 g carbohydrate, 1.6 mg iron, 159 RE vitamin A, 0.8 mg vitamin E, 60 mg vitamin C, 49 mg calcium, 102 mg sodium.

Beaten Biscuits

MAKES 1½ DOZEN

My mother developed this recipe, which is based on a turn-of-the-century recipe and made easier by using a food processor. These biscuits are flatter and crisper than the traditional biscuits.

3 cups flour	**⅓ cup unsalted butter**
¾ teaspoon sugar	**¾ cup to 1 cup milk**
½ teaspoon dried dill	

Preheat the oven to 350°F. Sift together the flour, sugar, and dill into a large bowl. Using two knives, cut the butter into the flour. Add just enough milk to make a very stiff dough. Turn the dough out onto a lightly floured board, and knead until soft and pliable.

In a food processor fitted with the metal blade, with the motor running, drop the dough piece by piece into the chute and process until the dough blisters, about 10 minutes.

On a floured board, roll the dough to ½-inch thickness. Cut circles with a 2-inch biscuit cutter and place on ungreased cookie sheets. Prick each one with a fork and bake for 20 minutes, or until the biscuits are golden. Serve warm or wrap in plastic and refrigerate up to 1 week.

NUTRIENTS PER BISCUIT: 117 calories, 2 g protein, 4 g fat, 17 g carbohydrate, 0.8 mg iron, 39 RE vitamin A, 17 mg calcium, 6 mg sodium.

the high-potassium diet

12

Potassium is essential to good health. It plays a role in fluid balance, helps the heart beat regularly, and aids in muscle contraction and the transmission of nerve impulses.

Fortunately, potassium is found abundantly in food. A diet based on the Healing Food Guide provides between 2700 to 4000 milligrams of potassium daily, a healthy amount for most people. We need at least 2000 milligrams of potassium each day.

Who Should Eat a High-Potassium Diet?

Numerous studies show that a potassium-rich diet helps lower blood pressure. It is possible that a potassium-rich diet can reduce or even eliminate the need for blood pressure medication. The elderly and ill people often have low levels of potassium in the blood due to poor diet, chronic diarrhea, or overuse of laxatives, and/or vomiting. If the patient suffers from any of these, or is taking a medication that affects blood pressure, he or she may need to follow a high-potassium diet.

It is very difficult to get too much potassium, since normally we excrete any our bodies don't need. People taking high blood pressure medications that "spare" potassium, however, can't get rid of excessive amounts of it. People with kidney disease also may not be able to efficiently remove excess potassium from the blood. If your patient takes blood pressure medications or has kidney disease, check with the health care provider. Too much potassium can cause heart failure.

What to Eat on a High-Potassium Diet

Plan menus based on the Healing Food Guide, taking special care to serve the recommended number of servings from the Protein, Calcium, and Vegetable and Fruit groups. Because potassium leaches into cooking water, focus on cooking methods that conserve liquids, such as stewing, baking, or steaming.

- *Protein Group:* While meat, fish, and poultry supply from 75 to 150 milligrams of potassium per ounce, beans supply even more—one cup of baked beans supplies 500 to 1000 milligrams. Just one tablespoon of peanut butter provides 100 milligrams and one egg, about 65 milligrams. Eight ounces of tofu contain 300 milligrams of potassium.

- *Calcium Group:* Skim, low-fat, and whole milk contain about 400 milligrams of potassium per cup. Yogurt has half that amount, and cheeses such as American and Cheddar about 170 milligrams per ounce. Cottage cheese contains 1000 milligrams per cup. Green leafy vegetables weigh in at about 150 milligrams per half cup. Be sure to use the cooking or canning water from vegetables too.

- *Vegetable Group:* One half cup of most vegetables supplies from 140 to 280 milligrams of potassium. Again, use the cooking water; save it to make vegetable soup. Vegetable juices contain as much potassium as whole vegetables.

- *Fruit Group:* All fruits and juices are good sources of potassium. Apricots, dates, melons, papayas, plantains, pomegranates, prunes, and raisins are superb sources, with at least 250 milligrams per half cup. One medium banana contains about 450 milligrams.

- *Grain/Starch Group:* One serving from this group provides only 30 to 80 milligrams of potassium.

- *Fat/Oil Group:* The most potent potassium source in this group is the avocado, with 1000 milligrams per medium fruit (even though they are a fruit, avocados are quite high in fat—hence, their assignment to this group). Butter and margarine contain only 5 milligrams of potassium per teaspoon.

- *Other Foods:* Seasonings and Condiments: In general, these foods are poor sources of potassium. Spices and herbs contribute only 20 to 50 milligrams of potassium per teaspoon. Honey, jelly, and marmalade contain just 10 to 70 milligrams per tablespoon. Likewise, mustard, catsup, and barbecue sauces contribute little potassium.

- *Beverages:* Little potassium is found in most beverages, including coffee, tea, and water. Fruit drinks and powders made from small amounts of fruit juice do contain some potassium, but nowhere near the amounts found in a 100 percent juice product.

POTASSIUM SUPPLEMENTS AND SALT SUBSTITUTES

Do not use potassium supplements or salt substitutes (which contain potassium instead of sodium) without checking with the health care provider. Salt substitutes contain 1500 to 2800 milligrams of potassium per teaspoon—enough to dramatically increase blood levels in some people. The resultant condition, called hyperkalemia, can lead to cardiac arrest. People with kidney disease are at greatest risk for this problem.

Salmon with Fettuccine

MAKES 2 SERVINGS

Salmon is cut into bite-sized pieces for easier eating and greater appeal. Substitute swordfish or halibut if you like.

Juice of 1 lime

1 clove garlic, chopped

¼ cup olive oil

Pinch of pepper

8 ounces salmon fillets, cut into 1-inch cubes

½ pound fettuccine, cooked

2 tablespoons salted butter, softened

¼ cup fresh coriander or flat-leaf parsley leaves

In a shallow dish, combine the lime juice, garlic, olive oil, and pepper. Add the salmon cubes, cover, and marinate in the refrigerator for 1 hour. Turn occasionally.

Arrange the salmon on a microwave-safe plate. Cover with plastic wrap or a glass lid and cook for 2 minutes on high. Rotate the fish for even cooking, moving the pieces in the center to the outside. Cover and cook on high for 90 seconds more. Let rest, covered, for 3 minutes to complete cooking. The fish should be hot and firm to the touch.

Toss the fettuccine with the butter, coriander, and any of the salmon's cooking juices. Arrange on a platter and top with the fish. Serve immediately. Cover leftovers and refrigerate up to 3 days.

NUTRIENTS PER SERVING: 980 calories,* 37 g protein, 52 g fat,* 90 g carbohydrate, 5.4 mg iron, 162 RE vitamin A, 27 mg vitamin C, 40 mg calcium, 690 mg potassium.

*Calorie and fat content includes all of the marinade. For each 1 tablespoon marinade that remains in the dish, subtract 100 calories and 13 grams fat from the analysis.

Winter Chowder

MAKES 4 SERVINGS

The flavors of potassium-rich turnips, carrots, and potatoes complementone another and become even more pronounced when they are cooked together as in this hearty chowder. Use evaporated skim milk to reduce fat if desired.

1 onion, chopped

1 clove garlic, chopped

1 tablespoon unsalted butter

3 carrots, peeled and diced

1 large baking potato, peeled and diced

1 small turnip, peeled and diced

1 cup canned chicken broth or Poultry Stock (page 248)

One 13-ounce can evaporated milk

In a heavy saucepan over low heat, cook the onion and garlic in the butter until the onion is translucent, about 2 to 3 minutes. Stir in the vegetables and broth, cover, and simmer until the vegetables are tender when pierced with a fork, about 10 minutes.

Add the milk, stir, and cook, covered, until the chowder is heated through, about 5 minutes more. Serve hot. Cover and refrigerate leftovers, up to 3 days.

NUTRIENTS PER 1-CUP SERVING: 268 calories, 11 g protein, 12 g fat, 33 g carbohydrate, 1.2 mg iron, 1622 vitamin A, 0.6 mg vitamin E, 26 mg vitamin C, 308 mg calcium, 984 mg potassium.

Garden Casserole

MAKES **6** SERVINGS

This meatless main dish is high in both protein and potassium. The colored peppers and strips of bright carrot cooked on top of golden polenta make a beautiful combination.

2 cloves garlic, chopped

1 tablespoon olive oil

1 carrot, peeled and sliced into
    thin strips

1 red bell pepper, cored, seeded,
    and thinly sliced lengthwise

1 onion, thinly sliced

4 cups water

1 1/2 cups yellow cornmeal

1 teaspoon salt (optional)

1 cup whole-milk ricotta cheese

2 ounces mild Cheddar
    cheese, grated

Preheat the oven to 325°F. Lightly oil a 2-quart baking dish. In a medium saucepan over low heat, cook the garlic in the olive oil for 1 minute. Add the vegetables and sauté until softened but still a bit crisp but not completely cooked, about 3 minutes. Set aside.

In a large heavy saucepan, bring the water to a boil. Gradually stir in the cornmeal and salt and bring to a boil, then reduce the heat to very low and cook, stirring frequently to prevent lumps, until the polenta thickens, 15 to 20 minutes.

Pour the polenta into the baking dish and stir in the ricotta until evenly combined. Spread the mixture evenly over the bottom of the dish. Top with the grated cheese and sprinkle the sautéed vegetables over the cheese. Bake for 25 minutes, or until the vegetables just start to brown and the cheese is melted. Cut into squares and serve hot. Cover leftovers and refrigerate up to 3 days.

NUTRIENTS PER SERVING: 312 calories, 13 g protein, 12 g fat, 36 g carbohydrate, 2.3 mg iron, 449 RE vitamin A, 0.8 mg vitamin E, 12 mg vitamin C, 174 mg calcium, 253 mg potassium.

Sweet Sausage, Apple, and Squash Casserole

MAKES 4 SERVINGS

One serving of this casserole provides almost one half of the RDA for potassium. It is very versatile and makes an excellent breakfast, light lunch, or side dish.

1 small acorn or butternut squash, peeled, halved lengthwise, seeded, sliced

4 medium apples, cored and sliced

1 small onion, chopped

2 cloves garlic, chopped

1 tablespoon canola oil

8 ounces Italian sweet sausage, cut into ½-inch slices

1 cup apple cider or apple juice

Preheat the oven to 325°F. Lightly oil a 1-quart baking dish. In the bottom of the dish, alternately layer the apple and squash slices so that they lay flat in the dish.

In a large skillet, sauté the onion and garlic in the oil for 2 minutes on medium heat until the onion is soft. Add the sausage and cook, stirring, for 2 minutes more until the sides are browned. Drain off the fat.

Sprinkle the sausage mixture evenly over the squash and apples. Pour the cider over the sausage.

Bake for 45 minutes, or until the squash and apples are very soft. Serve hot. Cover leftovers and refrigerate up to 4 days.

NUTRIENTS PER SERVING: 419 calories,* 13 g protein, 48 g fat,* 47 g carbohydrate, 2.2 mg iron, 51 RE vitamin A, 1 mg vitamin E, 22 mg vitamin C, 83 mg calcium, 923 mg potassium.

*For each tablespoon of fat drained off, subtract 12 grams fat and about 100 calories from the nutrient analysis.

Fruit Puree

MAKES ¾ CUP (1 SERVING)

Use fruit purees to top fruit salads, ice cream, yogurt, or puddings, or mix with milk to make fruit shakes or stir into pancake batters or quick breads. In most cases the fruit should be peeled to avoid a gritty texture. Pureed apricots are an excellent source of potassium, with more than 300 milligrams per three-quarter cup; the same amount of pureed papaya yields 780 milligrams.

**1 cup peeled, seeded, and
chopped fruit**

1 tablespoon water

Combine the fruit and water in a microwave-safe dish, cover, and cook on high for 2 minutes. Stir and cook 1 minute more. Let rest for 2 minutes to complete cooking.

Puree the fruit along with its cooking juices in a food grinder, blender, or food processor. Cover and refrigerate up to 3 days or freeze up to 4 months.

NUTRIENTS PER SERVING (MADE WITH APPLES): 91 calories, 0.5 g fat, 23 g carbohydrate, 0.3 mg iron, 6.8 RE vitamin A, 8.5 mg calcium, 150 mg potassium.

Tricia's Chutney

MAKES 2 CUPS

My friend Tricia spends a lot of time in the Caribbean, where tropical fruits are an integral part of the cuisine. Chutney is an easy, low-fat way to get potassium. Try this with any cooked meat, Chicken Dijon (page 129), or even Baked Fish Fillets (page 138).

1 papaya, peeled, seeded, and cut into ½-inch dice

½ red bell pepper, cored, seeded, and cut into ½-inch dice

1 cup diced pineapple, preferably fresh

1 small red onion, minced

2 tablespoons golden raisins

⅓ cup sugar

1½ tablespoons red wine vinegar

¼ teaspoon ground cinnamon

¼ teaspoon ground ginger

Combine all of the ingredients in a 1-quart microwave-safe dish. Cook, covered, on high for 3 minutes. Stir and cook for 3 minutes more. Stir, allow to cool, and serve warm. Cover and refrigerate up to 3 days.

NUTRIENTS PER ½ CUP: 203 calories, 3 g protein, 1 g fat, 47 g carbohydrate, 1 mg iron, 40 RE vitamin A, 5 mg vitamin E, 92 mg vitamin C, 50 mg calcium, 386 mg potassium.

the low-
protein diet

13

The body always needs some protein, but when the liver or kidneys are diseased or damaged, too much protein can be toxic. The challenge of a low-
protein diet, then, is to get enough protein without overburdening the body's
ability to metabolize it. Medical conditions that dictate a low-protein diet
also frequently limit sodium, potassium, phosphorus, and fluids. If a low-
protein diet is recommended for your patient, plan it with the help of the
health care provider and a registered dietitian to incorporate any limitations
necessary. Use this chapter to supplement the information you get from the
health care team.

The RDA for protein for women is 44 grams, for men, 63 grams. Low-protein diets generally contain no more than this recommended amount, about 40 to 60 grams a day. Yet because most people eat about twice as much protein as they need, most patients must significantly change their food choices if they need to decrease protein intake.

Menus based on the Healing Food Guide provide about 80 grams of protein. To reduce protein to levels prescribed by the health care provider, the number of servings from the Protein, Calcium, and Grain/Starch groups must be reduced.

Who Should Eat a Low-Protein Diet?

People with acute or chronic kidney disease and advanced liver disease, such as cirrhosis, often must follow a low-protein diet. Phosphorus, potassium, sodium, and fluids may also need to be restricted.

Scientists are also investigating whether a low-protein diet may help prevent the progression of some forms of kidney disease. All types of kidney and liver ailments, however, do not require a low-protein intake. In fact, some liver conditions may need plenty of protein for healing. Therefore, one should adopt a low-protein diet only under the recommendation of the health care provider.

What to Eat on a Low-Protein Diet

Ask the health care provider for the amount of protein your patient should eat daily. Then modify the Healing Food Guide to limit servings from each group to stay within the prescribed amount of protein. If other nutrients such as phosphorus, sodium, potassium, and fluids are restricted, work closely with the health care team to plan the diet. Chapters 11 and 12, on sodium and potassium, will also help you learn more about food sources of those nutrients.

MEETING NUTRIENT NEEDS ON A LOW-PROTEIN DIET

Low-protein diets generally do not provide enough calcium, iron, vitamin B_{12}, and zinc and may also be deficient in thiamin, riboflavin, and niacin. Check with the health care provider to see whether or not your patient needs a vitamin/mineral supplement.

- *Protein Group:* One ounce of meat, fish, or poultry, 1 egg, or ¹/₂ cup cooked beans supplies about 7 grams of protein. One half-cup of tofu contains 10 to 20 grams. Animal foods, which are complete proteins, contain all the essential amino acids the body needs for repair and maintenance and are the easiest way to get protein.

- *Calcium Group:* One half-cup of milk or yogurt contains about 4 grams of protein. One half cup of green leafy vegetables supplies approximately 1 gram of protein. Serve milk-based foods from this group rather than vegetables for complete protein.

- *Vegetable Group:* One half-cup of vegetables provides about 1 gram of protein.

- *Fruit Group:* Fruits contain about ¹/₂ gram of protein per ¹/₂ cup. Serve ample quantities of fruits to supply calories without raising the protein count.

- *Grain/Starch Group:* Foods in this group contain only small amounts of protein yet they accumulate quickly given the number of recommended servings. One slice of bread or ¹/₂ cup rice, cereal, potato, or pasta contains about 2 grams of protein.

- *Fat/Oil Group:* Most foods in this group, such as butter, cream, and oils, can be eaten in unlimited amounts. Indeed, they are a good source of needed calories but contain little, if any, protein. The exceptions are nuts and wheat germ—avoid them.

- *Other Foods:* Seasonings and Condiments: Sugar, jams, and jellies are all low in protein. Vinegar, herbs, spices, and meat tenderizers are also low in protein.

- *Beverages:* Coffee, tea, water, carbonated beverages, and fruit drinks contain no protein. Many carbonated beverages and fruit drinks contain added phosphorus; if your patient needs to limit phosphorus, read labels carefully. Avoid aspartame-sweetened drinks; it is made from protein. Avoid cereal beverages, such as Postum, and milk-based drinks.

The Protein Redistribution Diet and Parkinson's Disease

Research suggests that a protein-controlled diet may help reduce symptoms in some people with Parkinson's disease. The Protein Redistribution Diet was developed for that purpose; see Chapter 3 for more about its history and effectiveness. Before attempting this diet, however, discuss it with the health care provider.

If your patient decides to follow the Protein Redistribution Diet, limit protein to no more than 10 grams during the day. To stay within this limit, do not serve foods from the Protein Group and do not select any milk-based foods from the Calcium Group. Study the protein

A SAMPLE LOW-PROTEIN MENU

This menu contains 44 grams of protein. To provide extra calories, use protein-free foods such as jams, butter, mayonnaise, and sugar liberally. If your patient needs even more calories, supplement the diet with the "free" foods listed on page 273.

	Protein (g)	Calories
Breakfast		
4 ounces orange juice	0.9	56
1 poached egg	6	74
1 slice whole wheat toast	2.4	61
2 teaspoons butter		67
1 tablespoon jam		55
½ cup whole milk	4	75
Coffee or tea with 2 teaspoons sugar and 2 tablespoons cream	0.8	90
Lunch		
1 ounce ham	5	52
on 2 slices whole wheat bread	5	122
with lettuce and tomato	0.4	7
and 1 tablespoon mayonnaise	0.2	100
½ cup fruit cocktail	1.6	36
1 cup fruit drink (no phosphorus added)		117
Snack		
½ cup fruited yogurt	5	116
Dinner		
Beef Stir-Fry:		
1 ounce beef	5.6	49
with 1 cup Chinese vegetables	1.3	17
1 cup rice	4.3	205
1 tablespoon butter		100
Baked peach sprinkled with 1 teaspoon sugar and topped with 2 tablespoons whipped cream	0.3	60
Coffee or tea with 2 teaspoons sugar and 2 tablespoons cream	0.8	90
Total	44.2	1580

"FREE" FOODS

The following foods contain little, if any, protein, sodium, or potassium. They do contain calories, which your patient may need. Use these foods liberally if necessary.

Granulated sugar	Maple syrup
Hard candy	100 percent fruit popsicle
Jelly and jam	Italian water ice
Marmalade	Cool Whip
Jelly beans	Chewing gum
Honey	Gumdrops
Sour balls	

content of foods in the different groups to determine what you can serve. Onions, celery, and green pepper are so low in protein they may be eaten as snacks. Use hard candy and other protein-free foods from the list on page 273 to quell hunger and satisfy appetite. After the hour that has been established by the health care provider (usually 7:00 p.m.), protein-containing foods can be eaten in unlimited amounts. Aim for the minimum number of servings recommended from each food group listed in the Healing Food Guide, with emphasis on the Protein and Calcium groups.

The recipes in this chapter show you how to stretch high-protein ingredients to meet the requirements of a low-protein diet without sacrificing flavor and other nutrients. An emphasis on vegetables adds calories, bulk, and flavor. Grains are used in moderation, since each half-cup carries about 2 grams of protein. The recipes that incorporate meat are most appropriate for the person following a diet only moderately low in protein. For those requiring a long-term low-protein diet in the 40-to-60-gram range, modify the recipes by using special low-protein ingredients from one of the companies listed here. They carry a host of products such as low-protein bread, baking mixes, and macaroni as well as recipes for making nutritious, low-protein meals.

Special Low Protein Products

Breads, baking mixes and pastas contain small amounts of protein that add up to significant quantities considering the amounts of these foods we usually eat. But several companies offer low-protein alternatives to these favorite foods. Healthfood stores and specialty food catalogues often carry such products, but you can also order them directly by contacting the manufacturers.

Low-Protein Specialty Foods
Dietary Specialties, Inc.
P.O. Box 227
Rochester, NY 14601
For information and prices, call
716-263-2787; to place an order,
call 1-800- 544-0099

Kingsmill Foods Company, Ltd.
1399 Kennedy Road, Unit 17
Scarborough, Ontario
Canada, MIP 2L6 · 416-755-1124

Ener G Food
5960 First Avenue South
P.O. Box 84487
Seattle, Washington 98124-5787
800-331-5222 or 206-767-6660
In Washington, call: 1-800-325-9788

Pasta with Prosciutto

MAKES 4 SERVINGS

Prosciutto is very intensely flavored; a little bit goes a long way. Keep in mind that fresh pasta is usually made with eggs and will add significantly to the protein value if used instead of the spaghetti.

1 pound spaghetti, cooked

½ cup (1 stick) salted butter, melted

2 ounces prosciutto, finely minced

1 cup cooked fresh or thawed frozen small peas

1 cup half-and-half

¼ cup freshly grated Parmesan cheese

Grated nutmeg to taste

Preheat the oven to 400°F. Lightly oil a baking dish. Put the noodles in the dish. Pour the butter over the pasta and add the prosciutto, peas, half-and-half, and 3 tablespoons of the cheese. Toss well. Sprinkle with the remaining cheese and nutmeg and bake for 10 minutes. Serve hot. Cover leftovers and refrigerate up to 3 days.

NUTRIENTS PER SERVING: 757 calories, 23 g protein, 34 g fat, 91 g carbohydrate, 5.5 mg iron, 307 RE vitamin A, 1.8 mg vitamin E, 25 mg vitamin C, 194 mg calcium.

Beef Stir-Fry

MAKES 4 SERVINGS

Asian cultures traditionally use small amounts of meat in their dishes. Use this technique when trying to limit protein intake.

1 tablespoon cornstarch

½ cup canned beef broth or Beef Stock (page 249)

¼ cup sherry

1 tablespoon soy sauce

1 tablespoon plus 1 teaspoon canola oil

3 cloves garlic, chopped

2 teaspoons grated fresh ginger

1 cup chopped broccoli

1 carrot, peeled and sliced diagonally ½ inch thick

1 red bell pepper, cored, seeded, and diced

3 scallions, chopped

8 ounces beef sirloin, cut into ¼-inch cubes

2 cups hot cooked rice

In a shallow dish, combine the cornstarch, broth, sherry, and soy sauce and mix well. Add the beef and marinate for 20 minutes.

Remove the beef from the marinade, reserving the liquid. Set aside.

Heat 1 tablespoon of the oil in a large skillet over high heat. Add garlic and ginger and cook, stirring, for 1 minute. Add the broccoli, carrot, red pepper, and scallions and cook, stirring, until the vegetables are crisp and tender but still firm, 2 to 3 minutes.

With a slotted spoon, remove the vegetables from the pan and set aside. Add the remaining 1 teaspoon oil to the pan. Add the marinated meat and cook, stirring occasionally, for 5 minutes. Return the vegetables to the pan, add the reserved marinade, and cook until the meat is well done and the marinade thickens, about 5 minutes more. Serve over the rice. Cover and refrigerate leftovers up to 3 days or freeze in individual portions (without the rice) up to 3 months.

NUTRIENTS PER SERVING: 358 calories, 24 g protein, 11 g fat, 36 g carbohydrate, 4 mg iron, 568 mg vitamin A, 0.2 mg vitamin E, 38 mg vitamin C, 51 mg calcium.

Almost-Vegetarian Stew

MAKES 4 SERVINGS

A small amount of ground beef gives this dish a meaty taste without adding much protein.

1 onion, chopped

1 celery stalk, chopped

1 tablespoon canola oil

4 ounces ground beef

4 cups canned beef broth or
   Beef Stock (page 249)

1 bay leaf

One 32-ounce can crushed
   tomatoes

2 carrots, peeled and diced

¼ cup brown rice

In a large pot over medium heat, sauté the onion and celery in the oil until translucent, about 2 to 3 minutes. Add the beef and sauté until it is no longer pink. Add all the remaining ingredients and bring to a boil. Reduce the heat and simmer, uncovered, until the rice is tender, about 45 minutes. Cover leftovers and refrigerate up to 4 days or freeze up to 2 to 3 months.

NUTRIENTS PER SERVING: 227 calories, 11 g protein, 9 g fat, 26 g carbohydrate, 2.7 mg iron, 1250 RE vitamin A, 0.4 mg vitamin E, 43 mg vitamin C, 128 mg calcium.

Meatless Tomato Sauce

MAKES 6 CUPS

A great way to satisfy the vegetable requirement, this meatless tomato sauce is low in protein and fat. Use no-salt-added canned tomatoes if salt is an issue.

1 small onion, chopped

3 cloves garlic, chopped

1 carrot, peeled and chopped

2 tablespoons olive oil

Two 28-ounce cans peeled crushed Italian tomatoes

One 6-ounce can tomato paste

1 teaspoon dried basil

1 bay leaf

1/2 cup red wine

1 tablespoon sugar (optional)

In a large skillet over low heat, sauté the onion, garlic, and carrot in the oil for 2 to 3 minutes. Add the tomatoes, tomato paste, basil, bay leaf, and wine, and the sugar, if using. Cook, uncovered, for 1 hour until thickened, stirring frequently. Cover and refrigerate up to 4 days or freeze in 1-cup portions up to 4 months.

NUTRIENTS PER CUP: 146 calories, 4 g protein, 5 g fat, 20 g carbohydrate, 2.7 mg iron, 686 RE vitamin A, 0.1 mg vitamin E, 57 mg vitamin C, 127 mg calcium.

cooking without sugar

forget all the bad things you've heard about sugar. It does *not* cause obesity, diabetes, or hyperactive behavior in children. In fact, recent research shows that eating moderate amounts of sugar helps people meet recommendations to reduce dietary fat. What's more, a diet that contains moderate amounts of sugar usually contains plenty of vitamins and minerals too. The key word is *moderation.* There is no need to eliminate sugar if your patient enjoys it and does not have any medical reason to avoid it. Indeed, sugar often adds important calories and taste to foods that otherwise may lack appeal.

It was long thought that sugar played a critical role in diabetes. But in 1994, the American Diabetes Association issued findings that scientific evidence no longer justifies the longtime belief that sugar intake must be restricted by those who have diabetes. Read more about diabetes and diet in Chapter 3.

It is important to understand that any food that contains calories—regardless of whether they come from protein, fat, or carbohydrate—can contribute to the amount of glucose, or blood sugar, in the body. The absence of sugar in a food does *not* mean that the food will not affect blood sugar levels. Staying within a prescribed limit of calories is more important to diabetes than limiting sugar.

Most people with diabetes are advised by their health care team to follow a diabetic exchange diet, to be planned with the help of a registered dietitian. This plan for eating developed by the American Diabetes Association and American Dietetic Association is similar to the Healing Food Guide. For more information, contact either of these organizations (see Resources, page 340). People with reactive hypoglycemia should work closely with their health care provider.

Although rare, reactive hypoglycemia may require limited sugar intake. In this condition, blood sugar levels may rise after eating sugar, then drop to levels that cause shakiness, dizziness, and even fainting. Sugar tolerance among people with reactive hypoglycemia is very individual—some are sensitive to any amount of sugar, while others tolerate sugar in small amounts.

Who Should Eat a Sugar-Free Diet?

People with reactive hypoglycemia, which causes loss of the ability to regulate blood sugar levels, need to follow a diet controlled in sugar, other carbohydrates, and calories. Regulating these plays a key role in keeping blood sugar levels within a healthy range. People undergoing medical treatments that cause sweet foods to taste unpleasant may benefit from a sugar-free diet. People who have diabetes can certainly continue to eat sugar-free, but strict avoidance of sugar is no longer considered essential.

Sugar is not essential to healthy diets, and its elimination does no harm. Yet sugar-rich foods such as soft drinks, ice cream, or desserts may be vital during illness to keep calorie intake high when solid or traditional foods are refused.

What to Eat on a Sugar-Free Diet

The balanced diet outlined by the Healing Food Guide is suited to the person with reactive hypoglycemia, although the number of servings from each group should be planned with the assistance of a registered dietitian. The following list provides a closer look at foods within each group that may help or be problematic.

- *Protein Group:* Include a small amount of protein at breakfast to carry your patient through the morning. Try 1 tablespoon of peanut butter, 1 egg (2 to 3 mornings a week), 1 breakfast sausage, or 1 slice of cheese.

- *Calcium Group:* Limit portions to 1 cup of milk at any one meal. Limit chocolate milk, milk shakes, and sugar-sweetened yogurt.

- *Vegetable Group:* Limit vegetables with cheese or white sauces.

- *Fruit Group:* Consume as advised by your doctor. Limit fruit drinks, fruit juices, and fruit-flavored yogurt with added sugar. Select canned fruits without added sugar.

- *Grain/Starch Group:* Consume as advised by the health care team. Select whole grains and high-fiber cereals. Limit sweetened cereals.

- *Fats/Oils:* Use in moderation, since these are very rich in fat and calories. Except for whipped cream and salad dressings, these foods rarely contain sugar.

- *Other Foods:* Seasonings and Condiments: Use herbs and spices as desired. Catsup contains added sugar; limit to 2 tablespoons per meal unless otherwise advised by the health care team. Sugar substitutes such as NutraSweet, Sugar Twin, Sweet'n Low, and Equal are allowed.

- *Beverages:* Use coffee and tea without added sugar. Diet sodas are fine; limit sugar-sweetened drinks.

FOODS AND INGREDIENTS TO LIMIT WHEN LIMITING SUGAR

Some of the following foods and beverages may be consumed in limited amounts. Check with the health care team before including them in your patient's diet.

Alcohol (consult your physician)	Honey
Candy	Ice cream
Cereal (presweetened)	Jams, jellies, and marmalade
Chewing gum (regular)	Milk (chocolate, strawberry, or
Desserts, cakes, and cookies with	sweetened condensed)
frostings and fillings	Pastries
Dietetic foods	Pie
Dried fruits such as figs, dates, and	Pudding
raisins	Sherbet
Fructose	Soft drinks (sugar-sweetened)
Fruit drinks and punches sweetened	Sugar
with sugar	Syrup
Gelatin desserts (sugar-sweetened)	Yogurt (fruited or frozen)

This chapter includes recipes for desserts and snacks that contain no added sugar. For recipes for main dishes and vegetables, turn to Chapter 5.

When sugar is eliminated from baked goods and replaced with fruit, fruit juice concentrate, and fruit purees, the texture of the foods is softer and the taste may be somewhat less sweet. These baked goods, though, carry more fiber and nutrition than their sugar-sweetened counterparts.

Carrot Muffins

MAKES 18

The dab of cream cheese that tops these muffins makes them look rich and creamy. They are a tasty way to serve carrots.

2 cups all-purpose flour

2 teaspoons baking powder

1 teaspoon baking soda

1 teaspoon grated nutmeg

1 teaspoon ground cinnamon

3 large eggs

$\frac{1}{2}$ cup (1 stick) salted butter, softened

$\frac{3}{4}$ cup canned unsweetened crushed pineapple, drained

2 cups finely grated carrots

8 ounces cream cheese, softened

Preheat the oven to 350°F. Lightly grease 18 muffin cups. Combine all the dry ingredients in a bowl.

In a large bowl, beat together the eggs, butter, and crushed pineapple. Gently stir in the dry ingredients until blended. Stir in the carrots.

Pour the batter into the muffin cups and place 2 rounded teaspoons of the cream cheese on top of each muffin. Bake for 18 minutes, or until the muffins and cheese are lightly browned. Serve warm, or cover and refrigerate up to 7 days or freeze up to 3 months.

NUTRIENTS PER MUFFIN: 161 calories, 4 g protein, 13 g carbohydrate, 10 g fat, 0.9 mg iron, 460 RE vitamin A, 0.3 mg vitamin E, 2 mg vitamin C, 25 mg calcium.

Blueberry Cobbler

MAKES 4 SERVINGS

This great breakfast treat or dessert will satisfy your patient's sweet tooth without adding sugar to his or her diet. When peaches are in season, replace the berries with two cups sliced peaches.

2½ cups fresh or frozen unsweet-
    ened blueberries

1 teaspoon ground cinnamon

¾ cup all-purpose flour

¾ cup whole wheat flour

1 teaspoon baking powder

½ teaspoon baking soda

1 large egg

¼ cup canola oil

½ cup orange juice

2 tablespoons milk

Preheat the oven to 325°F. Lightly grease a 1½-quart baking dish. Toss the fruit with the cinnamon and pour into the dish.

In a small bowl, combine the dry ingredients. In a large bowl, with a fork, beat together the egg, oil, juice, and milk, until well blended. Add the dry ingredients and mix just until all the ingredients are moistened. Do not overmix. Pour the batter over the fruit.

Bake for 25 minutes, or until lightly browned on top. Serve warm, with plain yogurt if desired. Cover leftovers and refrigerate up to 4 days.

NUTRIENTS PER SERVING: 372 calories, 8 g protein, 51 g carbohydrate, 16 g fat, 2.4 mg iron, 38 RE vitamin A, 1.1 mg vitamin E, 24 mg vitamin C, 42 mg calcium.

Not-So-Traditional Apple Pie

MAKES ONE 9-INCH PIE (8 SLICES)

My husband made his first apple pie for Thanksgiving dinner at my parents' house. Halfway through baking, he confessed he had forgotten the sugar. No one even noticed.

1 recipe Easy Pie Crust (page 136) or a prepared pie crust

4 cups peeled, cored, and sliced apples

1 tablespoon fresh lemon juice or 1 tablespoon frozen apple juice concentrate

1 tablespoon all-purpose flour

1 teaspoon ground cinnamon

1 teaspoon grated nutmeg

Dash of ground cloves

Preheat the oven to 425°F. Divide the pie dough in half. On a lightly floured board, roll out half the dough to a 12-inch circle. Set into a 9-inch pie plate, prick the bottom with a fork, and bake for 10 minutes, or until lightly browned. Set aside to cool. Set the remaining dough aside. Turn the oven temperature to 350°F.

In a large bowl, combine all the remaining ingredients and gently stir until well combined. Pour the mixture into the pie plate.

Roll out the remaining dough to a 10-inch circle large enough to cover the pie. Fit the pastry over the apples, pinching the top and bottom crusts together to seal. Prick the top crust with a fork to release steam.

Bake for 50 minutes, or until the crust is golden. Serve with plain yogurt or, if your patient needs extra calories and protein, serve with a slice of Cheddar cheese. Cover and refrigerate leftovers up to 5 days.

NUTRIENTS PER SLICE: 294 calories, 4 g protein, 38 g carbohydrate, 15 g fat, 1.6 mg iron, 135 RE vitamin A, 0.3 mg vitamin E, 18 mg calcium.

Coconut Cashew Snack Cake

MAKES ONE 9- BY 13-INCH CAKE (12 SERVINGS)

Coconut and toasted cashews are two of my favorite foods. Here they are combined with banana for a subtly sweet cake.

1/3 cup canola oil	2 cups all-purpose flour
1 cup mashed ripe bananas	1 1/2 teaspoons baking powder
1/2 cup milk	1 teaspoon baking soda
3 large eggs	1 1/2 cups unsweetened flaked coconut
1/4 cup cashew butter (or substitute peanut butter)	1/2 cup chopped cashews

Preheat the oven to 325°F. Lightly oil a 9- by 13-inch pan. In a large bowl, with an electric mixer, beat together the oil and bananas. Beat the milk and eggs. Add the nut butter and mix.

In a medium bowl, combine the flour, baking powder, baking soda, and 1 cup of the coconut. Gently fold the dry ingredients into the wet ingredients. Do not overmix; a few small lumps are okay. Pour the batter into the pan.

Sprinkle with the chopped cashews and the remaining 1/2 cup coconut. Bake for 18 minutes, or until the nuts and coconut are lightly browned and a knife inserted in the center of the cake comes out clean. Serve warm or at room temperature. Cover and refrigerate leftovers up to 4 days or freeze up to 3 months. Reheat in a 350°F. oven for 5 minutes to toast the nuts.

NUTRIENTS PER SERVING: 248 calories, 6 g protein, 27 g carbohydrate, 14 g fat, 1.6 mg iron, 29 RE vitamin A, 0.9 mg vitamin E, 2 mg vitamin C, 27 mg calcium.

the low-
fat diet

the role fat plays in the health of your patient depends on the symptoms and illness being managed. In some cases, fat is a superb way to add calories. In other situations, it can cause painful side effects because of digestive problems. For most people, a moderate intake of fat creates no problems. And, in contrast to recommendations for healthy people, low-fat eating is not always appropriate for those with serious illnesses, because fat is the most efficient source of energy.

The person who has difficulty digesting fat is generally given a specific recommendation for fat intake based on his or her individual tolerance. The Healing Food Guide provides 40 to 60 grams of fat daily, depending on the foods selected. The low-fat diet used to treat malabsorption associated with problems such as celiac disease, cystic fibrosis, enteritis, pancreatitis, and short bowel syndrome provides only 25 to 50 grams. The diet designed to lower levels of fat and cholesterol in the blood gets about 25 to 30 percent of its calories from fat and limits cholesterol to less than 300 milligrams per day.

Who Should Eat a Low-Fat Diet?

Along with the conditions listed here, a low-fat diet may also be used in the treatment of gallbladder disease, reflux esophagitis (a serious form of heartburn), irritable bowel syndrome, and uncontrollable diarrhea. There is some evidence to suggest that a fat-controlled menu may also help people with multiple sclerosis.

Dietary recommendations for all healthy people over the age of two emphasize a low-fat diet to help control weight, prevent obesity, and reduce risk for heart disease and some types of cancer.

When heart disease or high cholesterol levels are a concern, saturated fats must be limited. When illnesses such as pancreatitis or other malabsorption syndromes are an issue, all fats, regardless of their source, should be restricted.

A low-fat diet may not be advisable, however, for anyone during serious illness or for the elderly. If food intake is low or appetite poor, eating high-fat foods is the best and most efficient way to get much-needed calories.

Know Your Fats

Fat is a nutrient as essential to a healthy body as protein and carbohydrate. It plays a critical role in many essential body functions, including cholesterol metabolism, the transport and absorption of fat-soluble vitamins, and the synthesis of vital hormones and body fluids.

Fats are classified into three types—saturated, monounsaturated, and polyunsaturated. Saturated fats, which generally stay hard at room temperature, tend to raise blood cholesterol levels. These fats are found primarily in animal foods, such as beef, poultry, lamb, pork, eggs, and dairy products. Some vegetable products, including palm oil and coconut oil, also contain saturated fat. Watch for these especially in commercially prepared baked goods. Monounsaturated and polyunsaturated fats help reduce blood cholesterol levels. Polyunsaturated fats are found in vegetable oils that remain liquid at room temperature, including corn, safflower, and sunflower oil, soft margarines, salad dressings, and mayonnaise. Monounsaturated fats are found in olives and olive oil, peanuts, and peanut oil and canola oil.

Cholesterol is a soft, waxy fatlike substance that plays a key role in the manufacture of estrogen and testosterone, vitamin D, bile, skin oils, and nerve- and brain-cell sheaths. Indeed, it is so essential that one organ, the liver, makes all of the cholesterol we need—about 1000 milligrams a day—to carry out these functions. A typical diet adds 400 to 500 more milligrams of cholesterol daily. While blood cholesterol levels are determined in part by heredity, they are also affected by diet. When too much cholesterol circulates in the blood, the risk of heart disease rises. One way to reduce blood cholesterol is to limit intake of fat and, for about one third of the population, to limit cholesterol intake. More than half the fat we eat comes from animal foods, such as meats and whole milk and cheese. Cholesterol is found only in foods derived from animal products. Fortunately, when we cut back on fat, cholesterol levels are usually lowered.

What to Eat on a Low-Fat Diet

- *Protein Group:* For a 25-gram fat diet, limit lean meat or meat substitutes to 5 ounces per day; for a 50-gram-fat-and-above diet, limit to 6 ounces. Lean meats include beef round, loin, sirloin, and chuck arm; pork tenderloin, center loin, and ham; all cuts of veal except ground; leg of lamb, loin, and foreshanks; poultry without skin; and most fish and shellfish. Avoid fried versions of all these foods. Check with the health care provider about use of eggs; some diets allow 3 to 4 a week, others restrict eggs to less than 1 per week. Beans, lentils, and tofu are low in fat. Peanut butter is high in fat; for a fat-controlled diet, consider 1 teaspoon of peanut butter as a serving of fat rather than of protein. Choose low-fat cheeses with 2 grams or less fat per ounce.

- *Calcium Group:* Use nonfat, skim, or 1% milk, evaporated skim milk, or buttermilk made from skim milk. Also try nonfat or low-fat yogurt, ice milk, sherbet, and low-fat frozen yogurt. Choose nonfat cottage cheese and other cheeses with 2 grams or less fat per ounce. All green leafy vegetables are low in fat.

- *Vegetable Group:* Avoid bathing vegetables in butter, margarine, oils, and rich sauces. Offer naturally low-fat vegetable juices. Olives and avocados are naturally high in fat and should be eaten in moderation.

- *Fruit Group:* Offer any fresh, canned, or frozen fruit.

- *Grain/Starch Group:* Read the labels to select only hot or cold breakfast cereals that contain 3 grams or less fat per serving. Offer all types of pasta and rice prepared without added fat. Choose whole-grain and white breads, rolls, English muffins, bagels, pita bread, baked tortillas, saltines, oyster crackers, matzoh, melba toast, flatbreads, pretzels, animal crackers, graham crackers, fig bars, ginger snaps, and other fat-free snack foods (check labels). Prepare potatoes without added fat; use skim milk when mashing, or top with nonfat yogurt or fat-free sour cream.

- *Fat/Oil Group:* On a 25-gram fat diet, do not use any fats or oils. On a 50-gram fat diet, 3 to 5 servings per day are allowed. Use primarily unsaturated fats. Vegetable pan sprays, fat-free salad dressings, and butter-flavored sprinkles, such as Butter Buds, help add flavor to low-fat cooking.

- *Other Foods:* Seasonings and Condiments: Use herbs and spices as tolerated. Although they add loads of fat-free flavor, some spices such as pepper and chili pepper can be irritating to sensitive stomachs. Jams, jellies, syrups, mustard, and catsup are fat-free.

- *Beverages:* Fruit drinks and juices, soft drinks, and coffee and tea served without milk or cream contain no fat. Serve hot cocoa made with skim milk.

LOW-FAT FOODS THAT SATISFY

Fat-free soups made from bouillon or broths from which you have skimmed the fat often provide comforting nourishment to the person who is ill and must keep fat intake low. If a cream soup is preferred, make it with skim milk or evaporated skim milk.

Creamy casseroles are also satisfying. Make casseroles with lean meat, fish, or poultry and low-fat cheese. Make your own low-fat white sauce using skim milk and flour (whisk together before heating).

Please your patient with low-fat desserts like cooked fruit, gelatin desserts, puddings made with skim milk, and angel food cake. Hard candies don't offer much nutrition beyond calories, but they don't contain fat either.

Oven-Fried Fish

MAKES 3 SERVINGS

This recipe contains only 6 grams of fat per serving. A fried version could have 40 or 50 grams of fat or more. Serve on a toasted roll with lettuce and tomato.

¹/₂ cup seasoned bread crumbs

1 teaspoon dried tarragon

1 tablespoon freshly grated Parmesan cheese

¹/₂ cup skim milk

1 pound fish fillets, such as cod, haddock, sole, or red snapper

1 tablespoon unsalted butter, melted

Lemon wedges

Preheat the oven to 400°F. Lightly oil a baking sheet. In a shallow dish, mix the bread crumbs with the tarragon and cheese. Pour the milk into another shallow dish. Dip each fillet into the milk, coat with the seasoned bread crumbs, and place in the baking dish.

Drizzle the melted butter evenly over the fish. Bake for 15 to 20 minutes, depending on the thickness of the fish, until it is firm and just flaky with a fork. Serve hot with lemon wedges. Cover leftovers and refrigerate up to 3 days.

NUTRIENTS PER SERVING: 248 calories, 31 g protein, 6 g fat, 14 g carbohydrate, 1.3 mg iron, 84 RE vitamin A, 2 mg vitamin C, 130 mg calcium.

Chicken Fajitas

MAKES 3 SERVINGS

This marinade tenderizes and flavors the chicken with just the right amount of spice.

1 tablespoon olive oil

2 tablespoons fresh lemon juice

¼ teaspoon chili powder

12 ounces skinless, boneless chicken breasts, cut into ½-inch strips

1 green bell pepper, cored, seeded, and sliced

1 red pepper, cored, seeded, and sliced

6 soft flour tortillas

Preheat the oven to 350°F. Lightly oil a baking dish. Combine the oil, lemon juice, and chili powder in a glass bowl. Place the chicken and peppers in the oil mixture, turn to coat, and refrigerate for 45 minutes.

Meanwhile, wrap the tortillas in foil and heat in the oven for 5 to 6 minutes. Set aside, wrapped, until ready to use. Turn the oven to broil.

Remove the chicken and vegetables from the marinade and arrange in the baking dish. Broil for 10 to 15 minutes, turning once, until the juices run clear when the chicken is pierced with a fork. Place an equal amount of the chicken and vegetables in each warm tortilla, roll, and serve. Cover leftover filling and refrigerate up to 2 days, or freeze up to 6 months.

NUTRIENTS PER SERVING: 606 calories, 52 g protein, 12 g fat, 52 g carbohydrate, 5 mg iron, 20 RE vitamin A, 20 mg vitamin C, 136 mg calcium.

Pasta with Tomatoes, Olives, and Capers

MAKES 4 SERVINGS

With the intense flavor of olives and distinct taste of capers, this sauce needs no more than one teaspoon of oil.

1 medium onion, chopped

3 cloves garlic, chopped

1 teaspoon olive oil

One 32-ounce can crushed tomatoes

6 Greek or other black olives, pitted and chopped

2 tablespoons capers

1 pound pasta, cooked

In a medium saucepan, sauté the onion and garlic in the oil until soft and translucent.

Add the tomatoes, olives, and capers. Stir and bring to a simmer, then cover, reduce the heat to low, and cook for 20 minutes. Uncover and simmer for 10 minutes more to reduce the sauce.

Pour the sauce over the pasta and serve. Cover leftovers and refrigerate up to 2 days.

NUTRIENTS PER SERVING: 520 calories, 17 g protein, 6 g fat, 99 g carbohydrate, 6 mg iron, 237 RE vitamin A, 0.12 mg vitamin E, 39 mg vitamin C, 122 mg calcium.

French Bakes

MAKES 2 SERVINGS

These unfried "fries" have the same crisp texture as French fries and less than half the fat. Leave the skin on for more flavor and fiber.

2 baking potatoes, peeled or scrubbed and cut into ¼-inch-thick slices

2 teaspoons canola oil

Salt to taste

Preheat the oven to 375°F. In a bowl, toss the potatoes with the oil until lightly coated.

Spread on a baking sheet in a single layer and bake for 20 minutes, turning once with a spatula. Cook until tender and browned. Sprinkle with salt and serve.

NUTRIENTS PER SERVING: 278 calories, 6 g protein, 5 g fat, 54 g carbohydrate, 2.3 mg iron, 3.8 mg vitamin E, 57 mg vitamin C, 21 mg calcium.

Summer Fruit Pie

MAKES ONE 9-INCH PIE (8 SLICES)

To satisfy a sweet tooth without blowing your patient's fat budget, I developed this terrific dessert that contains absolutely no added fat.

Meringue shell

3 large egg whites

¼ teaspoon cream of tartar

¾ cup confectioners' sugar

¼ teaspoon vanilla extract

Filling

2 cups blueberries or sliced strawberries

2 tablespoons brown sugar

1 tablespoon fresh lemon juice

Topping

2 large egg whites

¼ teaspoon cream of tartar

¼ cup confectioners' sugar

½ teaspoon vanilla

Preheat the oven to 275°F. Lightly oil a 9-inch pie plate. To make the meringue shell, in a mixing bowl, beat the egg whites with the cream of tartar until they start to thicken. Gradually add the confectioners' sugar and continue beating until the egg whites are stiff and shiny. Beat in the vanilla. Spread evenly into the pie plate. Bake for 1 hour and 10 minutes, or until the crust is dry and lightly browned. Set aside to cool. Increase the oven temperature to 350°F.

To make the filling, put the fruit in a bowl. In a saucepan over low heat, combine the brown sugar and lemon juice and cook, stirring, until the brown sugar melts, 1 to 2 minutes. Pour the brown sugar over the fruit and stir until the fruit is coated. Mound the fruit in the cooled meringue shell.

To make the topping, in a large bowl, beat together the egg whites and cream of tartar. When they start to stiffen, gradually add the confectioners' sugar and beat the whites until stiff peaks form. Stir in the vanilla. Spread in a ring around the edge of the pie, leaving the fruit exposed in the middle. Bake for 10 minutes, or until the meringue topping is golden. Serve immediately, topped with frozen low-fat yogurt if desired. The meringue will absorb the fruit juice and become soft if the pie sits, but it will still be delicious. Cover and refrigerate up to 3 days.

NUTRIENTS PER SLICE: 93 calories, 2.5 g protein, 0.1 fat, 21 g carbohydrate, 0.1 mg iron, 4 RE vitamin A, 6 mg vitamin C, 7 mg calcium.

Meringue Kisses

MAKES 12

Most cookies should be eaten in moderation on a low-fat diet, but these can be enjoyed without any guilt at all. Serve with fresh fruit or a cup of coffee.

2 large egg whites

1/4 teaspoon cream of tartar

1/2 cup confectioners' sugar

1 teaspoon vanilla

Preheat the oven to 250°F. Lightly oil a cookie sheet. In a large bowl, beat the egg whites until foamy. Add the cream of tartar and beat until the whites start to thicken. Gradually add the confectioners' sugar and beat until the whites are thick and shiny. Beat in the vanilla.

Drop the egg whites by the tablespoonful onto the cookie sheet and bake for 1 hour, or until lightly browned all over, dry on the outside, and still soft in the center. Turn the oven off and leave the meringues in the oven for 1 hour more to crisp. Let cool. Store in an airtight container up to 5 days.

NUTRIENTS PER COOKIE: 20 calories, 0.6 g protein, 4 g carbohydrate, 1 mg calcium.

Spiced Meringues: Add 1/4 teaspoon ground cinnamon and 1/4 teaspoon grated nutmeg to the egg whites before stirring in the vanilla.

Cocoa Meringues: Add 3 tablespoons cocoa powder to the egg whites before stirring in the vanilla.

cooking
milk-free

16

When illness affects the digestive tract, an intolerance to lactose, a milk sugar found in most dairy products, can develop. Often it's the result of damage to the villi, finger like projections along the intestinal wall that produce lactase, the enzyme responsible for breaking down lactose for digestion. When it's not broken down, lactose passes into the large intestine undigested, causing discomfort, including cramping, bloating, gas, and diarrhea.

Some people simply do not make enough lactase to handle the lactose they consume. This tends to be most common among African Americans, Hispanics, Indians (North and South American), Eastern European Jews, and Asians.

Most of the lactose in our diet comes from cow's milk, which must be restricted if your patient is lactose-intolerant. The restriction on lactose may be mild, or it may mean complete avoidance of any product containing lactose. Some lactose-intolerant people can have milk and foods made from milk if they are eaten in small amounts—for example, half a cup of milk at a time. Others can tolerate foods in which the lactose is for the most part already broken down, such as yogurt with live, active cultures and aged cheeses.

Who Should Eat a Lactose-Free Diet?

Lactose intolerance may accompany any disease or treatment for a disease that affects the digestive tract. Colitis, ileitis, surgery, and cancer and AIDS can lead to difficulties digesting lactose. If abdominal cramping or pain, gas, and/or diarrhea occur after eating foods such as milk, cheese, or ice cream, lactose may be the culprit.

To test for lactose intolerance, eliminate all lactose-containing foods. If symptoms improve, lactose intolerance may indeed be the cause. Once it has been identified as the problem, continue to avoid all lactose-containing foods until symptoms completely subside. Then serve small amounts of these foods to determine the patient's tolerance level. Start with servings one quarter of the size listed in the Healing Food Guide, and serve only one lactose-containing food at a time.

If all milk products must be avoided, your patient may risk deficiencies of calcium, vitamin D, and riboflavin. Try lactose-hydrolyzed products such as Lactaid milk or add lactase tablets to milk (see Resources, page 340). These products supply lactase to enable the body to break down lactose. Otherwise, if these are not tolerated, consider vitamin/mineral supplementation—talk to the health care provider.

Lactose intolerance is not the same as milk intolerance, or milk allergy. Milk intolerance often develops at a young age, and it is generally specific to milk from cows. Goat and soy milks can often be substituted to supply needed nutrition. Most children outgrow milk allergies, but if they are lactose-intolerant, they usually have the problem throughout life.

What to Eat on a Lactose-Free Diet

Eat according to the Healing Food Guide, avoiding the following foods. Although tolerance is highly individual, they contain enough lactose to cause unpleasant symptoms in many people. Check the ingredients list on food labels. If milk or lactose is present, it will be listed; lactate, lactalbumin, lactylate, lactic acid, and calcium compounds such as calcium lactate do *not* contain lactose. Some medications and vitamins may contain lactose.

Butter	Custard
Buttermilk	Ice cream and ice milk
Cheese*	Margarine made with skim-milk solids
Chocolate	Milk, cow and goat, in all forms (except
Chocolate milk	specially treated milk like Lactaid)
Cocoa mixes	Pudding
Cold cuts and hot dogs that contain	Sherbet
lactose (kosher varieties designated	Whey
"pareve" are lactose-free)	Yogurt*
Cream	

*Hard aged cheeses and yogurts with live, active cultures are often well tolerated. Cheeses such as American, ricotta, cream, and Neufchâtel contain smaller amounts of lactose that may be tolerated.

TIPS FOR COOKING WITHOUT MILK

When your patient can't tolerate milk, there are alternatives. Unsweetened coconut milk, soy milk, fruit juice, broth, and water can take the place of milk in many recipes.

- In soups and casseroles, replace the milk with broth, soy milk, or vegetable cooking water.

- In breads and rolls, use the cooking water from potatoes and vegetables instead of milk.

- Dilute nondairy creamers to half-strength and use as a milk substitute. For example, use $1/2$ cup nondairy creamer and $1/2$ cup water to replace 1 cup whole milk. Use full-strength nondairy creamers to replace cream in any recipe.

- In casseroles and baked goods, substitute mayonnaise for cream cheese or soft tofu for cottage cheese.

The recipes that follow are designed to allow the lactose-intolerant patient the pleasure of eating foods that usually contain milk as a primary ingredient.

Honey Custard

MAKES 6 SERVINGS

A superb source of protein, this custard can be a meal in itself if topped with fresh fruit. Serve it as a meal replacement when appetite is poor.

2 cups soy milk

¼ cup honey

½ teaspoon vanilla

Pinch of salt

2 large eggs, beaten

Grated nutmeg or ground cinna-mon to taste (optional)

Preheat the oven to 325°F. Lightly oil six 1-cup custard cups. In a large bowl, combine the soy milk, honey, vanilla, and salt and beat with a whisk or a spoon. Add the eggs and beat vigorously until well blended.

Pour an equal amount into each custard cup and set in a baking pan. Dust the custards with cinnamon if desired. Add hot water to come halfway up the sides of the cups. Bake for 20 minutes, or until the custards are slightly browned on top and a knife inserted in the center comes out clean. Serve warm or cold. Cover and refrigerate up to 3 days.

NUTRIENTS PER SERVING: 142 calories, 6 g protein, 20 g carbohydrate, 5 g fat, 1.2 mg iron, 51 RE vitamin A, 0.4 mg vitamin E, 18 mg calcium.

Berry Berry Tapioca

MAKES 4 SERVINGS

My mother always made tapioca as a special treat on sick days.

2 cups pure fruit juice, such as orange, grapefruit, or apple

3 tablespoons quick-cooking tapioca

¼ cup sugar

1 large egg, beaten

¼ teaspoon salt

1 cup fresh or thawed frozen whole blueberries or mashed strawberries

In a heavy saucepan, combine the fruit juice, tapioca, sugar, egg, and salt. Allow to stand for 5 minutes.

Place the saucepan over medium heat and bring to a boil, stirring constantly. Cook until the tapioca starts to thicken, about 5 minutes. Remove from the heat and set aside for 10 minutes. It will thicken as it cools. Fold in the fruit and serve warm. Cover leftovers and refrigerate up to 3 days.

NUTRIENTS PER SERVING: 167 calories, 3 g protein, 37 g carbohydrate, 2 g fat, 0.6 mg iron, 52 RE vitamin A, 0.4 mg vitamin E, 67 mg vitamin C, 24 mg calcium.

Milk-Free Eggnog

MAKES 1½ CUPS

I like this best when made with banana and apple juice, but try any combination of fruit and juice you like. For extra fiber, leave the peels on thin-skinned fruit such as peaches, but remove them if using kiwi, papaya, or other thick-skinned fruit.

¼ cup egg substitute   **½ cup pure fruit juice**

½ cup cut-up fruit

Combine all the ingredients in a blender and puree until smooth. Serve over ice. Cover leftovers and refrigerate up to 2 days. Reblend before serving.

NUTRIENTS PER SERVING (MADE WITH BANANAS AND APPLE JUICE): 144 calories, 6 g protein, 28 g carbohydrate, 2 g fat, 1.4 mg iron, 97 RE vitamin A, 0.2 mg vitamin E, 7.6 mg vitamin C, 32 mg calcium.

Better Than Cheesecake

MAKES ONE 9-INCH CHEESECAKE (10 SLICES)

Wonderfully light, protein-rich tofu replaces cream cheese in this easy-to-assemble cheesecake.

Crust

1¼ cups finely crushed ginger snaps and graham crackers

6 tablespoons margarine, melted

3 tablespoons sugar

Filling

2 pounds firm tofu

2 tablespoons fresh lemon juice

2 tablespoons poached fresh peaches, canned, chopped

2 tablespoons honey

2 teaspoons vanilla

½ cup sugar

Preheat the oven to 375°F. To make the crust, in a small bowl, combine the cookie crumbs, margarine, and sugar. Press the crumbs evenly over the bottom and 1 inch up the sides of a 9-inch springform pan. Bake for 5 minutes and set aside to cool. Reduce the oven temperature to 350°F.

To make the filling, combine all the ingredients in a food processor and puree until smooth. Pour the batter into the crust and bake for 30 minutes, or until a knife inserted in the center comes out clean. Let cool before serving. If desired, top with fresh fruit or Fruit Puree (page 266). Cover and refrigerate up to 3 days.

NUTRIENTS PER SLICE: 325 calories, 15 g protein, 33 g carbohydrate, 17 g fat, 10 mg iron, 81 RE vitamin A, 0.1 mg vitamin E, 2 mg vitamin C, 191 mg calcium.

Mom's Applesauce Cake

MAKES ONE 8-INCH TWO-LAYER CAKE (10 SLICES)

This cake is a family favorite. I use margarine, rather than butter. Butter contains small amounts of lactose.

3 cups all-purpose flour

2½ teaspoons baking powder

¼ teaspoon salt

1 cup (2 sticks) margarine, softened

2 cups sugar

4 large eggs, separated

1½ teaspoons vanilla

1 cup soy milk

Buttercream Frosting

½ cup (1 stick) margarine, softened

½ cup confectioners' sugar

1 teaspoon vanilla

1 cup chunky applesauce

Preheat the oven to 350°F. Lightly oil two 8-inch cake pans. Sift together the dry ingredients.

In a large bowl, cream together the margarine and sugar until light and fluffy. Beat in the egg yolks one at a time. Beat in the vanilla. Add the flour mixture gradually, alternating with the soy milk, and blend mix until smooth. Don't overmix.

In a separate large bowl, beat the egg whites until they form stiff peaks. Gently fold them into the batter. Pour the batter into the pans and bake for 30 minutes, or until a cake tester inserted in the center comes out clean. Cool the cakes in the pans on a wire rack for about 10 minutes, then remove the pans and allow to cool completely.

Meanwhile, make the frosting. In a medium bowl, cream together the margarine and confectioners' sugar until light and fluffy. Add the vanilla. Wrap leftovers in plastic wrap and refrigerate for up to 3 days.

Spread one cake layer with the chunky applesauce. Top with the second layer and spread with the buttercream frosting.

NUTRIENTS PER SLICE: 446 calories, 7 g protein, 37 g carbohydrate, 30 g fat, 2 mg iron, 373 RE vitamin A, 19 mg vitamin E, 27 mg calcium.

Sweet Pumpkin Muffins

MAKES 12

Whenever possible, I try to use carrots, squash, and pumpkins in my baked goods. Not only do they taste good but they are full of beta carotene, which is believed to reduce the risk of certain cancers and heart disease.

1¾ cups all-purpose flour

1½ teaspoons baking powder

2 large eggs, beaten

2 tablespoons canola oil

¼ cup granulated sugar

¼ cup packed brown sugar

¾ cup soy milk

1 teaspoon ground cinnamon

1 cup pumpkin puree, fresh or canned

Preheat the oven to 400°F. In a large bowl, sift together the flour and baking powder and set aside.

In another large bowl, combine the eggs, oil, sugars, soy milk, cinnamon, and pumpkin and stir until smooth. Gently fold the pumpkin mixture into the flour mixture. Do not overmix. Pour into 12 lightly greased muffin cups and bake until lightly browned, about 18 minutes. Serve warm. Store cooled muffins, wrapped in plastic for up to 3 days in the refrigerator.

NUTRIENTS PER MUFFIN: 146 calories, 4 g protein, 24 g carbohydrate, 4 g fat, 1.2 mg iron, 472 RE vitamin A, 2 mg vitamin E, 174 mg calcium.

Fettuccine with Tofu Sauce

MAKES 4 SERVINGS

Without cheese, traditional Italian pasta dishes seem impossible. Here is proof that they're not.

1 tablespoon olive oil

1 small onion, chopped

6 cloves garlic, chopped

1 pound soft tofu

³/₄ cup canned chicken broth or Poultry Stock (page 248)

¹/₄ cup white wine

¹/₂ pound mushrooms, chopped

¹/₂ teaspoon dried oregano

³/₄ cup Greek or other black olives, pitted and chopped

1 pound fettuccine, cooked

Salt and pepper to taste

1 small tomato, chopped, for garnish

In a heavy skillet over low heat, warm the oil. Add the onion and garlic and cook until the onion is translucent, 2 to 3 minutes. Add the tofu, chicken broth, wine, mushrooms, oregano, and ¹/₄ cup of the olives and cook, covered, for 5 minutes.

Remove the tofu mixture to a blender and puree until smooth. Season the sauce with salt and pepper to taste.

Pour the sauce over the fettuccine and garnish with the tomato and remaining olives. Serve immediately. Cover leftovers and refrigerate up to 3 days.

NUTRIENTS PER SERVING: 500 calories, 23 g protein, 71 g carbohydrate, 15 g fat, 5 mg iron, 27 RE vitamin A, 0.4 mg vitamin E, 11 mg vitamin C, 181 mg calcium.

Vegetable and Meat Lasagna

MAKES 8 TO 10 SERVINGS

A lasagna without cheese? I decided to try this out on my children, who are the harshest food critics. They love traditional lasagna, so I knew it was a winner when they asked for a second helping.

1 tablespoon olive oil

2 cloves garlic, chopped

1 pound spinach, cleaned, trimmed, and chopped, or frozen chopped spinach, thawed and drained

1 pound soft tofu

1/2 pound lean ground beef

3 cups Meatless Tomato Sauce (page 277)

1 large egg

1/2 pound lasagna noodles, cooked

1/2 cup chopped pitted black or green olives

Preheat the oven to 350°F. Lightly oil a 9.5- by 13.5-inch lasagna dish. Heat the oil in a large heavy skillet over low heat. Add the garlic and sauté for 1 minute. Add the spinach, cover, and cook, stirring occasionally, until the spinach is soft and wilted, about 3 minutes. Add the tofu and mash with a fork. Toss with the spinach until combined. Remove to a bowl and set aside.

Wipe out the skillet with a paper towel and return it to the heat on medium heat. Add the ground beef and cook, breaking up any large lumps of meat, until no longer pink, about 10 minutes. Drain the fat, add the tomato sauce, and bring to a simmer. Reduce the heat to low and cook for 5 minutes.

Meanwhile, add the egg to the spinach mixture and mix well.

Spread 1/2 cup of the tomato sauce in the bottom of the lasagna pan. Add a layer of noodles and top with half of the spinach mixture, 1 cup of the sauce, and the chopped olives. Top with another layer of noodles and repeat the layering, ending with a layer of sauce on top.

Cover with aluminum foil until the sauce bubbles and bake for 30 minutes. Let sit for 5 minutes. Serve warm. Cover leftovers and refrigerate up to 3 days or freeze up to 6 weeks.

NUTRIENTS PER SERVING: 343 calories, 18 g protein, 33 g carbohydrate, 15 g fat, 5 mg iron, 737 RE vitamin A, 1.8 mg vitamin E, 44 mg vitamin C, 64 mg calcium.

Autumn Soup

MAKES 4 SERVINGS

This soup is delicious served hot or cold.

5 carrots, peeled and sliced

¼ cup plus 1 tablespoon water

2 tablespoons margarine

2 tablespoons all-purpose flour

2 cups soy milk

1 cup nondairy creamer
   (or cream if tolerated)

In a heavy saucepan over medium heat, combine the carrots and water and cook until the carrots are tender, about 5 minutes. Set aside.

Melt the margarine in the top of a double boiler. Add the flour and slowly stir in the soy milk. Cook for 10 minutes to thicken. Add the carrots and cooking liquid. Cook, uncovered, stirring occasionally, until the sauce thickens, about 45 minutes.

Remove the mixture to a blender and puree. Return to the pan over low heat, add the nondairy creamer, and stir until the soup is heated through. Cover leftovers and refrigerate up to 3 days.

NUTRIENTS PER SERVING: 207 calories, 5 g protein, 22 g carbohydrate, 12 g fat, 1.3 mg iron, 260 RE vitamin A, 4.5 mg vitamin E, 8 mg vitamin C, 31 mg calcium.

White Sauce

MAKES 2 CUPS

Chicken broth and a whisked egg replace milk in this classic sauce. For an egg-free version, replace the broth and egg with three-quarter cup soy milk and one-quarter cup water.

2 tablespoons margarine

2 tablespoons all-purpose flour

2 cups canned chicken broth or Poultry Stock (page 248)

1 large egg yolk

Melt the margarine in a small heavy saucepan over low heat. Stir in the flour and cook for 2 minutes. Stir in the chicken broth and cook for 1 minute.

In a small bowl, whisk the egg. Gradually add ¼ cup of the warm sauce, whisking, return to the saucepan. Cook, stirring until the sauce thickens, about 5 minutes more. Cover leftovers and refrigerate up to 3 days.

NUTRIENTS PER ½ CUP: 92 calories, 2 g protein, 3 g carbohydrate, 8 g fat, 0.4 mg iron, 114 RE vitamin A, 4 mg vitamin E, 13 mg calcium.

water, water everywhere

UNDERSTANDING THE
FLUID-RESTRICTED DIET

following a fluid-restricted diet can be difficult for both the patient and the caregiver. At first, controlling fluid intake seems simple—just limit liquids. But it also means limiting all foods that contain liquid and any foods that become liquid once swallowed. Any food (except oils) that is fluid at room temperature is considered a liquid.

A healthy adult normally consumes from 1500 to 2800 cc (cubic centimeters) or milliliters of fluid a day. On a fluid-restricted diet, patients are often limited to 1500 cc, the amount of fluid lost on average every day via the skin, lungs, and urine. The idea is to meet the body's needs without adding extra fluid.

Who Needs a Fluid-Restricted Diet?

Fluid-restricted diets are most often prescribed to manage kidney disease or to control ascites, a condition in which fluid collects in the abdomen, or edema, fluid retention that is frequently related to liver disease.

Unless specifically advised by a physician, never restrict the patient's intake of liquids. The body needs fluids to perform vital metabolic processes.

What to Have on a Fluid-Restricted Diet

Control the intake of all foods that are liquid, that melt, or that supply significant amounts of fluid once eaten. These include ice cream, frozen yogurt and similar frozen desserts, gelatin, pudding, soup, juice, milk, yogurt, coffee, tea, soft drinks, water, and ice. In some cases, fruits with a high water content, such as watermelon, must be restricted. Check with the health care provider. Solid foods such as meats, bread, and vegetables are not considered significant sources of liquid.

240 cc = 1 cup
180 cc = $^3/_4$ cup
120 cc = $^1/_2$ cup
80 cc = $^1/_3$ cup
60 cc = $^1/_4$ cup
15 cc = 1 tablespoon

A day's fluid intake on a fluid-restricted diet might look like this:

	cc
16 ounces (2 cups) water	480
4 ounces orange juice	120
$^1\!/_2$ cup pudding	120
$^1\!/_3$ cup ice cream	80
1 cup soup	120
12 ounces soda	350
$^3\!/_4$ cup cranberry juice	180
2 tablespoons syrup from canned fruit	30
Total	1490

nurturing and nourishing a sick child

18

Every parent worries when his or her child is sick. And what better way to show love and concern than with food? Paying attention to the little details, such as serving soup at just the right temperature or using a favorite cup, comforts and nurtures a sick child. Whatever the special touches, use them to make eating more appealing. Sick children recover more quickly when they are well nourished, and you'll take comfort in the fact that they're eating.

Every parent should expect to encounter common childhood illnesses such as colds, flu, and chicken pox. The Healthy Feeding Guide for Kids and the recommendations given here for managing symptoms that can occur during illness apply to children with these routine illnesses. If your child has a serious illness such as cancer, diabetes, or kidney disease, you will want to develop an eating plan with the help of the pediatrician or pediatric dietitian to meet the nutrient challenges of the illness.

Much of the information in other chapters, such as the need for fiber and protein and the special diet modifications discussed in Chapter 3, The Nutrition Prescription, may be just as pertinent for kids as for adults, but talk to your health care provider before applying these recommendations to your child's diet. The information in this chapter and throughout the book is not meant to replace a pediatrician's recommendations.

Managing Common Symptoms

Fever, vomiting, diarrhea, and constipation frequently accompany childhood illness. Always discuss prolonged symptoms with your child's health care provider, and request specific, individualized advice based on your child's condition. Use the following information to supplement advice from the health care provider.

Fever

Fever usually means that the immune system is fighting an infection. It drives the metabolic rate up and increases calorie and fluid requirements, with the potential for weight loss and dehydration when fever is prolonged.

During a routine doctor's visit, discuss the normal temperature for your child, and when a temperature means you should call the doctor. Normal temperatures can vary according to the age of the child. Keep a thermometer on hand, and practice using it before you need it in an emergency.

Let your child's appetite guide you regarding foods to offer when fever strikes. Don't worry too much about balanced nutrition—serve what's appealing. Fluids are almost instinctively preferred; even when other foods are refused, be sure to offer calorie-rich fluids such as sodas or fruit juices. Avoid calorie-free drinks such as diet sodas and sugar-free lemonade. If a full- or clear-liquid diet is recommended, see Chapter 7. The recipes for liquid meals in that chapter may also help.

Vomiting

Vomiting can be just an unpleasant experience, or it can be serious. Call the health care provider if your child has blood in his or her vomit or vomits four times in two hours, or if the vomiting is accompanied by fever, diarrhea, and/or abdominal pain.

Immediately after an episode of vomiting, withhold all foods, including liquids. If your child is on medication, ask the health care provider about withholding it too. Elevate the child's head, and loosen his or her clothes. When vomiting appears to have stopped, offer a small amount of clear liquid at room temperature. Ice chips may also be well tolerated. Avoid milk products temporarily.

Dehydration is one of the major nutritional problems that occur as a result of vomiting. Weight loss may also occur because foods cannot be kept down. Prolonged vomiting must be managed carefully under the guidance of the health care provider.

When vomiting has subsided and your child is able to hold down clear liquids, the doctor may recommend the BRAT diet. At first, offer this menu of bananas, rice, apples, and toast in small amounts. As your child is able to tolerate more food, move on to a more varied diet. If vomiting recurs, go back to clear liquids—and keep the doctor informed.

Diarrhea

Alert the health care provider if diarrhea is accompanied by severe abdominal pains or if it is prolonged. Check with the health care team about when you should become concerned about diarrhea lasting too long.

A clear liquid diet is commonly recommended when diarrhea is a problem, but do not keep a child on clear liquids for more than twenty-four hours without consulting the health care provider. If diarrhea persists, a milk-free diet may help (see Chapter 16). Fatty foods may also exacerbate the problem. Avoid fried foods and rich sauces.

Excessive amounts of fruit juice, particularly pear and apple juice, which contain large amounts of sorbitol (a form of sugar that is not well absorbed by children or adults), may cause diarrhea in some children. Researchers at Connecticut Hartford Hospital were able to stop unexplained diarrhea in half of a group of toddlers just by eliminating the juice they usually consumed. This doesn't mean juice isn't suitable for healthy children, only that if your otherwise healthy child has diarrhea, you might try cutting out juice. Offer water instead. To meet the need for vitamin C, offer fruit such as oranges or grapefruits.

Constipation

If your child strains or passes blood during a bowel movement, constipation may be the cause. Constipation is frequently brought on by diet, medication, or even supplements such as iron. The dietary prescription is simple: Consume plenty of fiber and fluids.

Fiber-rich foods include fruits and vegetables (especially when unpeeled) and whole-grain or bran-enriched breads and cereals. Try baked beans, green beans, broccoli, carrots, fruits with peels, such as peaches, pears and apples, and dried fruits like raisins and prunes. In general, juices are not a good source of fiber. Read more about high-fiber eating in Chapter 10.

Most children meet their fluid needs by drinking when thirsty. But if constipation is a problem, pay closer attention to the amount of fluid your child consumes. Encourage him or her to drink plenty of water; it's a healthy habit to start early in life. If constipation persists, discuss the problem with the health care provider.

The Healthy Feeding Guide for Kids

This guide differs from the Healing Food Guide, page 18, only in that it lists foods from each group that children find most appealing. For a more complete list of foods, refer to the Healing Food Guide. You can use the recipes in the preceding chapters to fulfill the requirements outlined here. Encourage your child to eat at least the minimum number of servings from each group every day. Older children may need the larger number of servings; younger children may require smaller portions.

It is important to remember that a child does not have the same eating patterns or capacity as an adult. Because of the difference in body size alone, children can run short on important nutrients. They become dehydrated more quickly because their fluid reserves are smaller. Because children are growing rapidly and using lots of iron in the process, they face a higher risk than adults for iron deficiency, and the typical child's diet falls short on iron intake. Or, if a child does not eat plenty of fruits and vegetables and drink milk, his or her diet is likely to be low in vitamins A and C and calcium. During illness, these nutrients play critical roles in resisting infection and promoting healing.

Sick children aren't very different from sick adults, however, when it comes to the desire to eat. If your child refuses to eat, refrain from getting into food struggles. Think about why your child may not be eating well. Is he or she too tired? Fatigue interferes with interest and ability to eat. A nap before meals can help boost appetite. Loss of appetite is not uncommon just before a virus or stomachache reveals itself. If your child refuses a particular food one day, offer it the next. If he or she won't eat enough protein foods at mealtime, offer a protein-rich snack later. If your child wants more foods from one group than others one day, balance the choices over several days or a week. Do distractions keep your child from focusing on eating? Many children are slow, easily distracted eaters. Allow plenty of time for meals and snacks and eliminate common mealtime disruptions such as toys, arguments, playmates, and phone calls.

While I always recommend feeding a sick child his or her favorite foods, often these all fall into the fried food or high-fat categories. As with adults, sick children need plenty of calories, and fat is an efficient way to get them without having to eat large amounts of food. When your child recovers, return to a more prudent diet that includes favorite high-fat foods only occasionally. Just be sure to balance high-fat choices with low-fat items. For example, if you serve fried fish sticks, offer carrot sticks, melon balls, and whole-grain bread too.

Protein Group

2 to 3 servings daily

SERVING SIZES: Age 1 to 5, ¹/₂ to 2 ounces; age 6 to 18, 2 to 3 ounces

Foods include beef patties, tuna, fish sticks, chicken, peanut butter, chili, baked beans, and cheese.

Calcium Group

3 to 4 servings daily

SERVING SIZES: Age 1 to 5, ¹/₂ to 1 cup (total per day to equal 2 cups); age 6 to 18, 1 cup

Foods include yogurt, flavored milk, custard, pudding made with milk, and vegetables topped with cheese sauce.

Vegetable Group

2 to 5 servings daily

SERVING SIZES: Age 1 to 5, 1 to 5 tablespoons (1 tablespoon per year of age); age 6 to 18, ¹/₂ cup

Foods include carrot sticks, raw broccoli florets, vegetable juice, and cookies or muffins made with vegetables.

Fruit Group

2 to 4 servings daily

SERVING SIZES: Age 1 to 5, ¹/₃ to ¹/₂ cup; age 16 to 18, 1 medium piece fruit, ¹/₂ cup chopped, canned, or frozen fruit, ³/₄ cup fruit juice

Foods include fresh fruit cups, melon balls, orange slices, and 100 percent fruit juices.

Grain/Starch Group

6 to 11 servings daily

SERVING SIZES: Age 1 to 5, $^{1}/_{2}$ to 1 slice bread or $^{1}/_{4}$ to $^{1}/_{2}$ cup rice, cereal, or other starchy foods; age 6 to 18, 1 slice bread, $^{1}/_{2}$ cup serving rice, pasta, or hot cereal, or $^{3}/_{4}$ to 1 cup cold cereal

Foods include raisin bread, bagels, cereal, noodles, crackers, and rice.

Fat/Oil Group

3 to 8 servings daily

SERVING SIZES: All ages, 1 tablespoon salad dressing or mayonnaise or 1 teaspoon butter, margarine, or cooking oil

Foods include margarine, butter, salad dressing, oil, mayonnaise, cream.

Meeting Your Child's Nutrition Needs

· Follow the Healthy Feeding Guide for Kids to plan meals.

· Keep a record of what your child eats for several days. If any food groups turn up missing, plan how you can include them in meals and snacks.

· Keep track of your child's weight.

· Read up on how to manage symptoms that interfere with eating, such as diarrhea (page 203) and vomiting (page 204).

· Supply plenty of fluids when fever or diarrhea occurs.

· If your child complains of feeling tired, ask the health care provider to check the iron levels in his or her blood. Read about fatigue, page 201.

Supplying Iron

Iron-deficiency anemia is the most common nutrition problem for kids. Infants, children, and adolescents need more iron than adults to support their tremendous growth. When iron intake does not keep pace with needs, iron-deficiency anemia develops. Fatigue and impaired immune systems can result. An adequate iron intake during illness is especially critical.

If your child is iron-deficient:

- Serve foods rich in iron. Excellent source
  try. Ready-to-eat iron-fortified cereals, wh
  green leafy vegetables, and dried fruits an

- Check the nutrition facts panel on food labe
  in the ingredients list of cereals and grains.

- Offer meat, fish, or poultry at every meal; eve

- Serve vitamin C–rich foods such as orange juic
  C enhances the absorption of some types of iro

- If your child likes tea, do not serve it in large am
  tion.

- Avoid antacids; they may inhibit iron absorption.

Does Your Child Need Vitamin/ Mineral Supplements?

Children and adolescents with poor appetites or chronic medical conditions may benefit from a supplement that contains approximately 100 percent of the Recommended Dietary Allowances (RDA) of vitamins and minerals appropriate to their age. There is no one such supplement, however, that completely meets all needs. For example, most tablets supply less than the RDA for calcium and magnesium—fitting the full RDA of these into a pill would make the pill too big to swallow.

Remember that vitamin/minerals supplements do not replace food. They are meant to be exactly what their name implies—supplements. Discuss the need to boost your child's nutrient intake with the health care provider or pharmacist.

Watching Water Intake

Water, juice, fruit pops, milk, ice cream, and pudding all add up to meet the body's need for fluid. When fever, diarrhea, or vomiting occurs, pay particular attention to your child's fluid intake.

onsider the reasons you are doing so. Is it to quench thirst or to
and fruit drinks supply calories, but they can also dull appetite if
a meal. Water quenches thirst just as well.
ing juices, look for those that contain vitamin C. Orange and grapefruit juice
sources. Other juices such as apple and cranberry are frequently fortified with
n C. Fruit drinks "made with real fruit juice" may be poor sources. Check the label and
noose those that contain 100 percent of the RDA for vitamin C.

These guidelines for fluid intake are based on recommendations from Children's Hospital in Boston. Ask the doctor for specific fluid recommendations for your child. If applicable, read more about the fluid-restricted diet in Chapter 17.

Child's Weight (in pounds)	Total Fluid/24 Hours (in cups)
7	2
12	$3^1/_3$
21	5
26	6
35	7
44	8
63	$9^1/_2$
99	$10^1/_2$

Protein and Calories

How much protein and calories a child needs should be determined on an individual basis. A large active child needs more calories than a small quiet child. Some medical conditions or surgery may increase the need for protein. The information below, adapted from the Recommended Dietary Allowances, refers to general needs for these nutrients. Ask the health care provider if your child's needs differ. Also see Chapter 4 to learn more about the protein content of foods.

Age	Protein (in grams)	Calories
1 day to 6 months	13	650
6 to 12 months	14	850
1 to 3 years	16	1300
4 to 6 years	24	1800
7 to 10 years	28	2000
11 to 14 years (boys)	45	2500
11 to 14 years (girls)	46	2200
15 to 18 years (boys)	59	3000
15 to 18 years (girls)	44	2200

SPECIAL MEALS FOR SICK DAYS

When kids are sick, simple treats and comforts often add up to feeling better. Although most kids want to feel grown up, even an eight-year-old might not refuse being spoon-fed when ill. Very young children may want to drink from bottles. Try these other ideas to make meals special.

- Serve meals in bed or in front of the television.
- Serve juice or fluids in a special cup—even one of Mommy's best!
- Serve drinks with a funny straw.
- Make a get-well card and tuck it under the plate or in the napkin.
- Place a fresh flower on a bed tray.
- Use a fancy cloth napkin instead of paper.
- Serve pretty garnishes like orange twists, pineapple slices, or maraschino cherries. Serve sweet drinks with cherries.
- Sprinkle colored jimmies on pudding or oatmeal.
- Light a candle on the table or put a birthday candle in a muffin.

the path
less traveled

do you know people who swear that they've never felt better since they started a macrobiotic diet? Have you heard stories of miraculous recoveries because of vitamin therapy? Do friends recommend meditation to speed healing? Do you wonder if you should encourage your loved one to try such alternative therapies?

The answer is yes and no. Nontraditional therapies often become appealing when conventional treatment fails; they can provide a course of action when traditional therapy offers no hope. Chronically ill people are seeking alternative therapies in record numbers today, indicating that these treatments are filling a need not met by traditional medicine.

While it is important to keep an open mind about the potential of such therapies, do not blindly accept a nontraditional approach to nutrition and health care without examining it carefully. "First do no harm" applies to all therapies, traditional or nontraditional.

Do not be surprised if the health care professionals you regularly work with view new therapies with skepticism. Such suspicion stands in the way of quick assimilation of new ideas, but it does not block them entirely. It actually serves to weed out theories that do not hold up to scientific scrutiny and helps build a solid research base supporting those theories that do hold up.

Consider the relationship between diet and heart disease. In the early 1970s, some of the best medical doctors in the country challenged the notion that diet was a cause of the high rate of heart disease in this country. But eventually, painstaking research revealed that too much saturated fat could indeed raise blood cholesterol levels and affect one's risk of heart disease. Now doctors routinely test blood cholesterol levels and recommend diet as the first step in treatment to prevent or reverse heart disease.

In another example, early in the 1980s, it was suggested that babies born to women who had had adequate intakes of folic acid prior to conception ran a lower risk of certain types of birth defects. Although it was initially challenged, this theory was proven true through careful, time-consuming studies. Folic acid supplementation for all women of child-bearing age is now recommended by several leading health organizations.

However, not all theories pan out. Two studies, funded in part by the National Cancer Institute, do not support the popular belief that vitamin C aids cancer treatment. The first study looked at the effect of vitamin C in people with advanced cancer. It found that vitamin C was no more useful than a placebo. It did not improve survival rates or relieve symptoms.

The second study evaluated the effectiveness of vitamin C in treating patients with colon or rectal cancer who had not received chemotherapy. It, too, found vitamin C to be ineffective. Because these and other studies have provided no evidence that large doses of vitamin C help fight cancer, the nutrient is not recommended as part of traditional cancer treatment.

Personal testimony alone is not enough to validate a theory. Valid treatments must be documented through science to help ensure standards of care. Standards of care put into practice treatments that truly improve quality of life.

Does this mean that alternative therapies should be avoided until science proves it? Not always. It does mean that you should exercise caution when pursuing any treatment that grossly varies from what is considered usual and accepted.

How to Evaluate Nutrition Therapies

Alternative therapies frequently emphasize nutrition more than conventional therapies do. Since many health care providers do not pay much attention to diet, this is not surprising. Still, many of these therapies don't live up to their claims.

The first step in determining the validity of a nutrition therapy is to know its source. The term *nutritionist* has no legal definition. A person selling vitamins in a drugstore and a person with a Ph.D. in biochemistry can both use the name. In the medical profession, registered dietitians are most commonly considered the most reliable nutrition experts. The title registered dietitian certifies that the bearer passed a rigorous examination that ensures competency in the field of nutrition.

In many states, nutritionists or dietitians are licensed as the preferred providers of nutritional care. Indeed, for a practitioner to receive reimbursement for nutrition services, many insurance companies require such licensure. It's one guarantee for you, too, that you are dealing with a qualified nutrition professional and that you can trust the information you receive from him or her.

Also scrutinize therapies on the basis of what is recommended. Nutrition therapies should emphasize food to meet the body's needs. Requirements for basic nutrients such as protein, carbohydrates, fat, and essential vitamins and minerals must not be overlooked.

Further, nutrition therapies should be highly individualized, based on the disease and its symptoms. If a therapy ignores nutritional problems such as fat intolerance, diarrhea, and weight loss, it may actually speed the progression of problems by causing malnutrition.

The nutritionists who recommend an arsenal of enzymes, vitamins, minerals, or extracts are practicing medicine, not nutrition therapy. If they sell these supplements at a profit, suspect their motives for prescribing them. You should also question their credentials if they always find a "problem" they can cure, have "inside" knowledge "suppressed" by other health professionals, blame the patient for failure of the therapy, or will not consult or cooperate with other health care professionals.

This chapter describes several alternative nutrition therapies you may encounter. If you have questions about other therapies, there are several sources to ask: your health care provider, a registered dietitian from your hospital, or the National Center for Nutrition and Dietetics at 1-800-366-1655.

Vitamin and Mineral Therapy

Massive doses of vitamin and mineral supplements cannot cure a disease unless it is caused by deficiencies of the nutrients in the supplements. Nor do pills replace food—food contains a multitude of important nutrients and other essential components not found in pills.

Still, there is a place for supplements in many people's diets, especially when ill. Studies show that multivitamin preparations can reduce the rate of infection and boost the immune system.

While the diagnosis of a serious or chronic illness may warrant the need for vitamin/mineral supplements, the path to finding the best choices is often curved and twisted. There are no widely accepted guidelines to steer you toward responsible selection and use of supplements.

The Center for Science in the Public Interest, a Washington, D.C.–based consumer group, and the *University of California at Berkeley Wellness Letter* recently made similar recommendations about the safe and responsible use of vitamin/mineral supplements. For most nutrients, they recommend taking no more than 100 percent of the RDA daily.

The brands of multivitamins that come closest to providing a proper balance of nutrients include Centrum, Theragram-M, Unicap M, and Unicap T—or any store brand that replicates the formulas used in these brands. Indeed, there is little difference between brand-name and generic vitamins—except the price!

When vitamins and minerals are taken as recommended here, they rarely if ever cause problems. When taken in large doses, however, the risk of harmful side effects rises.

Supplements of the antioxidants vitamin C, vitamin E, and beta carotene have been advocated in the hope of fighting such serious ailments as cancer and eye and heart disease. However, in 1994, a Finnish study published in the *New England Journal of Medicine* released startling results suggesting that beta carotene supplements may actually increase the risk of lung cancer and adversely affect the heart. The same study found that supplements of vitamin E reduced the risk of prostate cancer but increased the risk of hemorrhagic stroke. These results have caused nutritionists to rethink the current advice regarding supplementing with antioxidants. Antioxidants are still important to health and disease prevention, but until further studied, obtain them in the safe and natural way—through the food you eat. Or when taking a supplement do not exceed 100 percent of the RDA. People with intestinal, kidney, or liver diseases may run the greatest risks. In particular, they should avoid massive doses of vitamins A, B$_6$, D, E, C, niacin, and iron. Evaluate your own and your patient's use of supplements according to the information in the following section. No one should take potentially toxic doses of supplements.

Can I Overdose on Vitamins and Minerals?

When it comes to vitamins and minerals, more is not always better. Indeed, too much can create significant problems.

Nutrient	RDA	Potential Side Effects of Daily Toxic Doses
Vitamin A	Women, 800 RE (4000 IU) Men, 1000 RE (5000 IU)	More than 50000 IU may cause headaches, vomiting, liver damage, even birth defects in pregnant women
Vitamin C	Adult, 60 mg	Higher doses may cause diarrhea and stomachache
Vitamin D	Adult, 5 mcg (200 IU) Under age 25, 10 mcg (400 IU)	More than 45 mcg may cause kidney and heart damage in young children
Vitamin E	Women, 8 mg (12 IU) Men, 10 mg (15 IU)	More than 800 IU may cause diarrhea and headaches
Vitamin B$_6$	Women, 1.6 mg Men, 2 mg	More than 25 mg may cause numbness of extremities
Selenium	Women, 55 mcg Men, 70 mcg	More than 5 mg may cause hair loss; higher doses may cause nausea, diarrhea, fatigue
Zinc	Women, 12 mg Men, 15 mg	More than 50 mg may hinder copper absorption; over 80 mg may lower "good" HDL cholesterol; more than 150 mg may impair immune response

The Macrobiotic Diet

The macrobiotic diet is part religion, part dietary way of life. It was founded by George Ohsawa, author of *Zen Macrobiotics,* and was popularized in this country in the 1960s by Michio Kushi.

In general, the theory revolves around the idea of selecting foods based on their ability to restore balance—yin and yang—in the body, not according to their nutritional properties. Whole grains, particularly brown rice, are considered near-perfect foods, and macrobiotic meals consist primarily of whole grains.

Vegetables, soybeans or soybean foods such as tofu, and soups based on seaweed, beans, grains, or vegetables make up the rest of macrobiotic meals. Beverages include herbal tea, water, and fruit juice. Fish may be eaten a few times a week, but meat, butter, eggs, poultry, and milk products are avoided. Vitamin/mineral supplements are discouraged. The theory also says it is essential to chew each bite fifty times before swallowing.

Because the Calcium and Protein food groups are entirely or almost entirely proscribed, a macrobiotic diet may not supply the additional protein and calories an ill person needs. Furthermore, if appetite is poor, the emphasis on plant foods—and the high volume of food intake that means—can lead to protein-calorie malnutrition in a seriously ill person. Macrobiotic diets may also be low in riboflavin, niacin, calcium, and vitamins B_6, B_{12}, and D.

What's more, there is no proof that a macrobiotic diet can cure cancer, AIDS, or any other disease. Although many people swear the diet has helped them, the American Cancer Society groups macrobiotic diets with other unproven methods. It states that if not properly planned, a macrobiotic diet may not provide adequate nutrition.

If you intend to incorporate the macrobiotic diet into your patient's treatment, do not overlook potential nutrition problems. Know the limitations of this regimen. Very importantly, keep track of weight. A weight loss of even a few pounds indicates that not enough food is being consumed, and your patient is at risk of becoming malnourished.

The Yeast-Free Diet

Many species of *Candida* (yeast) live in different areas of the body—the mouth, throat, intestines, and, in women, the vagina. Proponents of the yeast-free diet believe that some people are sensitive to *Candida albicans* and suffer from its overgrowth, called *Candidiasis.* They believe the overgrowth causes a variety of symptoms, including post-nasal drip, fatigue, fluid retention, food cravings, depression, and headaches.

On the yeast-free diet, all foods containing yeast are avoided. These include yeast breads, aged cheese, vinegar, alcohol, mushrooms, and other foods. In its initial stages, the diet restricts many carbohydrates, such as sugar, white flour, and fruits and milk, in the belief that these foods provide nourishment for the yeast.

With careful planning, a yeast-free diet can meet nutritional needs. The diet, however, significantly complicates food selection, which can be daunting when one is faced with other stresses and demands on time.

Many people claim a yeast-free diet makes them feel better, but the improvement could be related to a number of reasons. The placebo effect—which means that something works because the patient expects it to work—is one reason. Another is that people may actually improve their diets because they are paying greater attention to the foods they select. Still, there is no scientific support that *Candida albicans* causes the sort of problems that are popularly linked to it, nor is there evidence that a yeast-free diet solves the problems.

The American Academy of Allergy has issued a statement discrediting the *Candida* hypersensitivity theory. If you intend to experiment with a yeast-free diet, inform your doctor first.

Herbal Therapy

Are herbs effective in treating illness? Your guess is as good as mine. Many people swear by *Echniacea purpurea,* an herb purported to be effective in treating cold symptoms. Herbal teas such as chamomile are credited with curing upset stomachs. Unfortunately, herbal medicines are not regulated by the Food and Drug Administration. This means there are no standards for labeling. Consumers and practitioners can't be guaranteed that the herb product they buy contains what they expect it to, nor whether it does what it is reputed to do.

Few studies of the effectiveness of herbal remedies exist, and the studies that have been conducted show little promise. For example, *Pau d'arco* tea, made from the inner bark of one type of evergreen tree, has been credited with fighting cancer, anemia, rheumatism, and other ailments. But studies of the effectiveness of *Pau d'arco* tea as a cancer treatment do not indicate that it lives up to the claims.

Unfortunately, there is little economic incentive for the big pharmaceutical companies—which sponsor most of the drug research—to investigate herbal remedies. As a result, questions regarding their safety and curative powers will probably go unanswered for the time being. Just remember: Although herbs are touted as safe and natural, Mother Nature bestowed some of her plants with toxic ingredients, and they should be approached with caution.

Indeed, all herbal remedies are not harmless. Chaparral, an herb from the leaves of the creosote bush, is said to slow aging and keep skin healthy. Since 1992, six people taking this herbal remedy developed acute, toxic hepatitis.

In the absence of regulatory control of herbal products, it is impossible to make safe recommendations about their use. And without studies, their efficacy cannot be validated. Proceed very carefully if you intend to use herbs. Keep the health care provider informed.

The Kelley Malignancy Index and Ecology Therapy

The American Cancer Society frequently receives inquiries about the effectiveness of the Kelley therapy. It was originally promoted by William Donald Kelley, an orthodontist, as a treatment program he credited with curing his own cancer. The therapy includes nutrition supplements, body "detoxification" (purges, fasts, enemas), and neurologic stimulation "to reactivate the nerve enervation and spiritual attitude." The Kelley Research Foundation has also developed the Kelley Malignancy Index, which is claimed to be an early cancer detection system.

The American Cancer Society has found no evidence that this therapy results in any objective improvement in cancer symptoms, or that the Kelley Malignancy Index is an effective tool to diagnose cancer.

The Gerson Method

The American Cancer Society frequently receives questions about the therapy called the Gerson method. It is claimed to detoxify the body by boosting the immune system, and it is available at a clinic in Tijuana, Mexico.

The treatment calls for drinking about thirteen glasses of vegetable juice daily, with supplements of linseed oil, thyroid, niacin, pancreatic enzymes, and more. Injections of raw liver extract are given, but little or no animal protein is eaten. Salt, oil, coffee, berries, nuts, drinking water, and all bottled, canned, refined, preserved, and frozen foods are prohibited.

There is no scientific evidence to support the belief that the Gerson therapy helps cure cancer. In fact, patients have been admitted to San Diego hospitals suffering from blood poisoning believed to be the result of the liver injections. Serious infections and even deaths have been reported due to the use of the coffee enemas that are part of the therapy. The American Cancer Society strongly urges individuals with cancer not to use this dangerous treatment.

The Mind-Body Connection

Worry, anxiety, fear, and anger are all typical human emotions. If any one becomes overwhelming, however, not only do we become unhappy and uncomfortable, but our stress levels increase and affect our risk of developing or exacerbating illness.

Just learning of a serious illness ranks high on the list of situations that provoke stress. On the scale known as the Social Readjustment Rating, personal injury or illness rates number six out of forty-three life events. Serious illness causes more stress than being fired from a job, getting married, retiring, or experiencing the death of a close friend. Stress can cause loss of appetite and trigger vomiting and diarrhea. It can raise blood pressure and reduce immune system effectiveness.

Fortunately, effective stress management can improve all these symptoms. In a remarkable study published in 1991 by Dr. James Strain, a psychiatrist, it was reported that elderly men with broken hips who discussed their troubles with a mental health counselor healed faster than those who did not.

In another study, women with metastatic breast cancer who received psychotherapy to help with pain, anxiety, and depression lived longer, with better quality of life, than those who did not. And in a Yale University School of Nursing study, people with poor appetites as a result of cancer were able to eat more and gain weight by practicing simple relaxation techniques before eating.

There is no one path to relieving stress, but some of the many ways include hobbies, exercise, and prayer. Meditation, muscle relaxation, creative visual imagery, massage therapy, biofeedback, and individual and group psychotherapy are other ways.

Do not be afraid to seek help to manage stress, both yours and your patient's. Stress management is equally important for the patient, the family, and the caregiver. Ask the health care provider for a referral to a counselor. See Resources, page 340, for information on support groups.

drug and food
interactions

do not underestimate the effects food and drugs have upon each other. The interactions between the two are so numerous, it is impossible to list them all. Drink milk with Tetracycline and its effectiveness is canceled. Take Naprosyn on an empty stomach and a stomachache will occur. Eat too many green leafy vegetables and the anticoagulant action of the blood-thinning drug Coumadin is squelched.

In addition, the risk for a food and drug interaction is greatest for children and the elderly. Likewise, someone who has been taking a particular medication for a long time, or who takes several medications, runs an increased risk. Poor diet or an illness that affects the digestive tract also may create problems by interfering with drug absorption.

Drug-nutrient interactions occur in several ways. In some situations, medication affects the absorption of nutrients. Laxatives increase the rate at which food passes through the body and may reduce absorption of glucose, protein, and sodium. Because it acts as a physical barrier and solvent for fat-soluble vitamins, mineral oil interferes with absorption of the fat-soluble vitamins A, D, E, and K, calcium, and phosphorus.

Antacids that contain aluminum can decrease vitamin A absorption, and antacids that contain magnesium can cause diarrhea. Cholesterol-lowering medications such as Cholybar, Questran, and Colestid reduce blood cholesterol levels by preventing the reabsorption of bile acids. But this effect can also result in deficiencies of iron, folic acid, and fat-soluble vitamins. Broad-spectrum antibiotics can upset the gastrointestinal tract, causing irritation and diarrhea. Because they destroy intestinal flora that make vitamin K, a nutrient that helps blood coagulation, these antibiotics can also cause uncontrollable bleeding in people who have a condition called hypoprothrombinemia.

Drugs can also affect the way nutrients are used by the body once they are absorbed. The anticancer drug methotrexate and the antibiotic trimethoprim prevent folic acid from being converted to its active and usable form within the body. Isoniazid, used to treat tuberculosis, can bind vitamin B_6, creating a deficiency, making supplementation necessary.

What's more, drugs may cause nutrients to be excreted in excessive amounts. Diuretics cause potassium loss. Chronic and high doses of aspirin can lead to losses of vitamin C and potassium.

In turn, foods may affect the efficacy of drugs. Specific foods are the culprit in some cases, such as milk with tetracycline. In others, any food may delay, although not reduce, the absorption of drugs such as acetaminophen, amoxicillin, cimetidine, and digoxin. Still other drugs are not absorbed as well if taken with food. Ampicillin, Vibramycin, tetracycline, erythromycin stearate, and isoniazid, among others, should be taken on an empty stomach.

Chemotherapy agents deserve special mention. These drugs often cause nausea, vomiting, diarrhea, loss of appetite, sore mouth, and constipation. The risk for developing these side effects increases according to the length of treatment, dosage, and the individual's tolerance. Some cancer specialists believe that good nutrition helps reduce the negative side effects of chemotherapeutic drugs. For more information about chemotherapy, side effects, and nutrition, request the publication *Chemotherapy and You: A Guide to Self-Help During Treatment* from The National Cancer Institute (see Resources, page 340).

The potential risk of food and drug interactions is real and often overlooked. Don't assume that the doctor or pharmacist will alert you to potentially significant risks, particularly if more than one doctor is prescribing medications. Follow these tips to reduce your patient's risk.

- Keep a list of all medicines (including over-the-counter remedies) taken, and inform all health care providers.

- Ask the health care provider and pharmacist about potential side effects and interactions.

- Pay attention to the warning labels on medication packages.

- Read the package inserts that come with prescription medications.

- Use only one pharmacy to fill prescriptions, and establish a relationship with the pharmacist. Pharmacists are often better informed about side effects and interactions than physicians.

- Consult the *Physician's Desk Reference.* This technical guide to medications is found in every library, although most libraries also have more consumer-friendly manuals that explain how to take medications.

- Inform the health care provider of all side effects.

Reducing the Risk of Drug-Food Interactions

To reduce the chances that your patient will suffer nutrient deficiencies or less-effective medications because of food-drug interactions, ask the health care provider and pharmacist these questions.

- When should medication be taken: morning, night, twice a day?

- Should the medication be taken with water?

- Should the medication be taken with food on an empty stomach?

- Are there any foods that will enhance or impede the drug's effectiveness?

- Does the medication have a sedative effect?

- Will the medication interact with over-the-counter drugs, such as cold medicines or vitamin-mineral supplements?

- Does drinking alcohol affect the drug?

- Will other prescription medications taken affect the way this one works?

Food Interactions with Commonly Prescribed Drugs

These commonly prescribed drugs interact with foods and/or nutrients. The list is not comprehensive; many other drugs also interact with food. Confirm these instructions with your pharmacist or doctor to make sure they are appropriate for your patient.

AMOXICILLIN: Antibiotic. Take with food to minimize potential gastrointestinal effects such as nausea, vomiting, or diarrhea.

CAPOTEN: Antihypertensive. Take one hour before meals; avoid potassium salt-substitutes.

CECLOR: Antibiotic. Take on an empty stomach; avoid alcohol.

DARVOCET: Analgesic. Avoid alcohol.

ELAVIL AND ENDEP: Antidepressants. Avoid alcohol; increase milk intake to supply riboflavin.

ERYTHROMYCIN: Antibiotic. Check with your doctor.

GLYBURIDE AND GLYPIZIDE: Diabetes medication. Follow balanced diabetic diet; avoid alcohol.

HCTZ (HYDROCHLOROTHIAZIDE): Diuretic. Take with food to minimize potential gastrointestional effects; eat high-potassium diet; avoid natural licorice.

KEFLEX: Antibiotic. Take on empty stomach; avoid alcohol.

LANOXIN: Antiarrhythmic. Take on empty stomach; eat potassium-rich diet. Avoid natural licorice.

PHENYTOIN: Anticonvulsant. Take with food; avoid alcohol; increase fiber and fluid in diet to avoid constipation; eat diet rich in folic acid.

PROPRANOLOL: Antiarrhythmic. Take with meals.

TAGAMET: Antisecretory, antiulcer drug. Take with food.

TETRACYCLINE: Antibiotic. Take 1 hour before or 2 hours after meals; do not eat or drink dairy products for 1 hour before and after taking.

TRIAMTERENE: Diuretic. Take with food; avoid potassium supplements, salt substitutes, and excessive intake of potassium-rich foods.

WARFARIN: Anticoagulant. Maintain consistent vitamin K intake, avoid excess amounts of green leafy vegetables, garlic, onions.

XANAX: Antianxiety. Avoid alcohol.

CHEMOTHERAPY SIDE EFFECTS

ALKYLATING AGENTS: Busulfan, Cyclophosphamide, and Thiotepa can produce nausea, vomiting, sore mouth, and stomachache.

ANTIBIOTICS: Bleomycin, Doxorubicin, and Mithramycin may cause nausea, vomiting, and inflammation of the stomach and a sore mouth; some antibiotics decrease absorption of iron and calcium.

ANTIMETABOLITES: 5-Fluorouracil, 6-Mercaptopurine, and methotrexate may cause nausea, vomiting, diarrhea, and liver disorders; methotrexate can interfere with folic acid and decrease absorption of vitamin B_{12} and fat.

HORMONES: Prednisone, Fluoxymesterone, and Tamoxifen can cause increased appetite, sodium and fluid retention, stomach upset, glucose intolerance, potassium wasting, osteoporosis, and negative nitrogen balance.

ESTROGENS: Diesthylstilbestrol and Megestrol acetate may cause nausea, vomiting, appetite loss, and high blood calcium levels.

DNA SYNTHESIS INHIBITORS: Cisplatin may cause nausea, vomiting, low levels of blood magnesium, potassium, and zinc, and kidney toxicity. Hydroxyurea may cause nausea and increase blood levels of urea nitrogen. Procarbazine can cause nausea and vomiting. Vinblastine and Vincristine can cause nausea, vomiting, and constipation.

Resources

AIDS/HIV

Centers for Disease Control
Center for Infectious Disease
AIDS Program
Atlanta, GA 30333

National AIDS Information
    Clearinghouse
National A-I-C
P.O. Box 6003
Rockville, MD 20850
1-800-458-5231

National AIDS Network
Washington, DC 20003
202-546-2424

Task Force on Nutrition Support in AIDS
Wang Associates, Inc.
19 West 21st Street
New York, NY 10010

Alzheimer's Disease

Alzheimer's Association National
    Headquarters
919 North Michigan Avenue
Suite 1000
Chicago, IL 60611-1676
1-800-272-3900

Recommended Reading

Donna Cohen, *The Loss of Self: A Family
    Resource for the Care of Alzheimer's
    Disease and Related Disorders.* New
    York: Norton, 1988.

Miriam K. Aronson, *Understanding Alz-
    heimer's Disease.* New York: Scribner's,
    1988.

Cancer

National Cancer Institute
Bethesda, MD 20892
NCI Cancer Information Service
1-800-4-CANCER
In Hawaii, on Oahu, call 524-1234

American Cancer Society
1599 Clifton Road NE
Atlanta, GA 30329
404-320-3333

Recommended Reading

*Chemotherapy and You: A Guide to
    Self-Help During Treatment.* Available
    from the National Cancer Institute.

Michael Lerner, *Choices in Healing:
    Integrating the Best of Conventional and
    Complementary Approaches to Cancer.*
    Cambridge, MA: MIT Press, 1994.

Larry LeShan, *Cancer as a Turning Point.* New York: Dutton, 1990.

Bernie Siegal, *Love, Medicine, and Miracles* (1986), and *Peace, Love, and Healing* (1989). New York: Harper & Row.

Children

American Academy of Pediatrics
141 Northwest Point Road
P. O. Box 927
Elk Grove Village, IL 60007

Children's Liver Foundation
76 South Orange Avenue
Suite 202
South Orange, NJ 07079
1–800–526–1593

Diabetes

American Diabetes Association
National Center
P.O. Box 25757
1660 Duke Street
Alexandria, VA 22313
1–800–232–3472

American Dietetic Association
216 West Jackson Boulevard
Suite 800
Chicago, IL 60606–6995
1–800–877–1600

Joslin Diabetes Foundation Inc.
One Joslin Plaza
Boston, MA 02215
617–732–2400

Juvenile Diabetes Foundation
International
432 Park Avenue South
New York, NY 10016
212–889–7575

The National Diabetes Information
Clearinghouse
P. O. Box NDIC
Bethesda, MD 20892
301–654–3327

Digestive Diseases

National Digestive Disease Information
Clearinghouse
P. O. Box NDDIC
Bethesda, MD 20892

Crohn's Ileitis and Colitis Foundation
444 Park Avenue South
New York, NY 10016–7374
212–685–3440

Heart Disease

American Heart Association National
Center
7320 Greenville Avenue
Dallas, TX 75231

National Heart, Lung, and Blood
Institute Information
Center/Publications
4733 Bethesda Avenue
Suite 530
Bethesda, MD 20814

Kidney Disease

American Association of Kidney
Patients
100 South Ashley Drive
Suite 280
Tampa, FL 33602
813–223–7099

American Council of Transplantation
700 North Fairfax Street
Suite 505
Alexandria, VA 22314
703–836–4301

National Kidney and Urologic Disease
   Information Clearinghouse
P. O. Box NKUDIC
Bethesda, MD 20892
301–468–6345

National Kidney Foundation Inc.
30 East 33rd Street
New York, NY 10016
1–800–622–9010

Polycystic Kidney Research Foundation
922 Walnut Street
Kansas City, MO 64106
816–421–1869

Lung Disease

The American Lung Association
1740 Broadway
New York, NY 10019
212–319–8700

Mind/Body

Mental Health Information
The American Psychiatric Association
APA Division of Public Affairs
1400 K Street NW
Washington, DC 20005
Write for free information on mental
   health problems.

American Psychological Association
750 First Street NE
Washington, DC 20002–4242
Send a self-addressed stamped enve-
   lope for free information on mental
   health problems.

The National Association of Social
   Workers
750 First Street NE
Washington, DC 20002
202–408–8600
Write for a list of practitioners in your
   area.

The American Association for Marriage
   and Family Therapy
1100 Seventeenth Street NW
10th Floor
Washington, DC 20036
1–800–374–2638

Self-Help Groups

The American Self-Help Group
   Clearinghouse
St. Clares–Riverside Medical Center
25 Pocono Road
Denville, NJ 07834
201–625–7101

Recommended Reading

Norman Cousins, *Anatomy of an Illness*.
   New York: W. W. Norton, 1979.

Gerald Epstein, *Healing Visualizations*. New
   York: Bantam, 1989.

Dennis Jaffe, *Healing from Within*. New
   York: Knopf, 1980.

Lawrence LeShan, *How to Meditate*.
   Boston: Little Brown, 1974.

Martin Seligman, *Learned Optimism: How
   to Change Your Mind and Your Life*.
   New York: Pocket Books, 1990.

Food Safety

Meat and Poultry Hotline
   1–800–535–4555

Consumer Information Center
574-X
Pueblo, CO 81009
Write for a free copy of *Safe Food*.

Specialty Food and Eating Products

Enrichments for Better Living Catalogue
P.O. Box 579
145 Tower Drive

Hinsdale, IL 60521

1–800–323–5547

This catalogue carries over three hundred items to make daily tasks easier. It contains products such as extra-long straws and utensils with oversized handles to make eating easier. A free copy is available upon request.

Beano Drops

AK Pharma Inc.

P.O. Box 111

Pleasantville, NJ 08232

1–800–257–8650

Food enzyme drops

Thick-It

Original Diafoods

2525 Armitage Avenue

Melrose Park, IL 60160

1–800–333–0003

A product used to thicken foods to make swallowing easier.

Artificial Saliva

The following companies make products for people who have decreased saliva production. Contact your local pharmacy or the company for more information.

Salivart Spray

Westport Pharmaceutical

P.O. Box 816

Westport, CT 06881

Saliv-Aid

Copley Pharmaceutical, Inc.

398 West Second Street

Boston, MA 02127

Lactase Products

Lactaid, Inc.

P.O. Box 111

Pleasantville, NJ 08232

Lactaid Hotline

1–800–257–8650

Kremers-Urban Company

P.O. Box 2038

Milwaukee, WI 53201

Lactase tablets.

Winthrop Consumer Products

Glenbrook Laboratories

Division of Sterling Drag, Inc.

90 Park Avenue

New York, NY 10016

Dairy-Ease tablets and lactase-treated milk.

Bibliography

General References

Alpers, D. H. *Manual of Therapeutics.* 2nd edition. Boston: Little, Brown & Company, 1990.

Dietitian's Patient Education Manual. Gaithersburg, MD: Aspen Publishers, 1994.

Goodhart, R. S., Shils, M. E., and Young, V. R., eds. *Modern Nutrition in Health and Disease.* 7th edition. Philadelphia: Lea and Febiger, 1988.

Manual of Clinical Dietetics. 4th edition. Chicago: American Dietetic Association, 1992.

National Research Council. *Recommended Dietary Allowances.* 10th edition. Washington, DC: National Academy of Sciences, 1989.

Robinson, C. H. et al. *Basic Nutrition and Diet Therapy.* New York: Macmillan Publishing Company, 1993.

Whitney, E. N. *Understanding Nutrition.* 5th edition. St. Paul, MN: West Publishing Company, 1990.

Chapters 1 and 2

Jacobson, M. *Safe Food: Eating Wisely in a Risky World.* Los Angeles: Living Planet Press, 1991.

Kant, A. et al. "Dietary Diversity in the U.S. Population, NHANES II, 1976–1980." *Journal of the American Dietetic Association* 91 (1991): 1526–31.

"Multistate Outbreak of *Salmonella poona* Infections—United States and Canada, 1991." *Journal of the American Medical Association* 266 (1991): 1189–90.

Chapter 3

AIDS/HIV

Butterworth, R. F. "Thiamin Deficiency in AIDS." *Lancet* 338 (1991): 1086.

Cimoch, P. J. "Treating Wasting and Malnutrition in HIV/AIDS Patients." *Nutrition and the M.D.* 19 (1993): 1–3.

DeBruyne, L. K. "Nutrition and AIDS." *Nutrition Clinics* 6 (1991): 1–11.

"Improving Appetite in AIDS Patients." *Nutrition and the M.D.* 19 (1993): 6–7.

Tang, A. M. et al. "Dietary Micronutrient Intake and Risk of Progression to Acquired Immunodeficiency Syndrome (AIDS) in Human Immunodeficiency Virus Type 1 (HIV-1)–Infected Homosexual Men." *American Journal of Epidemiology* 11 (1993): 937–51.

Weaver, K. "Reversible Malnutrition in AIDS." *American Journal of Nursing* 91 (1991): 24–31.

Alzheimer's Disease

Neri, L. C. "Aluminum, Alzheimer's Disease, and Drinking Water." *Lancet* 338 (1991): 390.

Smith-Clagett, M. "Nutritional Factors Relevant to Alzheimer's Disease." *Journal of the American Dietetic Association* 89 (1989): 392–396.

Still, A., and Kelley, P. "On the Incidence of Primary Degenerative Dementia Versus Water Fluoridation Content in South Carolina." *Neurotoxicology* 1 (1980): 125.

Arthritis

Biquaoette, J. et al. "Nutritional Adequacy of Diet and Supplements in Patients with Rheumatoid Arthritis Who Take Medication." *Journal of the American Dietetic Association* 87 (1987): 7–8.

Gilman-Wolman, P. "Management of Patients Using Unproven Regimens for Arthritis." *Journal of the American Dietetic Association* 87 (1987): 1211–14.

Kjeldsen-Kragh, J. et al. "Controlled Trial of Fasting and One-Year Vegetarian Diet in Rheumatoid Arthritis." *Lancet* 338 (1991): 899–902.

Cancer

Bloch, A. S. *Nutrition Management of the Cancer Patient.* Rockville, MD: Aspen Publishers, Inc., 1990.

Coronary Heart Disease

"Second Report of the Expert Panel on Detection, Evaluation, and Treatment of High Blood Cholesterol in Adults." National Institutes of Health Publication No. 93–3096. September 1993.

Diabetes

The Diabetes Control and Complications Trial Research Group. "The Effect of Intensive Treatment of Diabetes on the Development and Progression of Long-term Complications in Insulin-Dependent Diabetes." *New England Journal of Medicine* 329 (1993): 986–993.

Diseases of the Digestive Tract

Inflammatory Bowel Disease

Diet for Inflammatory Bowel Disease. "Diet Therapy/Obesity Update." *Nutrition and the M.D.,* Vol. 14, May 1988: 7–8.

Irritable Bowel Syndrome

Mullin, G. E. "Irritable Bowel Syndrome and Food Allergies." *Journal of the American Medical Association* 265 (1991): 1736.

Ulcers

Kumar, N. et al. "Effect of Milk on Patients with Duodenal Ulcers." *British Medical Journal* 293 (1986): 666.

Kumar, N. "Do Chillies Influence Healing of Duodenal Ulcers?" *British Medical Journal* 288 (1984): 1803–4.

Rydning, A. et al. "Prophylactic Effect of Dietary Fibre in Duodenal Ulcer Disease." *Lancet* 2 (1982): 736–39.

Geriatric Conditions

Chandra, R. K. "Effect of Vitamin and Trace-Element Supplementation on Immune Responses and Infection in Elderly Subjects." *Lancet* 346 (1992): 1124–27.

Ham, R. J. "Indicators of Poor Nutritional Status in Older Americans." *American Family Physician* 45 (1992): 219–28.

Tkatch, L. et al. "Benefits of Oral Protein Supplementation in Elderly Patients with Fracture of the Proximal Femur." *Journal of the American College of Nutrition* 11 (1992): 519–25.

Kidney Disease

Curhan, G. C., et al. "A Prospective Study of Dietary Calcium and Other Nutrients and the Risk of Symptomatic Kidney Stones." *New England Journal of Medicine* 328 (1993): 883–88.

Multiple Sclerosis

Douglas, J. B. "Nutrition Practices of Patients with Multiple Sclerosis." *Journal of the Canadian Dietetic Association* 49 (1988): 246.

"Low-Fat Diet and Multiple Sclerosis." *Nutrition and the M.D.* 17 (1991): 1.

Ransohoff, R. M. et al. "Vitamin B$_{12}$ Deficiency and Multiple Sclerosis." *Lancet* 335 (1990): 1285–86.

Swank, R. L, et al. "Multiple Sclerosis: The Lipid Relationship." *American Journal of Clinical Nutrition* 48 (1988): 1387–93.

Swank, R. L., and Dugan, B. B. "Effect of Low Saturated Fat Diet in Early and Late Cases of Multiple Sclerosis." *Lancet* 336 (1990): 37–39.

Parkinson's Disease
Karstaedt, P., and Pincus, J. H. "Protein Redistribution Remains Effective in Patients with Fluctuating Parkinsonism." *Archives of Neurology* 49 (1992): 149–51.

Lieberman, D. A. "Nutritional Management of the Patient with Parkinson's Disease." *Topics in Clinical Nutrition* 4 (1989): 1–6.

Paré, A. et al. "Effect of Daytime Protein Restriction on Nutrient Intakes in Free-Living Parkinson's Disease Patients." *American Journal of Clinical Nutrition* 55 (1992): 701–7.

Pincus, J. H., and Barry, K. "Influence of Dietary Protein on Motor Fluctuations in Parkinson's Disease." *Archives of Neurology* 44 (1987): 270–72.

Pincus, J. H. "Protein Redistribution Diet Restores Motor Function in Patients with Dopa-Resistant 'Off' Periods." *Neurology* 481 (1988): 481.

———. "Dietary Protein Enhances Effectiveness of L-dopa in Late Parkinson's Disease." *Nutrition and the M.D.* 18 (1992): 1–4.

Surgery
Bistrian, B. "Protein Status of General Surgical Patients." *Journal of the American Medical Association* 230 (1974): 858.

Haydock, P. A., and Hill, G. L. "Impaired Wound Healing in Surgical Patients with Varying Degrees of Malnutrition." *Journal of Parenteral and Enteral Nutrition* 10 (1986): 550.

Mughal, M. M. "The Effect of Nutritional Status on Morbidity After Elective Surgery for Benign Gastrointestinal Disease." *Journal of Parenteral and Enteral Nutrition* 11 (1987): 140–43.

Young, M. E. "Malnutrition and Wound Healing." *Heart and Lung* 17 (1988): 60–69.

Chapter 5
Mensink, R. P., and Katan, M. B. "Effect of Dietary Trans Fatty Acids on High-Density and Low-Density Lipoprotein Cholesterol Levels in Healthy Subjects." *New England Journal of Medicine* 323 (1990): 439–45.

Chapter 8

Menashian, L. et al. "Improved Food Intake and Reduced Nausea and Vomiting in Patients Given a Restricted Diet While Receiving Cisplatin Chemotherapy." *Journal of the American Dietetic Association* 92 (1992): 58–61.

Chapter 18

American Academy of Pediatrics Committee on Nutrition. *Pediatric Nutrition Handbook.* 3rd edition. Elk Grove Village, IL: American Academy of Pediatrics, 1993.

Chapter 19

Vitamin and Mineral Therapy

Bendich, A. "Vitamin C and Immune Responses." *Food Technology* 41 (1987): 112–14.

——, and Machlin, L. J. "Safety of Oral Intake of Vitamin E." *American Journal of Clinical Nutrition* 48 (1988): 612–19.

Block, G. "Vitamin C and Cancer Prevention: The Epidemiologic Evidence." *American Journal of Clinical Nutrition* 53 (1991): 270–82.

Lachance, P. "Dietary Intake of Carotenes and the Carotene Gap." *Clinical Nutrition* 7 (1988): 118–22.

Liebman, B. "The Ultra Mega Vita Guide." *Nutrition Action HealthLetter,* January/February 1993, pp. 7–9.

Moertel, C. G. et al. "High-Dose Vitamin C Versus Placebo in the Treatment of Patients with Advanced Cancer Who Have Had No Prior Chemotherapy." *New England Journal of Medicine* 312 (1985): 137–41.

"Our Vitamin Prescription: The Big Four." *University of California at Berkeley Wellness Letter* 10 (1994): 1–2.

Schardt, D. "Vitamins 101—How to Buy Them." *Nutrition Action HealthLetter,* January/February 1993, pp. 5–6.

Smigel, K. "Vitamin E Moves Onstage in Cancer Prevention Studies." *Journal of the National Cancer Institute* 84 (1992): 996–97.

Wittes, R. E. "Vitamin C and Cancer." *New England Journal of Medicine* 312 (1985): 178–79.

——. "Antioxidants: Surprise, Surprise." *Nutrition Action HealthLetter,* June 1994, p. 4.

Macrobiotic Diet, Yeast-Free Diet, Herbal Therapy, Kelley Malignancy Index, and Gerson Method

Dwyer, J. T. et al. "Unproven Nutrition Therapies for AIDS: What Is the Evidence?" *Nutrition Today,* March/April 1988, pp. 25–33.

Dwyer, J. T. "The Macrobiotic Diet: No Cancer Cure." *Nutrition Forum* 7 (1990): 1–11.

Executive Committee of the American Academy of Allergy and Immunology. "*Candiasis* Hypersensitivity Syndrome." *Journal of Allergy and Clinical Immunology* 78 (1986): 271–72.

"Herbal Roulette," *Consumer Reports,* November 1995, 698–705.

Questionable Methods of Cancer Management: Nutritional Therapies. American Cancer Society, 1993, Atlanta, GA.

"Unproven Nutritional Remedies and Cancer." *Nutrition Reviews* 50 (1992): 106–18.

Mind-Body Connection

Campbell, D. F. et al. "Relaxation: Its Effect on the Nutritional Status and Performance Status of Clients with Cancer." *Journal of the American Dietetic Association* 84 (1984): 201–4.

Spiegel, D. et al. "Effect of Psychosocial Treatment on Survival of Patients with Metastatic Breast Cancer." *Lancet,* 334 (1989): 888–91.

Strain, J. et al. "Cost Offset from a Psychiatric Consultation-Liaison Intervention with Elderly Hip Fracture Patients." *American Journal of Psychiatry* 148 (1991): 1044–49.

Chapter 20

Trovat, A. "Drug-Nutrient Interactions." *American Family Physician* 44 (1991): 1651–58.

Index

Page numbers in *italics* refer to recipes.